THE STAGE CRAFT HAND BOOK

Daniel A. Ionazzi

BETTERWAY BOOKS
CINCINNATI, OHIO

The Stagecraft Handbook.

Copyright © 1996 by Daniel A. Ionazzi. Printed and bound in the United States of America. All rights reserved. No part of this book may be reproduced in any form or by any electronic or mechanical means including information storage and retrieval systems without permission in writing from the publisher, except by a reviewer, who may quote brief passages in a review. Published by Betterway Books, an imprint of F&W Publications, Inc., 4700 East Galbraith Road, Cincinnati, Ohio 45236. (800) 289-0963. First edition.

Other fine Betterway Books are available from your local bookstore or direct from the publisher.

06   05   04   03   8   7   6   5

Library of Congress Cataloging-in-Publication Data

Ionazzi, Daniel A.
     The stagecraft handbook / Daniel A. Ionazzi.—1st ed.
          p.   cm.
     Includes index.
     ISBN 1-55870-404-3 (pbk.: alk. paper)
     1. Theaters—Stage-setting and scenery—Handbooks, manuals, etc. I. Title.
PN2091.S8I65   1996
792′.025—dc20   96-22964
                                                                          CIP

Edited by Katie Carroll
Designed by Angela Lennert Wilcox
Interior illustrations by Daniel A. Ionazzi
Additional illustrations by Kevin Basham

METRIC CONVERSION CHART		
TO CONVERT	**TO**	**MULTIPLY BY**
Inches	Centimeters	2.54
Centimeters	Inches	0.4
Feet	Centimeters	30.5
Centimeters	Feet	0.03
Yards	Meters	0.9
Meters	Yards	1.1
Sq. Inches	Sq. Centimeters	6.45
Sq. Centimeters	Sq. Inches	0.16
Sq. Feet	Sq. Meters	0.09
Sq. Meters	Sq. Feet	10.8
Sq. Yards	Sq. Meters	0.8
Sq. Meters	Sq. Yards	1.2
Pounds	Kilograms	0.45
Kilograms	Pounds	2.2
Ounces	Grams	28.4
Grams	Ounces	0.04

DANIEL A. IONAZZI is currently a member of the UCLA School of Theater, Film and Television faculty, Director of Productions for the UCLA Department of Theater, and Production Manager for the Geffen Playhouse. Recently he produced the battle sequence in *Wellington's Victory* for the Los Angeles Philharmonic's Beethoven Spectacular at the Hollywood Bowl, *The Woman From Samos* and *Casina* for the J. Paul Getty Museum and *A Life of Crime* for ABC Entertainment and UCLA. Before joining UCLA in 1988, Mr. Ionazzi served in a variety of management capacities on Broadway, in regional theaters, national and international tours, and for a wide variety of special events. Some of his credits include: Production Manager and Technical Director for the Denver Center Theatre Company and Santa Fe Festival Theatre, Executive Director of the Colorado Stage Company, Director of Festivals and Events for The Denver Partnership, and Assistant Technical Director for The Juilliard School. In addition, Mr. Ionazzi has designed lights for productions around the country including *Henry IV Part I*, *The Three Sisters*, *Telling Time*, *Othello*, *Trojan Women*, *Misalliance*, *Night of the Iguana*, *Antigone*, *Amelia Lives* and *Jenufa*. Mr. Ionazzi is the author of *The Stage Management Handbook*.

My thanks to the UCLA School of Theater, Film and Television and the UCLA Scene Shop. Thank you, also, to Marsha Ginsberg and the students of her model-building class for the photos at the end of chapter four.

TABLE OF CONTENTS

CHAPTER 6

CONSTRUCTION TECHNIQUES . . . 109

CHAPTER 7

INSTALLATION AND RIGGING . . . 173

CHAPTER 8

STOCK SCENERY . . . 197

Stagecraft is a unique adaptation of common construction techniques to the temporary and illusory environment of the stage. What appears to be a solid masonry wall or a dense tropical forest will be transported away with the tug of a rope or the push of a cart, making way for the next scene or the next production. It is a part of the magic that can convey an audience to places they can only reach while in a theater.

Many of the basic construction techniques covered in this text have existed for years. With advances in technology and the development of new tools and materials, more sophisticated construction techniques have and will be adapted for use on the stage. However, the primary forces that stimulate the adaptation of these techniques remain very much the same. The basic factors in building scenery for the stage are cost, time, mobility and illusion. In the real world, there are items that are man-made and items that occur in nature. In the imaginative world of the theater, and in the minds of many talented designers, there are objects that exist only in and of the stage. Constructing these elements in an efficient and convincing manner is the goal of stagecraft.

Good scenery and good construction techniques have several basic characteristics in common. Good scenery is very economical in comparison to the real-life items it represents. Production budgets and theater sizes vary, but all theaters strive to keep their scenery investments contained. This is necessary because, to some degree or another, all scenery is disposable. Prior to the nineteenth century, stock sets were common; a theater would have a standard forest set or street scene that would be used, time and time again, for every production that required such a location. How-ever, as scenic practices changed and scenery became more specific to a particular script or production, stock scenery became less desirable. In the majority of cases, scenery is useful for only one production—with the general exception of scenery built for opera and ballet companies, which tend to maintain a repertory of productions they return to from time to time. But even here, new styles evolve, tastes change, new forms are developed or new ideas conceived, and the life of a particular scene design is limited to a few years at best. Some scenic items may have value as components of another set but, on the whole, the vast assortment of theatrical scripts and the even more diverse conceptual approaches to mounting a production have widely varying needs with regard to scenery.

Scenery must be lightweight. The need to change from one scene to another quickly and without the use of heavy equipment inspires the need for scenery to be lightweight and mobile. It also requires a high ratio of strength to weight in order to withstand the stress of use and handling. The structure onstage may look like and act like a house in its ability to support people standing on a porch or on a second story, but it is not a house. It is scenery and, if properly constructed, will meet these strength requirements and still be light enough to be removed from the stage during a ten-minute intermission.

Scenery must be compact. The stage, which houses the scenery, is of a limited size. Regardless of the demands of a particular script—even if it requires a representation of the landscape of the moon, a mountain in the Himalayas or the interior of Grand Central Station—the scenery must fit within the dimensions of the stage and accommodate the other technical elements of the production. In many instances, scenery must also fit into a truck for transportation or into limited storage facilities.

Scenery must be simple to construct. Skilled technicians are a valuable asset to any theater. These craftspeople will enhance the quality of your productions and ensure the efficient use of resources. However, the skill level of stage technicians, as well as their availability at a given time and location, is a cost consideration. Simple construction techniques reduce the learning curve and mitigate the need for highly skilled craftspeople.

Scenery construction techniques must be adaptable. The craftspeople and techniques employed to build a castle one day may be required to build a forest the next, and perhaps a place of fantasy that exists only in the mind of a character the day after. Adaptability is a factor that will be addressed throughout this text.

It is impossible within the pages of any one book to provide a construction process or solution for every scenic unit that you will encounter during a career in the theater, but this text will ensure a foundation from which to find your own solutions and a framework that will guide you along the path to those solutions. It is very important that the stage technician responsible for building the scenery be as imaginative and creative as the designer whose scenery is being built. This text will provide many standard and accepted practices for building common scenic units, but new ideas, creative solutions and new techniques are being developed every day. Experiment when the opportunity arises.

Keep these basic characteristics of good scenery in mind when developing construction methods; this will ensure the success of your stagecraft.

CHAPTER 1

A BRIEF HISTORY OF WESTERN SCENIC PRACTICES

Although this is not a history book, a general overview of the evolution of Western scenic practices provides an important perspective for stage technicians. For the sake of brevity, this account omits the ritual origins of theater and the wealth of styles and techniques developed and refined in other world cultures, some of which continue to this day. It confines itself to a more or less chronological look at what was going on with scenery during certain periods of Western theater history, and how it developed over time and influenced modern practices.

THE GREEKS

Our first significant information about scenery can be found with the Greeks. By the middle of the fifth century B.C., most theatrical presentations were performed in front of a *skene*, or scene building. The Greek word *skene* means "hut" or "tent," which may give you some clues to the origins of this structure and what was going on in the theater before this time. Initially, the skene was thought to be a temporary structure erected for the presentation of one of the many festivals that took place each year. As the use of this structure became more prevalent, it was adopted as part of the permanent theater facility.

We cannot be absolutely certain about the design of these early skenes, but generally they are considered to have been roofed structures with one or more doors or entryways set into a wall or colonnade. The actors performed in front of the skene, which served as a generic scenic background for all plays. There is some debate as to the existence of an elevated stage at this time. If it did exist, it may have been no more than a set of steps leading from the skene down to a performance area known as the *orchestra* (see Figure 1-1). Today the term *orchestra*, as it relates to theater architecture, refers to the principal seating area on the main floor of the theater.

Some research indicates the use of painted panels attached to the skene that were exchanged for other panels as required by changes of scene during the play. These panels, called *pinakas*, were strikingly similar in function to modern flats. A *flat* is ordinarily a wooden frame covered with fabric which is painted to represent a scene or portion of a scenic locale. (A number of alternatives to this general form have been developed as a result of new materials and techniques being used by theater technicians. A complete description of flat construction is provided in chapter six.) Another device used by the Greeks to shift scenery was the *periaktoi*.

FIGURE 1-1
The skene of a classical Greek theater

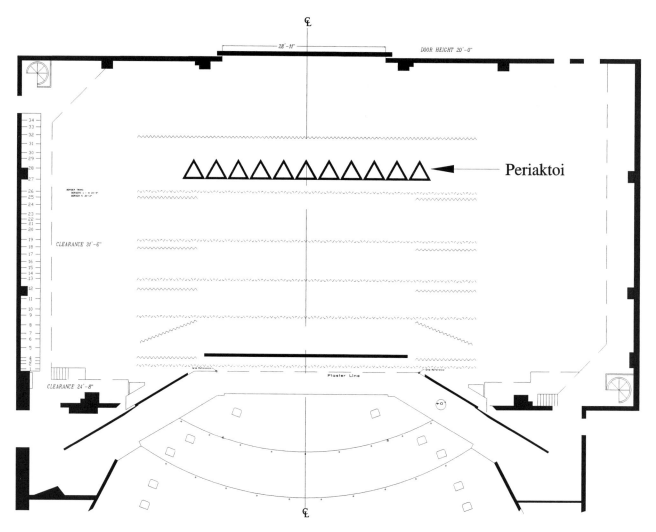

FIGURE 1-2
A wall of periaktoi used in a modern production of A Chorus Line

This item, constructed of three painted panels which formed a triangle in plan view, was revolved to reveal a new side whenever the scene changed. This concept still pops up in various applications today. Figure 1-2 illustrates a wall of periaktoi constructed of flats for a production of *A Chorus Line*.

Some theatrical machinery was in use at this time for the staging of special effects. An *ekkyklema* was a mechanism used for revealing a tableau. The exact form of the ekkyklema is not known with any certitude, but it may have been a platform, or wagon, which was rolled through one of the doors (or a revolve of some type) in the skene. A more dramatic and spectacular device was the *machina*. This crane-like apparatus was used to portray people in flight or hovering over the Earth. The *deus ex machina*, or "god machine," was usually employed to resolve the plot of the play through the intervention of the gods. The term is used today to refer to the unexpected appearance of a character who resolves the plot of the play.

In the Hellenistic Period, beginning with the reign of Alexander the Great in 336 B.C., a number of important changes took place. An eight- to thirteen-foot-high stage was customary. The front edge of this stage was supported by a facade known as the *proskenion*. Early versions of the proskenion appeared to be constructed of a series of columns that were notched to hold pinakas. At the rear of the raised stage was another facade, called the *episkenion*, which was initially fitted with one to three doors; later adaptations had as many as seven large openings (see Figure 1-3).

THE ROMANS

The Romans adapted their theater from the Greeks, and also employed a scenic background that was used for both comedies and tragedies. The Romans called the stage house the *scaena*; the facade of the stage house was known as the *scaena frons* (Figure 1-4). The scaena frons served as the ba-

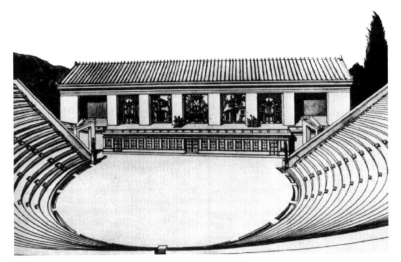

FIGURE 1-3
The proskenion of a Hellenistic theater

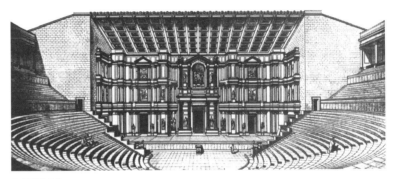

FIGURE 1-4
The scaena frons of the Roman theater

FIGURE 1-5
Mansions arranged along the medieval stage

sic scenic background and, like the skene of the Greeks, was architecturally detailed and included a series of doors that were used to represent different houses or a palace.

The periaktoi was also borrowed from the Greeks and was the principal device used to facilitate scene changes. A variety of mechanical devices were developed by Roman engineers for use in the theater, including elevators.

THE MIDDLE AGES

During the Middle Ages, scenery consisted principally of structures called *mansions* (Figure 1-5, page 11). The setting often consisted of a series of mansions arranged along the stage, around the performance space or, in some countries, incorporated into pageant wagons. Each mansion defined a specific location; as the actors moved from one mansion to the next, the scene changed. Special effects were of particular importance during this time. The role of the engineer, or mechanic, was considered crucial to the overall creation and success of the theatrical presentation.

THE ITALIAN RENAISSANCE

As was the case with all other art forms, the Italian Renaissance had an enormous influence on the theater—particularly scenery. The development of perspective drawing and its systemization around 1425 would find its way into the theater by 1480 and set in motion concepts for the design of theater facilities, scenic design techniques and staging practices that continue to this day. Many of the period's most influential architects and painters designed for the theater, bringing with them the knowledge, concepts, style and technique developed in their principal field of work.

In the early sixteenth century the *wing-and-drop system* was developed to take advantage of the new perspective techniques. Wing-and-drop system refers to a stage setting that employs a number of painted panels or flats that retreat from the front of the stage toward the rear along the sides of the performance space; at the rear of the stage is a painted drop that is positioned parallel to the front edge of the stage (see Figure 1-6). A *drop* is an unframed piece of fabric that is suspended from the stage rigging of the theater. The wings and drop were usually painted as one continuous scene with the perspective's vanishing point upstage center.

To facilitate the painting of this rather large picture, the wings and drop were set up in the theater and cords were stretched from the front of the stage to the vanishing point as guides for the artist. This process ensured that the perspective would be accurate and that the painted scene would blend smoothly from one panel to the next.

In the early seventeenth century, most settings were comprised of three components: side wings, borders and back shutters. The *borders* gave the illusion of a sky or ceiling. These were hung overhead between the wing panels and were painted to continue the scene depicted on the other panels. The *back shutters* were an adaptation of the drop that enabled changes of scene. Individual panels could slide past one another like a series of sliding doors to reveal the scene painted on the shutter behind.

This proved to be a very efficient way to quickly change scenes. To facilitate more rapid changes of scenery, the angled wings were eventually replaced by a series of panels that, like the back shutters, were positioned parallel to the front edge of the stage. These parallel wings were mounted in grooves at the top and bottom. A number of wings could be stacked one behind the other at each position and slid onstage or offstage to reveal a different painted scene. The position of each set of wings was chosen to ensure the illusion of the entire painted scene would not be interrupted by gaps between the panels. The parallel wings, in conjunction with the back shutters or a series of drops that could be raised or lowered, made changing scenes relatively quick.

Another system for changing scenery had developed in Venice by 1645. This system was called the *chariot and pole* (Figure 1-7, page 14). The scenic structure was the same painted panel used in the wing-and-drop system, but the method for changing the wings utilized a cart or wagon, the chariot, located under the stage. Attached to the chariot was a pole, or more accurately a wooden frame, which projected through a

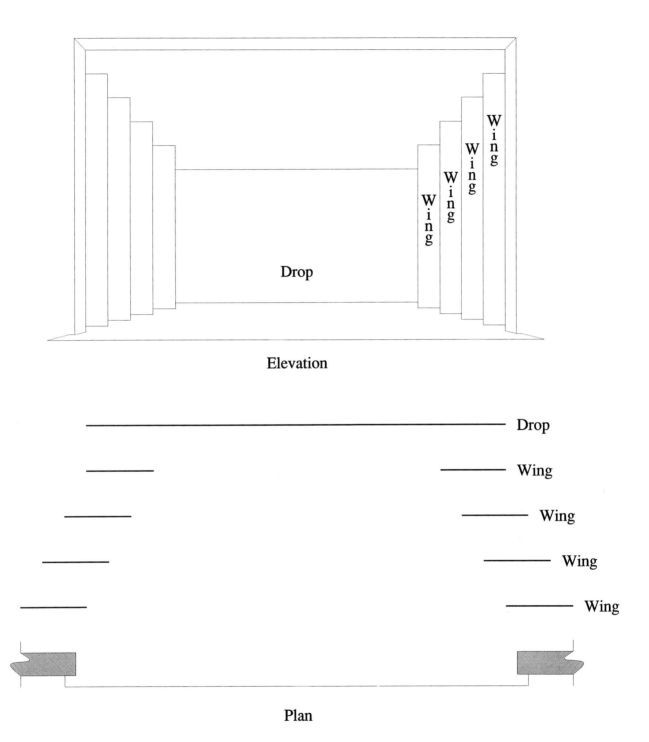

FIGURE 1-6
Elevation and plan of wing-and-drop scenic system

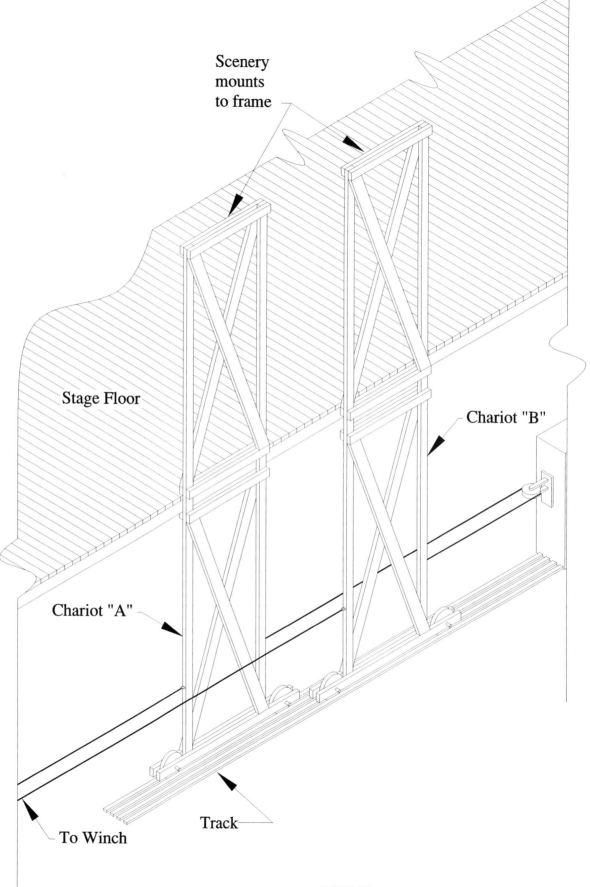

Scenery mounts to frame

Stage Floor

Chariot "B"

Chariot "A"

To Winch

Track

FIGURE 1-7
Chariot-and-pole scenic system

slot in the stage floor. The scenic panel was attached to this pole. A series of these chariots and poles were positioned to locate the scenic panels in onstage positions that were compatible with the perspective technique used to paint the scenery. The panel was brought onstage or offstage by wheeling the chariot along fixed rails until it reached the desired position. Using the chariot and pole, any number of scenes could be created by replacing the painted panels on the chariot and pole that was offstage while another set of panels was onstage for the current scene. Also, a number of chariots could be moved simultaneously through the use of pulleys and winches. The chariot-and-pole system remained in use until late in the nineteenth century. The painted panels that were part of wing-and-drop or chariot-and-pole systems are in essence a version of today's flats.

By the middle of the seventeenth century, the angled-wing version of the wing-and-drop system was almost entirely replaced by the parallel system. The shape of the theater was also being affected by perspective. The illusion of scenery painted in perspective was so revolutionary and so powerful that the architecture of the theater building began to change in order to fully exploit this technique. Since the design was in essence a huge painting, it seems only natural to frame the painting—and that is exactly what the Italians did. The Renaissance artist thought of space as finite, and so developed the *proscenium* as a means to restrict the view of the audience. This architectural frame, an adaptation of the Greek proskenion, helped maintain the illusion created by the scenery and masked, or hid, the mechanisms and offstage space required to support the scene changes and other aspects of production. The oldest surviving structure with a permanent proscenium arch is the Teatro Farnese (Figure 1-8), built in 1618 in Parma, Italy. This beautiful theater is considered by many to be the prototype of the modern theater.

FIGURE 1-8
The proscenium of the Teatro Farnese

The Italian Renaissance initiated another scenic practice which would, by the nineteenth century, be used extensively in the theater. In the late seventeenth century the first *box sets* were being used in Italy. A box set consisted of three walls and a ceiling (Figure 1-9, page 16). The open (fourth) wall was the side through which the audience viewed the play. The side walls would often have openings or gaps between them, which allowed for entrances and exits from the stage. The box set has become a staple of the theater and, in one form or another, illustrates the current method of representing realistic interiors onstage.

THE EIGHTEENTH, NINETEENTH AND TWENTIETH CENTURIES

By the beginning of the eighteenth century, most of the theaters of Western Europe had adopted the perspective scenic techniques developed during the Italian Renaissance. These techniques dominated theatrical production for the next 150 to 200 years. However, there were a few other trends that took hold during this time that are of interest for our purposes. Around 1703, Ferdinando Bibiena introduced angle perspective, *scena per angolo*. This evolution

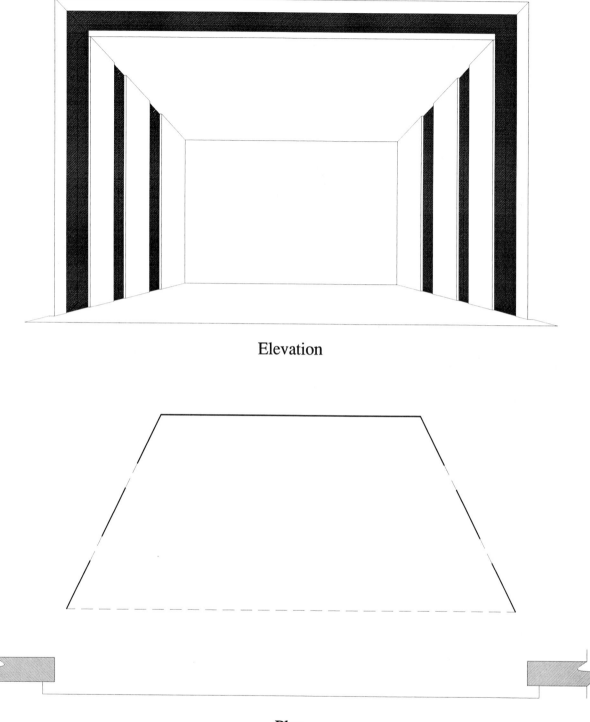

Elevation

Plan

FIGURE 1-9
Elevation and plan of a box set

of the central single-point perspective used two or more vanishing points at the sides of the setting or offstage entirely. With this technique, Bibiena was able to alter the perceived shape of the performance space, placing flats where required to make streets, hallways or passages project off in any direction. He also abandoned the common practice of scaling and positioning the scenery in accord with architecture of the auditorium. Under these conditions, the facing rows of buildings typically depicted in a single-perspective scene were completely visible, from ground floor to roof. Bibiena's scale was closer to reality. Structures situated downstage appeared to rise dramatically above the proscenium arch, well out of sightlines (see Figure 1-10).

Due in no small part to the exceptional artistry of Ferdinando Bibiena and his family, as well as other gifted designers working during this time, scenery and spectacle became increasingly more important in production, and theatrical sets began to increase in size. Prior to the mid-eighteenth century, most theaters maintained stock sets, which were used repeatedly, or staged performances in front of permanent facades or mansions. However, as scenery became more important, the use of new settings became more common and the scenery became specific to the text or production. There was also a growing interest in depicting real places, particularly local scenes. In the late eighteenth century, mood became a significant component of design, and the atmospheric qualities of light were emphasized.

Architecturally, theaters became bigger and the stage itself became very deep to emphasize the perspective of the scenery. The first indications of a thrust theater as we know it was seen at the Drury Lane in London in 1674. Paris saw independent scenic studios begin to replace the theater shops during the early 1800s; painted floorcloths were seen in Paris around 1846. In 1816, the Chestnut Theater in Philadelphia was the first theater to use gas lights

FIGURE 1-10
Example of scena per angolo

to illuminate its stage.

In the latter half of the nineteenth century, more space was provided to handle scenery effectively. Fly space and trap rooms were enlarged, and some theaters installed elevators. Of particular interest was the increasing use of three-dimensional scenic units such as stairs and platforms. This allowed for more interaction between the performers and the scenery. One of the influences of the perspective scenery techniques of the Italian Renaissance was also finally broken during this time when the concept of *free plantation* of scenery was implemented. This concept called for the scenery to be placed onstage ignoring the requirements of the wing-and-drop or chariot-and-pole scenic systems. The scenery, in essence, could be placed anywhere on the stage.

The turn of the century saw the beginnings of the modern theater and a number of significant technical innovations. Two men are generally considered to have paved the way for many of the theatrical practices that are considered standard today. Adolphe Appia (1862–1928) and Gordon Craig (1872–1966), working separately, developed many similar ideas about theater as an art form and the service this art form could provide to a modern society. While their ideas encompassed the whole of theater and its production, their innovations in scenic design were considerable. Appia championed the use of three-dimensional scenery (such as steps, ramps and platforms) in order to provide a transition between the horizontal plane of the stage floor and the vertical plane of upright scenery. This integration of the actor and the setting helped unify the theatrical elements into a more valuable whole. Appia differed from Craig in that he believed there should be a different setting for each locale in the script; Craig was interested in expressing the essence of the entire script in a single set. His efforts were focused on evoking a place and time in the audience's mind instead of literally representing such a place onstage. Both men led the way toward a more simplified decor, but a setting with greater plasticity.

The increasing emphasis on three-dimensional scenery inspired a number of technical innovations to handle the demands of shifting these heavier scenic units. Elevator stages were widely adopted as one means to accomplish rapid changes in three-dimensional scenery. A complete elevator system was installed in the Budapest Opera House in 1884. The Residenz Theatre in Munich, Germany, had a revolving stage in 1896, while the Royal Opera House in Berlin was using rolling platform stages around 1900.

Advances in lighting technology, the use of directional lighting and, ultimately, the development of stage lighting as design also began to change the nature of scenery. The theater of the Italian Renaissance, which had dominated theatrical production since the seventeenth century, had finally been challenged.

In the twentieth century, a number of literary and art movements had significant influence on theater production. New technologies eventually found their way into the theater to play their part in changing the way theater is produced and scenery is constructed. Other forms of entertainment such as film and television, which originally borrowed heavily from the theater, have made many contributions to the mix of techniques and practices which makes up modern stagecraft.

CHAPTER 2

THE STAGE

There are two minimum requirements for a theater: You need a space in which the actor can perform and a space from which the audience can watch. The essence of a good theater is the relationship between these two spaces. Usually, the actor's space is the stage and the audience space is the house. All other components of the facility are the result of cultural or technological needs and preferences. Spaces such as lobbies, rest rooms and various other public areas were developed as a result of social and cultural conditions. Technology and the need to provide support to the people working in the theater also played a part in increasing

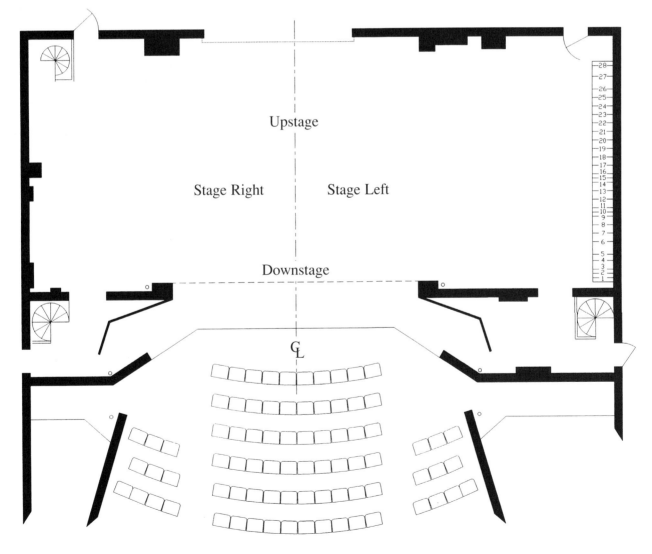

FIGURE 2-1 *Stage directions*

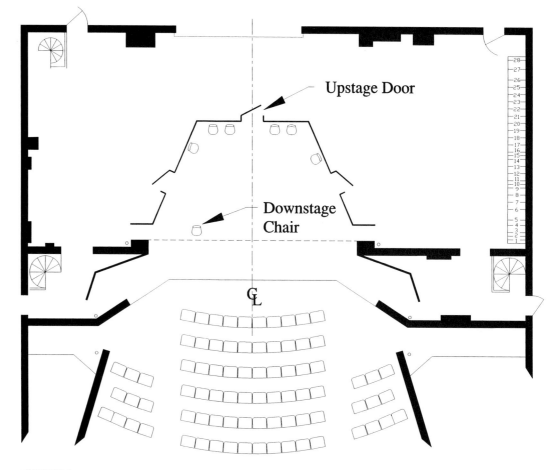

FIGURE 2-2
Using stage directions to identify location

the complexity of the theater and its stage. Today, with regard to the architecture of the stage, there is some common terminology that will aid in understanding this text and provide a foundation for your future work in the theater.

Stage directions are used to instruct actors, technicians and others working in the theater as to the location of a person or object, or their direction of travel. *Onstage* can refer to any location in view of the audience or the house. *Offstage*, or *backstage*, refers to parts of the stage which cannot be viewed from the house. Offstage is also used as a general indication that a person or object is not on the stage but perhaps in a dressing room or some other part of the building.

Once onstage, location or direction is indicated in general by the terms *upstage*, *downstage*, *stage left*, or *stage right*. To travel *upstage* is to move away from the audience. To travel *downstage* is to move toward the audience. An actor who is to move *stage left* moves to his left as he faces the audience. A move to the actor's right while facing the audience (that is, facing downstage) is to move *stage right* (see Figure 2-1, page 19).

Location can also be described with these stage directions. A door may be differentiated by its location onstage; the upstage door in Figure 2-2 is indicated by the arrow. Likewise, the position of a chair may be indicated as downstage right, as indicated in Figure 2-2. Another common stage direction is *center stage*. This direction is self evident and, when used in combination with the others (such as downstage center), can be quite specific.

The offstage left or right spaces of the theater are known as the *wings*. In fact, this term is often interchangeable with *offstage*, as in "The understudy is waiting in the wings."

FORMS OF THE THEATER

The physical form of today's stage has developed into four primary configurations that are more appropriately considered in the context of the actor/audience relationship than the actual physical shape of the stage. These four configurations are proscenium, thrust, arena and environmental. Figure 2-3 provides schematic illustrations for three of these configurations.

Proscenium

The proscenium form establishes an architectural frame between the audience and the actors. This frame is the window through which the audience views the play. The theater artist has a great deal of control over what the audience sees and how they perceive it when working in this form. Figures 2-4 and 2-5 on pages 22 and 23 illustrate the ground plan and centerline section, respectively, of a typical proscenium theater. (Drawings such as these are discussed in detail in chapter four.)

The ground plan also indicates the *sightlines* for this particular theater. Sightlines can be thought of as a kind of worst-case view of the stage that defines the extreme limits of the audience's view. Establishing sightlines is important for a number of reasons. Most importantly, can the audience see what you want them to see? Conversely, can they see what you do not want them to see? Sightlines are drawn from the perspective of the audience member with the most extreme view, or "worst" seat, up into the grid (typically the seat closest to the stage), left and right into the wings (extreme side seats) and down onto the stage floor (typically the highest seat in the house).

In the proscenium configuration, all the elements of the production are typically presented within the frame of the proscenium. This configuration can accommodate an enormous amount of stage machinery and equipment while keeping it upstage of the proscenium in the stage house—out of sight of the audience. With

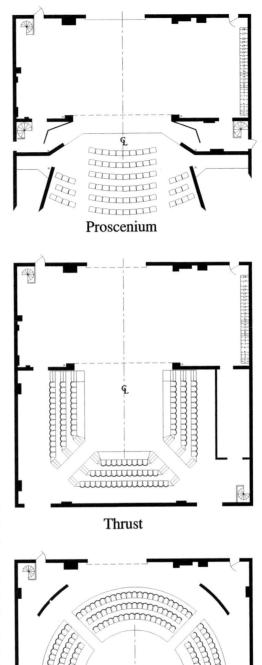

Proscenium

Thrust

Arena

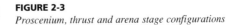

FIGURE 2-3
Proscenium, thrust and arena stage configurations

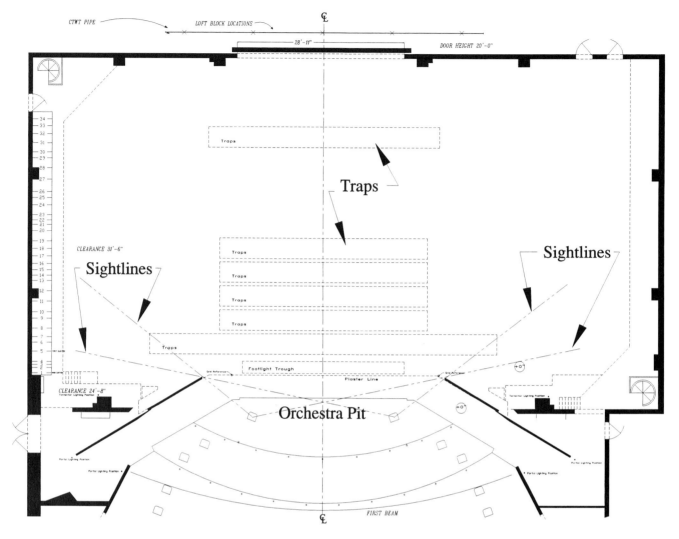

FIGURE 2-4
Ground plan of a proscenium theater

this equipment safely hidden behind the proscenium wall, the illusions of time and place can easily be maintained.

The single audience perspective inherent in this form has greatly influenced the manner in which scenery has been designed and constructed over the last 500 years. Scenery had to be finished on only one side: the side facing the audience. The limited viewing angles enable designers and craftspeople to manipulate the apparent size and shape of objects with two-dimensional techniques used in painting. (In fact, the form evolved in order to take advantage of the advent of perspective drawing). Other, more practical advantages to this stage form concern the techniques and devices employed to support the scenery. Since the upstage or offstage side of the scenery is hidden, these tech-

niques and devices can be essentially anything that fits the bill technically—with no need to worry about the look of the item.

Often, a proscenium theater will be constructed with a small extension of the stage projecting through the proscenium into the house. This extension is referred to as the *apron*. Also in front of the proscenium is the *orchestra pit*, if the theater is so equipped (see Figure 2-4).

In some theaters, the stage floor is *trapped*. This means that sections of the floor can be removed, or opened, to allow movement between the stage and the space below the stage, the *trap room*. Mechanical devices such as elevators can be used to facilitate this movement.

Upstage of the proscenium, over the stage, is the *grid*. The grid is the structural support for the equipment and machinery

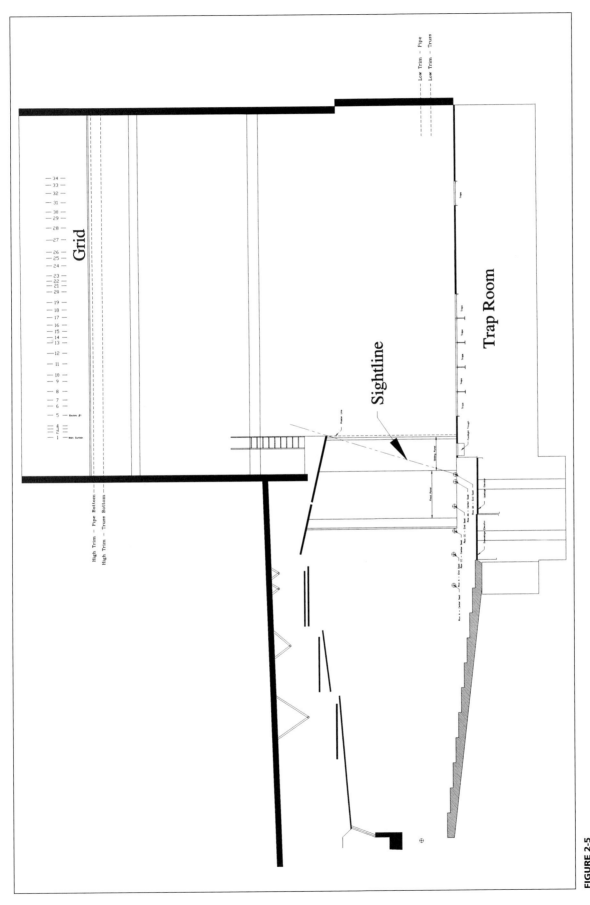

FIGURE 2-5
Center line section of a proscenium theater

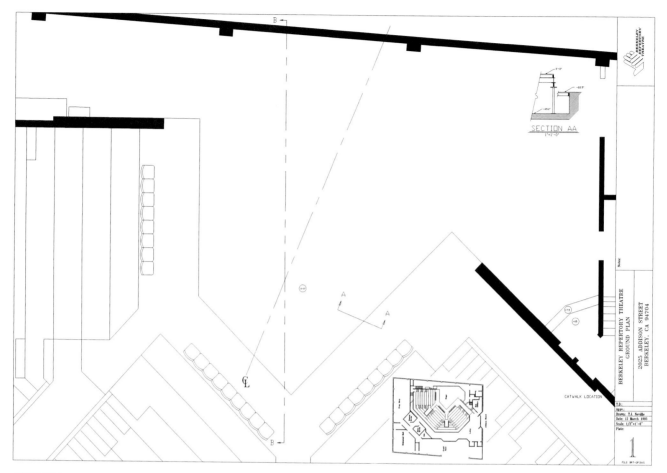

FIGURE 2-6

Ground plan of a thrust theater

used to hang or fly scenery, lights, and other design and technical elements of the production. The rigging used in association with the grid was originally adapted from the rigging used on ships to hoist and lower cargo and sails.

A variation of the proscenium stage is known as the *open stage*. In this form, the proscenium arch is obscured or eliminated, while the relationship between audience and actor is more or less the same.

Thrust

Around the middle of the twentieth century, theater artists began to search for a more intimate relationship between the actor and the audience. This search led to the reinvention or resurrection of two other physical configurations. The *thrust* theater is designed to break through the proscenium (or "fourth wall" as it is called), and "thrust" the actor out into the audience: No more imaginary wall or window to act

as a barrier between the actor and audience. The stage projects through the proscenium and provides the audience with a more intimate experience. Examine Figures 2-6 and 2-7. The ground plan shows the audience surrounding the playing space on three sides. From some perspectives, the audience acts as the backdrop for other members of the audience seated across the stage. The audience is now another part of the experience.

Note in the section of the thrust (Figure 2-7), the stage house still exists. In fact, the proscenium is still present, though visually neutralized. To the extent the scenic elements are positioned within the stage house, the design and construction techniques used in the proscenium form have applications in the thrust. However, the more extreme viewing angles of the audience require some adaptation, and items that are brought forward onto the thrust face two new requirements. First, they

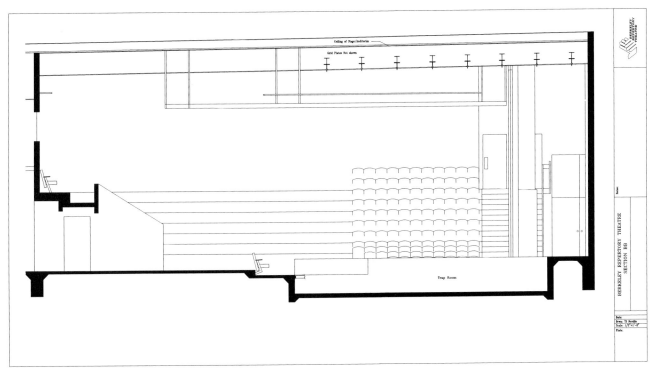

BERKELEY REPERTORY THEATRE
SECTION BB

Drwn: TJ Neville
Scale: 1/8"=1'-0"

must be three-dimensional, not only in form but also in finish. Second, the close proximity of the audience requires superior craftsmanship and construction techniques more in line with those used in residential construction trades.

Clearly the use of scenic items on the thrust stage is greatly curtailed as a result of the audience sightlines. It would not serve the play to create walls or other items that interfered with the audience's ability to see the production. This fact tends to focus the designer on prop items such as furniture, and scenic elements such as floors and perhaps ceiling structures, which establish character and add a sense of place to the set. Many thrust theaters also utilize a steeper pitch to the audience seating, thus emphasizing the stage floor as a background to the actors. Look again at Figure 2-7: Notice the angle of view for those seats near the rear of the house.

Arena

The desire to move toward an even more intimate relationship between the actor and the audience brought about the arena configuration. This form has the entire stage surrounded by the house. The proscenium is no longer present and the audience has a 360° view of the stage (see Figures 2-8 and 2-9, pages 26 and 27). As with the thrust configuration, scenery must accommodate the audience sightlines. Floors and overhead scenic elements are often the most significant traditional scenic items, while furniture and other dressing take on the lion's share of the task of setting the place and character of the action of the play.

Environmental

While the arena audience surrounds the stage, the stage surrounds the audience in the most contemporary concept, generically known as *environmental*. Theater artists continue to explore this concept, which places the audience into the environment of the play. Early examples of this concept endeavored to create settings within a theater with which the audience could interact. The usual theater seats were still available, but they were broken up into smaller groups and distributed around the theater. The performance space was also broken up and interwoven with the audience seating. In another

FIGURE 2-7
Center line section of a thrust theater

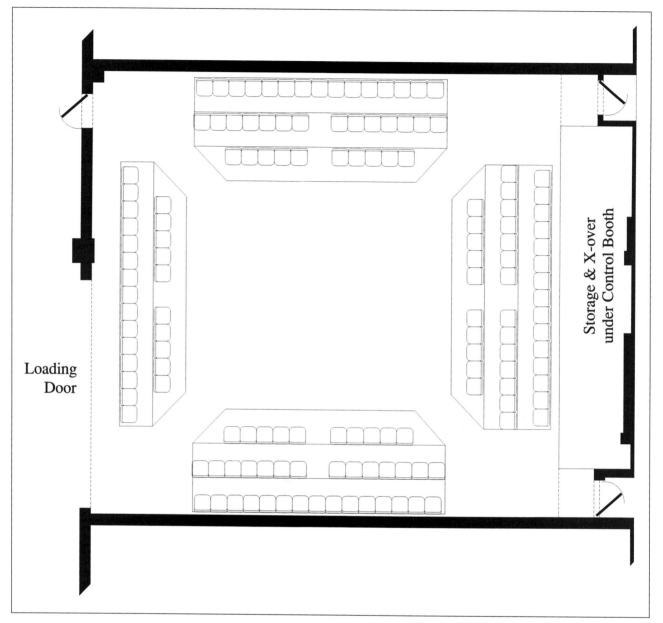

Loading
Door

Storage & X-over
under Control Booth

FIGURE 2-8
*Ground plan of
an arena theater*

example, some artists sought out nontraditional spaces, which they turned into theaters. These spaces are typically warehouses, factories or other open structures in which the performance space can be created.

The most recent manifestation of this approach has been the creation of theatrical events that invite the audience into the play as a guest to a gathering such as a wedding, funeral or dinner party. In one very popular example, the audience follows the character of their choice through the rooms of an Italian mansion—the kitchen, bedroom and parlor. The physical form of this theater can-

not be specifically defined; in fact, the majority of environmental productions do not take place in a traditional theater space but rather a space that can be made neutral, such as an airplane hanger, warehouse or armory, or a site-specific location such as a mansion, park, church or garage. The traditional separation of the actor's space from the audience's space is removed and the two are thrown together into the same space, blurring the lines between audience and actor, performer and voyeur. Often, seating is not available unless seating would normally be a part of the event being depicted.

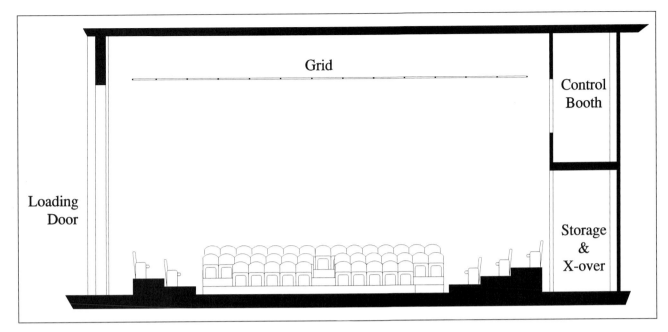

FIGURE 2-9
Center line section of an arena theater

THEATER EQUIPMENT

The equipment in a theater can vary widely from one facility to another. You will also find many variations of the basic equipment described here. In general, keep in mind the operating principles and you should be able to understand most of the equipment you encounter. However, before operating any equipment, be sure a qualified individual has briefed you on the system. I have found too many quirks in the systems I have encountered over the years to feel absolutely comfortable with an unfamiliar system.

Rigging Systems

Theater rigging is about as old as the theater itself. Its primary purpose is to fly or support scenery, or to create special effects. The *hemp system* is the oldest of the rigging systems still in use in today's theaters. While this system may have been replaced by more advanced and efficient systems, the basic principles, which have been adapted from the rigging used in sailing, still have significant value to the theater technician and should be thoroughly understood by anyone working with theatrical rigging of any sort.

In its simplest form, the hemp system is comprised of a natural fiber rope, typically ¾" manila (not hemp), which is attached to a scenic element onstage known as the *load* (see Figure 2-10, page 28). The rope then runs up to the theater's grid. It is necessary at this point for the rope to change direction toward offstage; this change of direction is accomplished by passing the rope around a pulley known as a *loft block* or *spot block*. The rope then continues offstage until it is over the location of the operator. It is then passed around another pulley known as the *head block* and down to the operator's position. At this location, a place to tie off the rope is required. This is usually the *pin rail*. With the system in place, a stagehand can pull on the rope and raise, or *fly*, the scenic item. When only one line is employed, it's called a *spot line*.

Larger scenic elements may require more than one line to ensure stability of the unit. In this case, a multiple-line hemp system can be used. The basic system is augmented with one or more additional ropes or lines. Each rope runs up from the load to its own loft block. The head block has multiple grooves or consists of a pulley, or sheave, for each of the lines. The ropes come down to the pin rail together. This multiple-line system is often used to rig *battens*. A batten is a pipe or wooden rail used to hang drops or other scenic

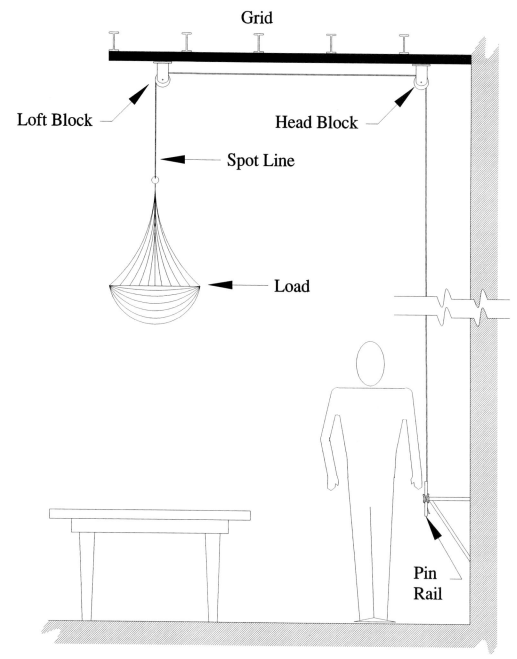

Grid

Loft Block

Head Block

Spot Line

Load

Pin
Rail

FIGURE 2-10
Typical arrangement for a hemp spot line

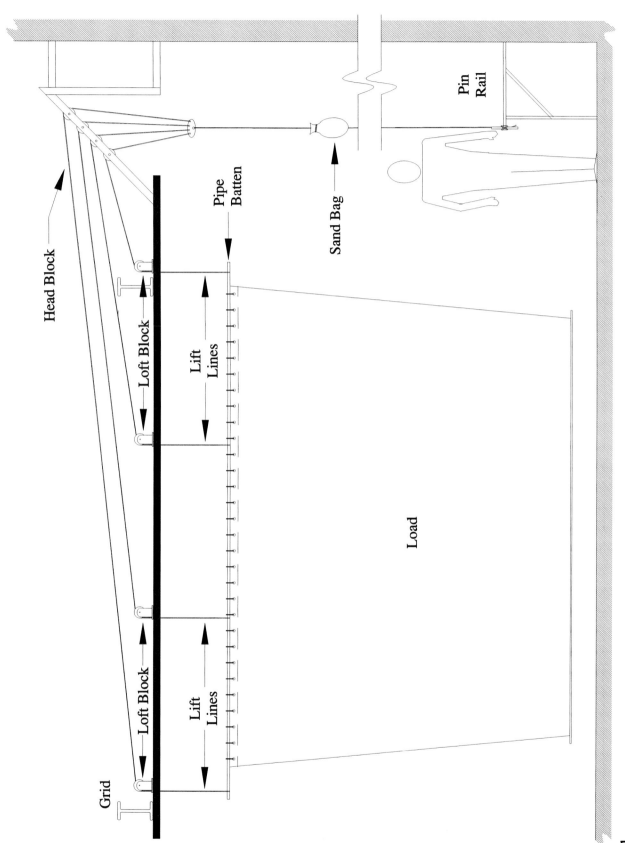

Head Block

Loft Block

Loft Block

Lift Lines

Lift Lines

Grid

Pipe Batten

Sand Bag

Pin Rail

Load

FIGURE 2-11
Multiline hemp & batten rigging system

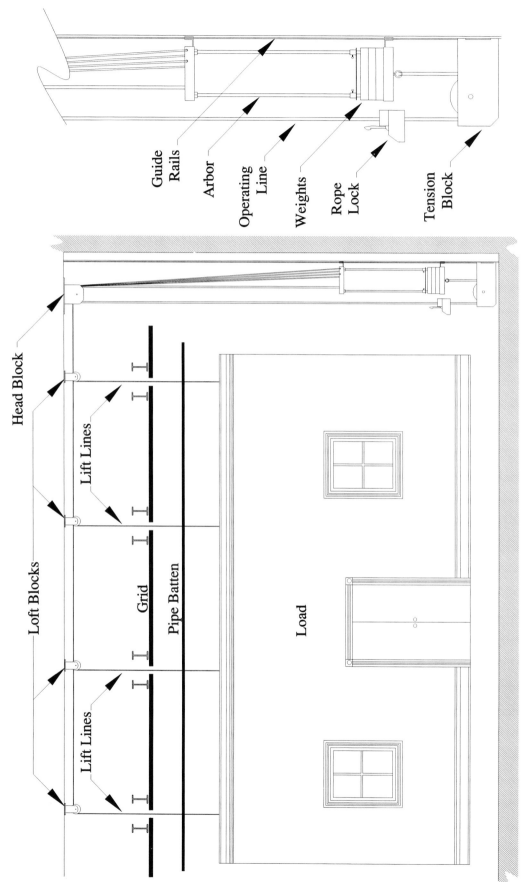

Guide Rails

Arbor

Operating Line

Weights

Rope Lock

Tension Block

Head Block

Lift Lines

Loft Blocks

Grid

Pipe Batten

Load

Lift Lines

FIGURE 2-12
Counterweight rigging system

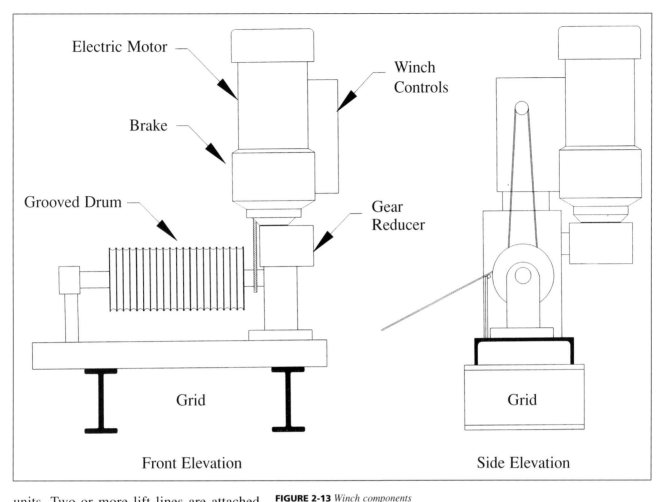

Electric Motor

Winch
Controls

Brake

Grooved Drum

Gear
Reducer

Grid

Grid

Front Elevation

Side Elevation

FIGURE 2-13 *Winch components*

units. Two or more lift lines are attached to the batten, as illustrated in Figure 2-11, on page 29.

When the weight of the load is more than a stagehand or two can comfortably lift, a sandbag is attached to the operating line, or hauling end of the rope, to counterbalance the load. This addition to the hemp system led to the development of the *counterweight system*. The modern counterweight system (Figure 2-12) uses wire rope instead of fiber rope for the lift lines, which are attached to a pipe batten onstage. After running through the loft blocks and a multigroove head block, the lifts lines terminate at an arbor that is designed to hold a stack of metal weights. These weights, the counterweights, are applied in sufficient numbers to equal the weight of the load being flown. Normally a theater stocks weights, often called *bricks*, in two or three different sizes. The maximum

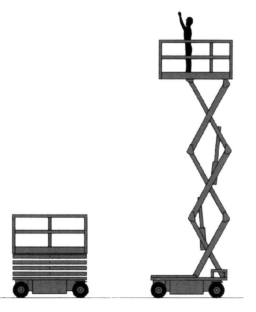

FIGURE 2-14 *A scissors lift*

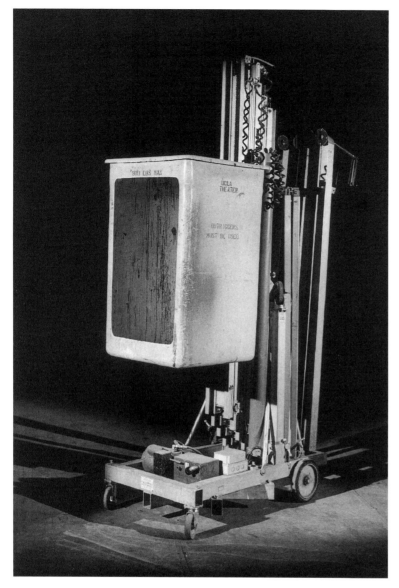

FIGURE 2-15
A personnel lift

cal rigging systems leads us to the current state of the art. The *motorized rigging system* has the capacity to eliminate the need to counterbalance the load and/or the need for strong stagehands. This evolution adds an electric winch the system in one of two predominant arrangements: The winch is either added into the counterweight system, providing the energy required to move the operating line, or it replaces the counterweight entirely, with a lifting capacity equal to or greater than the weight of the load.

The winch is comprised of several components, as illustrated in Figure 2-13, page 31. Fixed-speed winches operate at only one speed and are suitable for some theatrical applications where timing and positioning are not critical. A variable-speed winch is more versatile and can greatly enhance the level of production. With the addition of computer controls, the speeds and positions of several winches can be programmed and executed with the push of a few buttons.

Moving Floors
Another fairly common piece of theatrical equipment is the *elevator*. Simple mechanical versions have been in use for hundreds of years. Talented stage technicians have constructed elevators of one form or another to meet their specific production needs. Modern power elevators are often a part of the theater facility's permanent equipment. Typically, one or more elevators make up parts or all of the stage floor.

Through developments in other industries, a variety of self-contained and portable lift systems can be purchased or rented from some theatrical suppliers and most local construction equipment rental yards. These devices take many forms, such as the *scissors lift* illustrated in Figure 2-14, page 31, and the *personnel lift* in Figure 2-15, above left. However, these off-the-shelf systems may not afford you the level of control you may require for dramatic applications. Lifting capacity varies with the type and size of the unit, but a suitable

amount of weight is limited by the capacity of the system. The arbor's travel is guided by the use or wire rope guides or T-bar guide rails (the preferred option). A natural or synthetic (again, the preferred option) fiber *operating line* or *hand line* is attached to the top and bottom of the arbor, passing over the head block and under the tension block to form a continuous loop. The operating line also passes through a rope lock on the locking rail, which replaces the pin rail. Typically a theater will have a number of these counterweight sets permanently installed at intervals of six to twelve inches along a side wall of the stage.

The next step in the evolution of theatri-

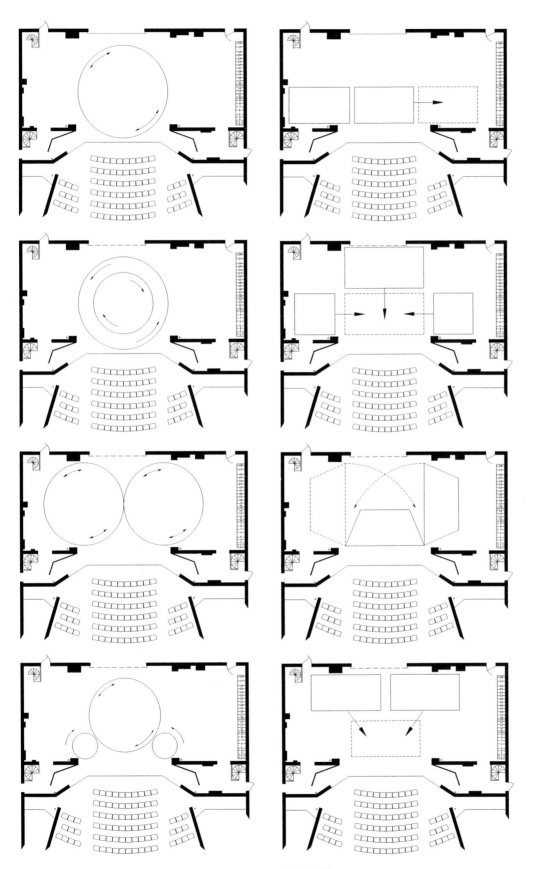

FIGURE 2-16
Common turntable configurations

FIGURE 2-17
Common wagon configurations

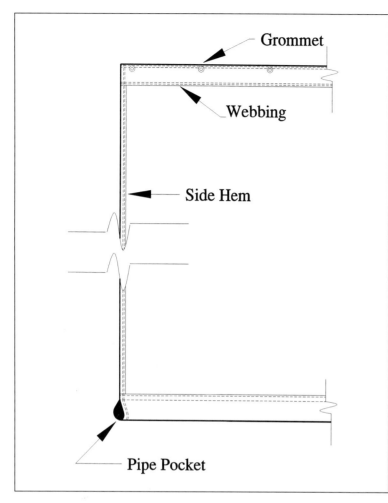

Grommet

Webbing

Side Hem

Pipe Pocket

FIGURE 2-18
A typical stock masking plan

sic form, a wagon is a platform on casters. More complex wagons can be designed and constructed to move in defined patterns, carry entire sets or glide onstage without the slightest indication as to how this happened. Figure 2-17, on page 33, illustrates some of the more common wagon configurations.

Masking

The term *masking* generally refers to an item used to block, or mask, the audience's view of the backstage space and equipment of the theater. Masking may be scenically representational or visually neutral to the audience.

Theaters commonly stock a set of neutral masking drapes comprised of three components, as illustrated in the stock masking plan in Figure 2-18. These three components are based on the wing-and-drop scenic conventions of the fifteenth century and are constructed like other two-dimensional scenic elements or as soft goods. *Legs*, like wings, are vertically oriented panels that can be constructed to any height or width to best suit the dimensions and standard use of the theater. *Borders* are horizontally oriented panels that are hung from overhead battens. The full-stage *drop* is often constructed as two panels that can be hung on a traveler track to open and close the drapes horizontally.

Black is the predominant color for masking drapes. The fabric of choice is velour, but other durable tight-weave fabrics can be (and are) used. All three components are typically constructed with webbing, grommets and ties along the top of the drape, with hemmed sides and a chain or pipe pocket at the bottom (see Figure 2-19).

Masking may also take the form of flats, as described in chapter six. The masking flats can be hard- or soft-covered as desired.

match can usually be found. Speed and positioning controls are not common in the local rental-yard variety. Take special care to thoroughly understand all safety and operating instructions and the working limits of these units.

Turntables are another device that may have been in use in the theater since the Greeks. The theatrical turntable is similar in function to turntables you may have seen in window displays or at car shows. They can be arranged in various configurations, as illustrated in Figure 2-16 on page 33. Their operation can also vary from manual to motorized and computer-controlled.

Wagons are very simple and versatile mechanisms, which, consequently, makes them very useful and common at every level of theater production. In its most ba-

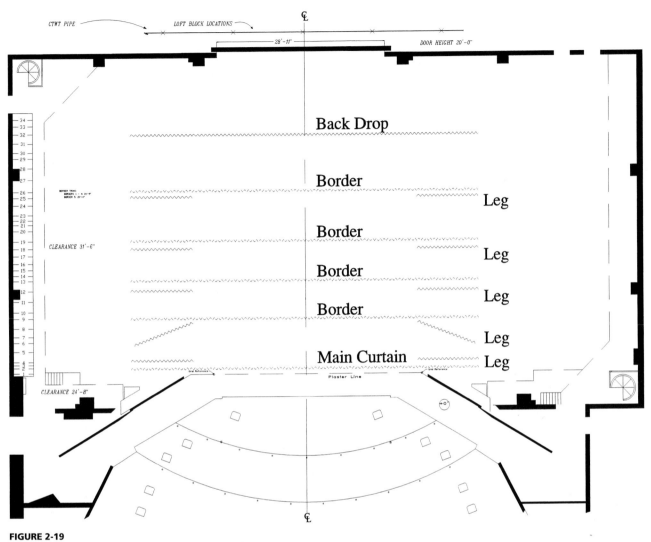

FIGURE 2-19
Standard masking construction for drops, legs and borders

CHAPTER 3

THE SCENE SHOP

FIGURE 3-1

The golden triangle representing the ultimate result of good construction techniques

Under ideal conditions, the scene shop should be organized and equipped to fabricate scenery with three objectives in mind. The shop should produce scenery of superior quality quickly and inexpensively. These objectives are commonly depicted along the three sides of a triangle as good, fast and cheap (Figure 3-1). The triangle is known as the "golden triangle" in the business, and the common adage is that the construction of scenery can meet any two of these characteristics, but all three are hard to come by. Certainly the craftspeople and their supervisors, who are responsible for the planning and construction of the scenery that comes into a shop, have a lot to do with meeting these objectives. However, this chapter will discuss some of the organizational and physical assets which may enhance the ability of a scene shop to have it all.

SHOP LAYOUT

The physical layout of the shop, including its dimensions and accessibility, is a significant factor in the shop's efficiency. Although modern scenery relies less and less on traditional flat construction, the basic construction pattern remains the same for scenery as it does for any other manufacturing process. Raw materials enter one end of the shop, and a finished set comes out the other. Along the way, a fairly typical sequence of procedures is implemented to transform wood, metal, fabric and other raw materials into a real-life version of the theatrical designer's vision.

This sequence begins with the technical planning and time and material estimates of the submitted designs. This is office work and requires the same tools and equipment as any business office. In addition to a drafting table (or two) and flat files or some other system for filing large drawings, the scene shop office should take advantage of the technology that has transformed the common office environment in the past few years. Computers, faxes and photocopiers have all found their way into modern scene shops; in fact, it is often hard to imagine how the work was done without these valuable tools. Communications have been made considerably more efficient as a result of fax machines, pagers, express mail, electronic mail, voice mail and the Internet. Material quotes and specifications are sent instantly by vendors via fax. Designers are paged for the answer that just can't wait. Revisions come by fax or overnight mail. Rehearsal reports and production-meeting notes are distributed by electronic mail. Blueprints are being replaced by photocopies as large-format photocopiers improve in quality. Computers are used not only to design and draft scenery, but also to provide material lists and cost estimates. Project scheduling is another task that can be expedited and controlled by computers. All of this is to say that the needs of a scene shop go beyond the tools and equipment used to convert construction materials into theatrical illusions. In laying out or designing and equipping a scene shop, do not overlook the needs of the shop office; this is a very important phase in the building process.

Once the designs have been approved for construction and the budget and schedule have been set, material acquisition is the next order of business. In terms of the shop layout, the storage of new materials

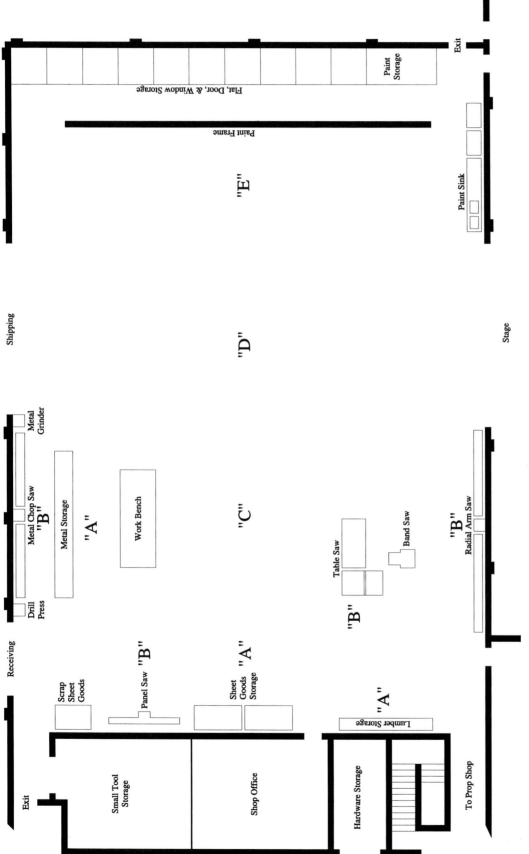

FIGURE 3-2
The scene shop of the UCLA School of Theater, Film and Television

is the first phase of the process on the shop floor. The raw materials storage facilities should have direct access from an exterior loading dock or receiving area (refer to the schematic in Figure 3-2, page 37, throughout this discussion). The area labeled *A* is the raw material storage area. New material should not have to cross the construction floor from receiving area to storage racks. Lumber is best stored flat. You will need sixteen feet to accommodate the standard length of stick or linear lumber. Sheet goods, such as plywood and Masonite, come in 4'-wide by 8'- or 10'-long panels. These materials are also best stored flat, but can be stored on edge if space does not permit. Steel, like board lumber, is stored flat and requires a 20'-long space to accommodate standard lengths.

The next step in the process is marking and cutting, or milling, of the raw material. The raw material storage area should feed directly into the area of the shop where the major power tools for crosscutting and ripping are located (area *B*). The radial arm saw, table saw and panel saw for wood, or the metal chop saw or horizontal band saw for steel, are typically the first tools used in the cutting process. These should be well-built stationary tools to enhance the quality of the work and extend the useful life of the tool. The size of this portion of the shop and the location of the stationary power tools should be such that the raw materials do not have to be turned or handled any more than is necessary as they come out of storage. A direct and unobstructed path to the tools should be the goal in laying out this portion of the shop.

Area *C* is for framing and fabrication of individual scenic elements. This space requires at least one large workbench or framing table (template table). The framing table should be large enough to accommodate the largest flats commonly built in the shop. A large table might be 6'-wide by 16'-long. A number of designs with varying features may be employed based on the individual preferences of the car-

penters using the table. The common feature among framing tables is a guide to establish a 90° corner when assembling flat frames.

The assembly of the individual scenic elements into larger set pieces is done in area *D*, which requires a sizable open floor space. In this area the pieces are fitted together, hardware is attached and finish detail is applied.

If space permits, the assembled set, or large portions of it, is moved to the paint area (*E*). This is the final stage of the construction process, where preparation for paint is handled and the final paint job is applied.

From here, the set is either moved onstage or shipped out to another location. The loading door to the theater should be very large to enable entire set units to roll into place onstage. Ideally, the orientation of the set in the paint area or trial setup area should be the same as its onstage position so the unit will not have to turn when loading it into the theater. The loading door to the exterior, for shipping, can be smaller since the set must break down to go into a truck.

The shop must accommodate storage facilities for tools, equipment, hardware and supplies. A number of other floor-standing power tools may be permanently located around the shop or mounted on casters for transportation to the place of use.

Stock Scenery Storage

This is a difficult concept to grapple with. Traditionally, when scenery was constructed primarily of flats, the reusability of these items was ensured. They required relatively little floor space and it made economic sense to keep them in stock. This is still the case in some theaters today. (This topic, along with recommendations for developing stock scenery, will be discussed in chapter eight.) As to storage, space is always at a premium in the scene shop. In a perfect world, the storage area for stock flats and three-dimensional weight-bearing units would be located adjacent to the assembly area of the shop. The presumption is that these pieces would enter the process having already gone through individual fabrication during their original construction.

TOOLS

Having the right tool for the job is one way to increase productivity and elevate the quality of the finished product. While a simple flat can be built with a few hand tools, there is an extensive array of tools available which can help achieve the objectives of the golden triangle. Useful tools for a scene shop fall into one of three categories: (1) stationary power tools, (2) portable power tools and (3) hand tools (nonpowered). The following section describes the most common tools in each category. However, this list is by no means exhaustive. New or improved tools come onto the market regularly and new techniques often spawn new tools. The diversity of portable power tools has greatly increased in recent years and continues to grow, particularly in the area of battery-powered or cordless tools. As with most things, the theater acquires tools that develop in other industries. Keep an eye out for new developments and maybe you will find something that works for you.

The ownership of tools is a question that requires some consideration as the shop is set up. Stationary power tools and most portable power tools should be the property of the scene shop in most circumstances. A professional shop employing professional carpenters would expect the carpenter to provide the majority of hand tools and even some frequently used portable power tools such as drills and screw guns. A college or university shop, or one that uses a number of volunteers, may need to stock necessary hand tools; the number of each item to be stocked is dependent on the normal contingent of volunteers or students.

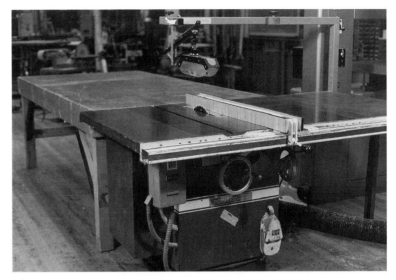

FIGURE 3-3
Table saw (blade guard removed for clarity)

Stationary Power Tools

There are at least five stationary power tools for working with wood that should be available in any reasonably equipped scene shop. The first four—the table saw, radial arm saw, panel saw and band saw—are all tools used for cutting. The fifth tool is a drill press. These tools add consistency, quality and speed to a shop's output, as well as enhance the safety of the work environment. The quality of these tools can vary widely, and often you get what you pay for. Purchase these tools for the long term; with proper maintenance they will last indefinitely. Quality tools will also produce better results. Look for stability and rigid construction. This will help maintain the long-term accuracy of the tool and ensure the tool will stand up to years of use. Also invest in tools that are sized and powered for your expected workload. You can find most of these tools in sizes that range from table models to behemoth mass-production models. The theater scene shop typically wants something in between. Home workshop models should usually be avoided in favor of industrial or professional versions.

Table Saw

The table saw has a circular blade mounted perpendicularly in a horizontal table. The saw blade can be adjusted as to height and

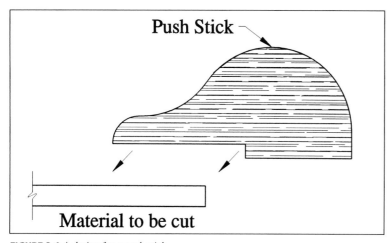

FIGURE 3-4 *A design for a push stick*

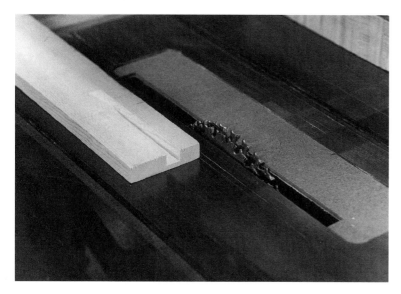

FIGURE 3-5
Dado blade mounted on a table saw and the resulting cut (blade guard removed for clarity)

angle in relation to the table. In general, set the height of the saw blade approximately ¼″ higher than the thickness of the material being cut. A rip fence, which acts as a guide for the material as it is pushed through the saw blade is mounted on the table. Cutting wood in the same direction as its grain is called *ripping*. A crosscut gauge is also available for cutting across the wood's grain. The gauge is guided by one of two grooves machined into the tabletop, and its angle in relation to the saw blade is adjustable from 90° to approximately 45°.

In operating a table saw, feed the material against the rotation of the saw blade. This eliminates the possibility that the saw will grab the wood away from the operator, pulling it into the blade under its own

power; enables the operator to better control the speed of the cut; and naturally holds the material down to the tabletop. This operation does produce a safety concern: The power of a table saw has the ability to kick back a piece of wood with enough force to seriously injure the operator—or a passerby. Never stand behind an operating table saw. As an operator, maintain a firm grip on the lumber at all times, and never force the material into the blade. This may cause the material to bind and will increase the likelihood of an accident. Always let the tool do the work; do not feed the material any faster then the saw can cut. A gentle, steady pace will generally provide excellent results. To avoid passing your hand too close to the blade, use a push stick like the one illustrated in Figure 3-4. The table saw should also be equipped with a safety cover for the saw blade. This device covers the blade and automatically rises to the height of the lumber as it is fed into the saw.

The table saw can use a variety of circular saw blades designed to cut with the grain or across the grain; combination blades are also available. The number of teeth per inch (tpi) determines the quality and speed of the cut. Generally, the more teeth per inch the finer the cut and the slower the feed rate. A carbide-tipped blade is more expensive but will hold its edge longer. A dado set can also be mounted on the table saw. This blade enables the saw to cut grooves wider than the normal blade width for dado joints (see Figure 3-5).

Radial Arm Saw (Crosscut Saw)
The radial arm saw is best suited for crosscutting, or cutting lumber to length. It employs a circular saw blade similar to the table saw blade, designed for crosscutting. The blade and motor are mounted on an arm that projects over the cutting surface. Ideally, this surface is extended 16′ to the left and right of the saw to accommodate a standard length of lumber. At the rear of

the cutting surface is a fence against which the material is positioned for cutting. The arm is set to provide a cut that is perpendicular to this fence. However, the arm can be adjusted to provide an angled cut, and the blade can be tilted for beveled cuts.

Unlike with the table saw, the material is held stationary on the radial arm saw table. The rotating blade is pulled along the arm and across the table to make the cut. The rotation of the blade presses the material against the fence. This also means that the blade can act like a wheel and drive across the material under its own power. Once again, the operator must be in control of the tool at all times. Do not let the saw move too quickly.

Many shops set up the fence of the radial arm saw so that it is calibrated in feet and inches. A *stop block* is attached to the fence at the desired length. This device allows for repetitive cuts of equal length to be executed without measuring each stick of lumber. The stop block clamps to the fence at the desired distance from the cutting edge of the saw. When the lumber is positioned against the fence and the stop block, the desired length is ensured.

Panel Saw

The panel saw is similar in concept to the radial arm saw but is sized to handle large panels of plywood or other sheet goods. The large saw table is turned up on edge just shy of vertical to conserve floor space. The saw blade and motor assembly are mounted on a rigid track that guides the saw over the width of the table. A crank is provided to drive the blade. A fence is mounted at the bottom of the saw table to support the sheet goods. Typically this saw is used only for 90° cuts. The panel saw uses the same type of circular saw blade as the table saw and radial arm saw. This saw is not absolutely necessary if the shop has a table saw. However, because the material is not moved during operation, it is much simpler and safer to use than a table saw when cutting sheet goods.

FIGURE 3-6 *Radial arm saw*

FIGURE 3-7 *Panel saw*

FIGURE 3-8 *Band saw*

FIGURE 3-9 *Drill press*

Band Saw

The three saws discussed above are all used to cut straight lines, whether ripping (with the grain), crosscutting (across the grain) or angled cutting. The band saw is designed to cut circles, arcs and other regular or irregular curves. The band saw uses a thin band of steel with saw teeth cut into one edge as its blade. The band is made into a continuous loop and mounted on two large wheels, one above the other. The saw blade is positioned vertically and passes through a table that can be angled to enable beveled cuts. The saw blade can be purchased in a variety of widths and tooth settings that will dictate the intricacies of the cut, among other things. The tighter the curve, the thinner the blade needs to be. The band saw can also be used for wood or metal, based on the type of blade. The *throat* of the band saw is the key to determining its capacity. The throat is the distance between the blade and the vertical support of the upper wheel.

Drill Press

The drill press cuts holes. The cutting tool is held vertically above the drill table. This cutting tool can take many forms, including twist drills, paddle bits and hole saws. The size of the hole is determined by the diameter of the cutting tool. The height and angle of the table are adjustable in relation to the cutting tool. When turned, a geared wheel drives the spinning cutting tool down through the material. The material is often clamped to the table in the desired position. The drill press can be used for cutting wood or metal, based on the type of cutting tool used and the speed at which the tool is turning.

Other Stationary Power Tools

A number of other tools in this category can greatly enhance the abilities of the scene shop. Many are designed for very specific milling functions required when higher quality work and finer detail are desired.

Belt/Disc Sander

The combination belt and disc sander provides two kinds of sanding surfaces. The disc portion of the tool is vertically mounted and adjacent to a small adjustable table that is positioned across the diameter of the disc; the table can be tilted up or down in relation to the disc. The sanding discs are self-adhesive and stick to the steel disc. They come in a variety of grits from fine to coarse, and are available for wood or metal work.

The belt portion of this tool is adjustable from horizontal to vertical. In the vertical position there is access to a small adjustable table to support the work. Sanding belts, like the sanding discs, can be purchased in varying degrees of coarseness.

Spindle Sander

A spindle sander uses various-diameter sanding drums to sand curved edges. The sanding drums are secured over the spindle, which projects up through the center of the work surface. The spindle oscillates up and down while rotating the sanding drum.

Lathe

A wood lathe is used to carve items such as furniture legs and railing spindles. The tool actually has no cutting blade of its own: It is designed to hold the material in the proper position and rotate or spin the material along its axis at the appropriate speed. Carving is achieved with various-size and -shape handheld gouges and chisels. These tools are held by the operator with the aid of an adjustable tool rest positioned alongside the spinning material.

Planer

A planer is used to mill the thickness of a piece of wood. From time to time, a project requires a thickness of wood that is not available as a stock item from the lumberyard. This tool makes it possible to plane the surface of the material to the desired thickness. It has a long cutting blade

FIGURE 3-10 *Belt/disc sander*

FIGURE 3-11 *Spindle sander*

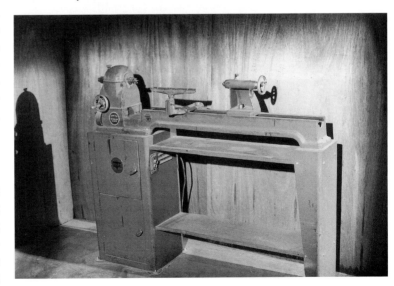

FIGURE 3-12 *Lathe*

FIGURE 3-13
Portable tabletop planer

FIGURE 3-14
Power miter box (blade guard raised for clarity)

mounted above the bed of the tool. The height of the blade is adjustable. This tool is self-feeding, so the operator's hands do not come into the cutting area of the tool.

Power Miter Box

This tool is designed to cut precise angles. It uses a circular saw blade mounted on a pivot behind the fence and over the bed of the saw. The motor and blade assembly can be rotated in relation to the fence to achieve the desired angle. The blade assembly is pivoted down to make the cut. Its compact size also makes it useful as a portable crosscut saw. A similar tool, known as a combination saw, also allows the blade to be tilted in relation to the bed. Compound miters can be made with this feature.

Shaper (Table Router)

A shaper is one of the most interesting tools in the shop. It is used to cut detailed contours into the face or edge of a piece of lumber, generally for moulding details. This tool has various-shape knives that can be used individually or together to cut the desired profile. The knives are stacked vertically on a rotating spindle that projects from the center of the shaper table. The height of the spindle is adjustable. A fence that has a cutout to accommodate the knife blades is used as a guide for the material. The material is fed against the rotation of the cutting knives.

An inexpensive substitute for a shaper uses a router mounted upside down to the bottom of a table with the bit projecting up through a hole in the center of the table. The capacity and shape are limited to the available router bits, but this can be a very useful alternative to the more expensive shaper.

Portable Power Tools

The most significant advances in tools of use to a theatrical scene shop have come along in this category. There seems to be a portable power-tool version of almost every stationary power tool or hand tool in existence. Traditionally, the majority of portable power tools are electric powered. Pneumatic (air-powered) tools have also been adopted by larger scene shops. The most recent development has been cordless tools, which are battery powered. Improvements in battery technology and the somewhat nomadic construction process of the theater have made these tools a good fit and a significant part of the inventory of a modern scene shop.

Drills

Electric hand drills are probably the most common portable power tool around. The most useful model for the scene shop is a ⅜″, variable-speed reversible drill. This tool meets most of the needs for drilling and can use the same types of cutting tools as the stationary drill press. It can also be used to drive screws when a screwdriver bit is used in place of a drill bit. A Phillips-head screw is typically used under these conditions. Cordless versions of this drill are very handy and very popular among scene technicians. They can be purchased with an extra battery and a charger to ensure continuous use throughout the workday. One battery can recharge while the other is being used in the tool. Most professional scenic carpenters own their own cordless drill. A ½″ electric drill is a useful addition for portable heavy-duty drilling.

Nailers/Staplers

A wide variety of powered nailers and staplers are available and applicable for use in scenery construction. Pneumatic tools are the most desirable for medium- to heavy-duty use. Electric staplers are usable for light-duty fabric applications.

Pneumatic tools are designed to drive either wire staples or nails. Staples come in varying widths and lengths, and should be chosen based on the required application. Pneumatic nailers are designed for driving almost any size nail, from brads to 3″-long common nails. Some special nail-

FIGURE 3-15 *Shaper*

ers are available for driving corrugated fasteners and other, more exotic, fasteners.

Saws

Power handsaws come in two general types and, with a couple of exceptions, are commonly powered by electricity. Circular saws come with blades ranging in size from four to eight inches. The blades are smaller versions of those used in a table saw or radial arm saw. Larger blades (up to sixteen inches in diameter) are available, but they are not very practical in most circumstances. A cordless version with a 3″ blade is available and can come in handy from time to time, but this tool is a bit of a luxury.

The other type of power handsaw has a

FIGURE 3-16
Portable drills from left—½″ electric drill, ⅜″ electric drill with Phillips head screw driver bit, battery powered cordless drill with Phillips head screw driver bit and charger assembly

FIGURE 3-17A *Pneumatic nailer*

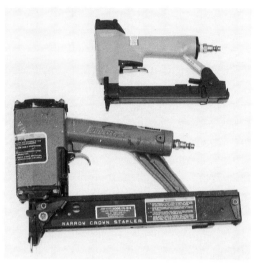

FIGURE 3-17B *Pneumatic staplers*

FIGURE 3-18A
Cordless 3" circular saw and 7¼" worm drive circular saw

FIGURE 3-18B
Reciprocating saws clockwise from top—electric tiger saw, electric jig saw, pneumatic jig saw

reciprocating blade. In this type, the blade moves up and down or in and out, depending on how you look at it. The most common form is a jigsaw. A wide variety of blades are available based on the type of material, including metal, and the quality of the cut. It is well suited for cutting irregular shapes and fine scrollwork. Electric and pneumatic models are common, and both work well.

A larger version of the reciprocating saw is known as the *tiger saw*, or simply as a reciprocating saw. This is a more powerful saw than the jigsaw, with a longer and wider blade for coarse cutting.

Grinders and Sanders

Grinders, generally used on metal, use an abrasive grinding wheel, or a grinding disc similar to sanding discs, which is available in varying grits. Electric models are most common, but pneumatic versions are available. The grinders and associated abrasive wheels or grinding discs are available in sizes from three to nine inches. The same tool can be used as a disc sander for wood when the appropriate sanding disc is mounted.

Belt sanders use a sanding belt three or four inches wide with a working length of about one foot, and are used primarily with wood.

Random orbit sanders (finish sanders or

FIGURE 3-19
Sanders clockwise from top—pneumatic disc sander, orbital sander, belt sander

FIGURE 3-20 *½" router*

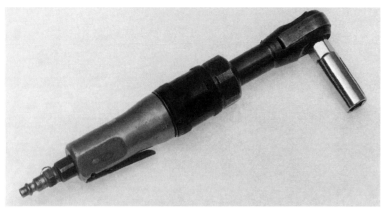

FIGURE 3-21
Pneumatic wrench

FIGURE 3-22
Power hand-held planer

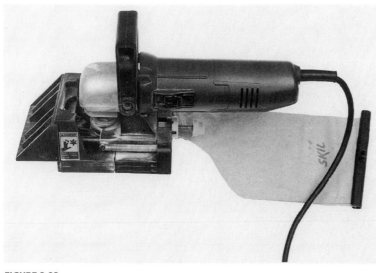

FIGURE 3-23
Biscuit cutter

palm sanders, as they are sometimes called) are used for final sanding. These tools are designed to operate in a manner that ensures a smooth surface free of any patterns left by the sanding process.

Routers

A router is a handheld version of the shaper. It comes in a few different sizes, and a large assortment of router bits are available. One of the most useful applications for a router employs a trim bit to trim the hard covering of a flat or platform back to its frame. Other bits are designed to cut edge details and moulding profiles.

Wrenches

Pneumatic wrenches are useful and time-saving tools for bolt installation or disassembly. They have interchangeable socket heads to fit the size bolt being used.

Power Planer

This is a handheld, power version of a hand plane. It is used most often to plane the edge of a piece of lumber.

Biscuit Cutter/Plate Joiner

This unique tool is designed to make very strong and invisible joints. The tool actually allows the operator to position and cut a pair of matching slots into the two pieces of wood to be joined. The appropriate size biscuit or plate is glued and inserted into the slots and the pieces are clamped together until dry. The resulting joint is very strong without the use of mending plates or metal fasteners.

Hand Tools

The following hand tools are recommended as a basic inventory for this category. In commercial or professional situations, the majority of these tools are owned by the individual carpenters working in the shop. In community theater and educational environments, these tools are supplied by the shop. As with power tools, the quality of hand tools varies. Again, look for tools that are well made and that are made for the kind of use you anticipate.

Measuring Tools

FIGURE 3-24 TAPE MEASURES
Retractable, locking, steel blade in lengths from six to over thirty feet.

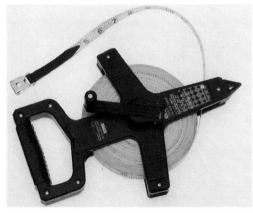

FIGURE 3-25 100-FOOT TAPE MEASURE
Long tape measure that comes in handy for positioning a set onstage, as well as for hanging and trimming scenery and masking. This tape should be made of cloth instead of steel so it will not break when someone steps on it.

FIGURE 3-26 COMBINATION SQUARE
Used for marking 45° and 90° angles.

FIGURE 3-27 FRAMING SQUARE
Used to mark and set 90° angles and to set the rise and tread of a stair carriage.

FIGURE 3-28 BEVEL GAUGE
Adjustable tool to check or copy angles. Useful in transferring an existing angle to a tool or new material.

FIGURE 3-29 LEVELS
Levels come in a variety of forms and are used to check for true horizontal or vertical position. The most useful form is a carpenter's level, which comes in 2' to 8' lengths. A line level clips on to a string for longer distances. A spirit level is a rather small version of a carpenter's level.

Measuring Tools CONTINUED

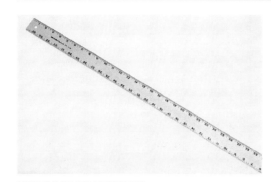

FIGURE 3-30 STRAIGHTEDGE
A long metal ruler, usually five or six feet in length, used most frequently for layout.

FIGURE 3-31 COMPASS
A tool that scribes circles.

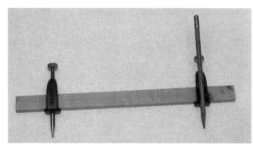

FIGURE 3-32 TRAMMEL POINTS
When used with a long piece of wood or metal, these devices form the working ends of a large compass.

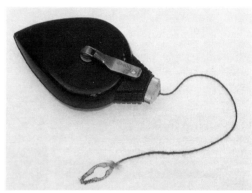

FIGURE 3-33 CHALK LINE (SNAP LINE)
An enclosed reel of string that is coated with powdered chalk. The chalk line is used to mark a straight line that is longer than your straightedge. The chalk line is stretched taut between two points and then pulled and released at the center, causing the line to snap back into position, depositing a line of chalk.

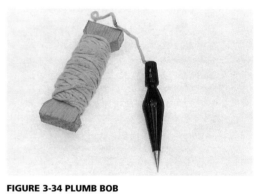

FIGURE 3-34 PLUMB BOB
A weighted piece of string used to establish a true vertical line or to transfer points vertically.

Cutting Tools

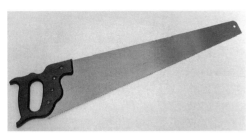

FIGURE 3-35 HANDSAW
Handsaws are designed for either ripping or crosscutting.

FIGURE 3-36 COMPASS OR KEYHOLE SAW
These saws have a short, tapered blade and are designed for cutting cricles and arcs, or cutting in tight places. The keyhole saw is smaller than the compass saw for use in cutting tighter curves.

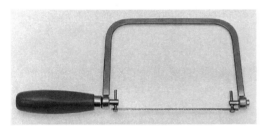

FIGURE 3-37 COPING SAW
This saw is designed for cutting irregular shapes. A very thin blade similar to a short section of a band saw blade is utilized.

FIGURE 3-38 HACKSAW
The hacksaw is a metal-cutting saw with a blade that looks like a one-foot section of a band saw blade.

FIGURE 3-39 BACKSAW
The backsaw is a fine-toothed crosscut saw with a stiffened back. A miter box is used as a guide for the saw when cutting angles or miters.

FIGURE 3-40 BOLT CUTTER
Scissors-like tool used to cut bolts or other small-dimension metal bar stock. Bolt cutters come in a variety of sizes, and are not to be confused with wire-rope cutters.

Cutting Tools CONTINUED

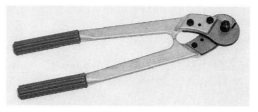

FIGURE 3-41 WIRE-ROPE CUTTER
This tool looks like a bolt cutter, but the cutting jaws are designed very differently to cleanly cut wire rope. Cutters come in a variety of sizes.

FIGURE 3-42 TIN SHEARS
Scissors used to cut thin sheet metal.

FIGURE 3-43 SCISSORS
Always handy to have around, fabric shears should not be used for cutting other materials

FIGURE 3-44 UTILITY KNIFE
This is a razor blade in a holder. Some are designed to be retractable, which is safer and increases the life of the blade. Utility knives are used for trimming muslin or canvas.

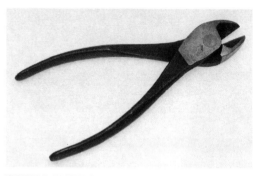

FIGURE 3-45 SIDE CUTTER
Used for cutting wire.

FIGURE 3-46 PIPE CUTTER
This tool clamps to the pipe and is rotated around the pipe while the pressure of the cutting wheel is increased until it cuts through the pipe.

Drilling Tools

Hand drills have been made virtually obsolete by electric and cordless power drills, but they are still available.

Planing Tools

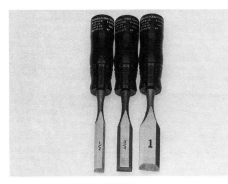

FIGURE 3-47 WOOD CHISELS
Hand carving tools with blades ranging from ¼" to as much as 3" wide. The wood chisel should be struck with a mallet, not a hammer.

FIGURE 3-48 COLD CHISEL
A chisel made for metalwork, available in limited sizes.

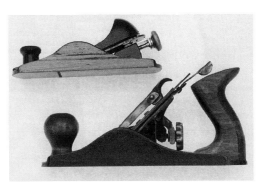

FIGURE 3-49 PLANE
These tools come in various shapes and sizes, depending on the job at hand. The small block plane is used for working the end grain or other narrow surfaces; the smooth plane is designed for larger surfaces. These tools require a fair amount of skill and patience, and are not often used in scenery construction—especially if modern sanders and other power tools are available.

FIGURE 3-50 RASPS AND FILES
These tools come in varying shapes, sizes and levels of coarseness. They are available for wood or metal.

Driving Tools

FIGURE 3-51 HAMMERS
Available in different weights and with either a curved or straight claw. The curved claw is well suited for pulling nails; the straight claw does not have quite the leverage of the curved claw, but is better at prying pieces of lumber apart.

FIGURE 3-52 BALL PEEN HAMMER
Used in metalwork; the ball end is used to form metal.

FIGURE 3-53 TACK HAMMER
Used to drive upholstery tacks.

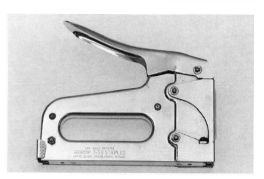

FIGURE 3-54 HAND STAPLER
A manual version of the pneumatic or electric stapler for upholstery and other fabric applications.

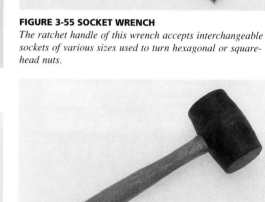

FIGURE 3-55 SOCKET WRENCH
The ratchet handle of this wrench accepts interchangeable sockets of various sizes used to turn hexagonal or square-head nuts.

FIGURE 3-56 MALLET
Mallets are available in a variety of shapes, sizes and materials. Rubber-head mallets are useful for protecting the surface of the object being struck. Some mallets are designed specifically to strike carving tools such as chisels.

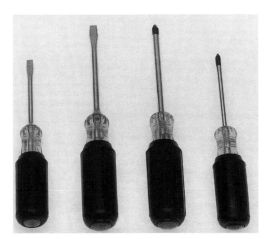

FIGURE 3-57 SCREWDRIVERS
A variety of sizes should be stocked in straight-slot and Phillips-head models.

FIGURE 3-59 ALLEN WRENCHES
Also known as hex keys, these are designed to turn Allen screws or bolts and are available in a range of sizes.

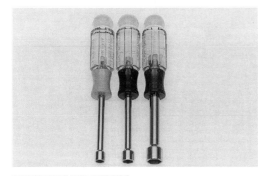

FIGURE 3-58 NUT DRIVERS
Similar in form to screwdrivers, but designed to turn a hex-head nut, these tools come in a range of sizes.

Gripping Tools

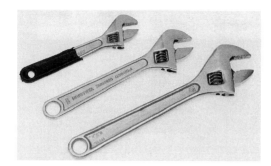

FIGURE 3-60 CRESCENT WRENCHES
An adjustable wrench for turning or holding nuts and bolts.

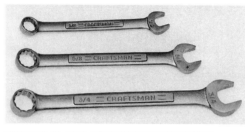

FIGURE 3-61 BOX- AND OPEN-END WRENCHES
Fixed-size wrenches for turning or holding nuts and bolts. They come in a variety of sizes.

FIGURE 3-62 VISE GRIPS
Adjustable, spring-loaded gripping tool; jaws are available in several different styles.

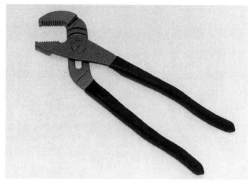

FIGURE 3-63 CHANNEL LOCKS
Adjustable gripping tool for nuts, bolts, small pipe fittings, etc.

FIGURE 3-64 PLIERS
Available in many forms, such as slip-joint, needle-nose, electrician's and side-cutting.

FIGURE 3-65 PIPE WRENCH
Large adjustable wrench designed to grip pipe.

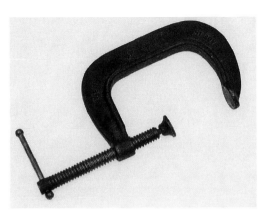

FIGURE 3-66 C-CLAMP
These clamps get their name from their shape. They come in a range of sizes.

FIGURE 3-68 VISE
Table-mounted device used for holding objects in place. Wood and metal versions are available, as well as a vise designed specifically for pipe.

FIGURE 3-67 BAR AND PIPE CLAMP
Holding pads are mounted on a long steel bar or pipe.

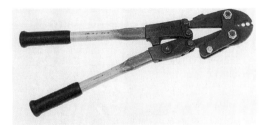

FIGURE 3-69 NICOPRESS TOOL
This tool is specially designed to crimp nicopress sleeves around wire rope. The crimping jaw is either designed for a specific size sleeve or has multiple crimping positions for small-diameter wire rope. A separate gauge is available to ensure the tool is compressing the sleeve to the proper dimension.

FIGURE 3-70 *Horizontal band saw*

FIGURE 3-71 *Chop saw*

Metalwork Tools

Steel construction is a significant element of modern scenic construction and its use requires some special tools and techniques. Some of the cutting, drilling and grinding tools described earlier can be used with blades, bits and abrasives designed for steel; however, there are a few additional tools that will make working with steel much easier and more efficient.

Horizontal Band Saw

This version of a band saw uses a blade, designed for cutting steel, which is mounted horizontally over a bed that includes a vise for holding the material in place. The cutting process is aided by a continuous flow of a lubricating cutting fluid directed to the cutting portion of the blade. Unlike the wood band saw, which is designed for cutting irregular shapes and curves, the horizontal band saw is the metal-cutting version of a radial arm saw. It is used to cut structural steel and pipe to length. An angled cut is also possible with this tool.

Chop Saw/Cutoff Saw

This tool uses the edge of an abrasive disc to cut material to length. It is equipped with a pump to lubricate the material during cutting.

Power Hacksaw

This is a power hand tool designed to cut metal. It uses a band saw-type blade and is commonly known as a portaband.

Grinders

Grinders are available in a variety of styles and configurations and are usable for woodwork or metalwork, as discussed earlier. Belt, disc and wheel versions all have their uses. If you plan to do a considerable amount of metalwork, stationary and portable metal working grinders should be dedicated for this purpose and separate from woodworking models.

Welding

The joining of metal is principally accomplished by the process known as *welding*. A number of machines are available for this process.

Gas Welding

Gas welding uses oxygen and acetylene gases mixed together in a welding torch to form a controllable flame. The flame is used to heat the joint of the components being welded and the filler rod, which supplies the metal for filling the bevels in the joint. The filler rods come 36″ long and range in diameter from ⅟₁₆″ to ⅜″. The alloy of the filler rod must match the alloy of the metal being welded.

Appropriate protective equipment, including welding goggles and gloves, is required during this process.

Arc Welding

Arc welding employs an electrical arc as the heat source for the welding process. The negative connecting cable, which terminates in a clamp, is attached to the work. The positive cable terminates in a hand grip with a clamp to hold the electrode or welding rod. The welding rod is formed of steel coated with the appropriate flux. When the arc is struck, the generated heat melts the material along the joint and deposits melted steel from the welding rod into the joint, forming the bond. The voltage is adjustable, based on the heat required to melt material of varying thicknesses.

Protective clothing and equipment are crucial to the safety of this process. A welding mask, along with gloves and clothing that covers all exposed skin, must be worn as protection from the ultraviolet light emitted by the welding process.

MIG

The MIG (metal inert gas) system is an improvement over the basic arc welder. A MIG welder uses a spool of wire in place of welding rods. The wire is automatically

FIGURE 3-72
Power hacksaw or Porta-band

FIGURE 3-73
Grinders—4″ grinder with grinding disc and 9″ grinder with wire brush

FIGURE 3-74 *Oxyacetylene torch*

FIGURE 3-75 *Arc welder*

FIGURE 3-76 *Mig welder*

fed through the tip of the welding gun, which also supplies an inert gas to the area of the weld during operation. The regulated atmosphere created by the infusion of gas during the welding process makes for a cleaner weld. The preferred choice for the gas when welding steel is a 75 percent argon and 25 percent CO_2 mixture. Straight CO_2 can be used, but the argon mixture produces a better weld. As with an arc welder, the voltage can be regulated to adjust to the thickness of the material. The speed of the wire feed must also be adjusted to ensure the proper amount of filler material is being supplied.

TIG

A TIG welder is in principle the same as the MIG welder; the difference lies in the use of tungsten as the inert gas.

MIG and TIG welders require personal safety equipment and clothing. Be sure the welding shield in the welding mask meets the needs of your particular use.

SHOP SAFETY

Avoiding accidents and injuries and establishing a safe working environment is a combination of knowledge, well-established and meaningful safety practices, proper equipment and the ability to recognize inherent safety hazards. Knowledge is the most significant preventive measure against accidents: *Never work beyond your capabilities.* A complete knowledge about the process and techniques required to complete the project you are undertaking, including the operation of the tools and equipment you will be using and the potential hazards you will encounter, is essential. This is not to say that you should never do anything you have not done before, but you must prepare yourself for the task. Learn how to use tools you are unfamiliar with and practice new construction techniques under controlled conditions before you feel the pressure to complete the job.

The first step in any encounter with a tool is to read the manufacturer's installation, operation, maintenance and cautionary instructions. This material will provide important information on the capabilities of the tool, its operational and safety features, and any health and safety hazards present as a result of its use. Understand what work the tool or equipment is designed to accomplish. Follow all maintenance recommendations to ensure the tool is functioning as designed. Replace defective parts immediately. Never disengage a tool's safety features. Limiters, blade guards and emergency stop switches are designed to prevent injuries. Misuse and abuse of tools is a significant cause of injuries. When you fully understand the ins and outs of a tool, test yourself and the tool under controlled conditions.

One note about safety features on some tools. You may from time to time encounter a blade guard or some other safety feature that impedes the safe operation of a tool rather than enhances it. If this is actually the case, and not a matter of your personal preference, do not disengage the safety feature. The tool has a design flaw and should be replaced or passed over for a better designed tool. Safety is a principal consideration in purchasing any tool.

All of this may sound like it pertains only to power tools, and focusing on these tools is justified in light of the serious injuries they can cause, but nonpower tools should also be treated with respect and caution. A screwdriver is not a pry bar, a wrench is not a hammer, and a utility knife is not a dart—yet people are all too often guilty of this kind of abuse.

Safety Rules and Procedures

Each shop should establish its own set of safety rules and procedures developed expressly to address the specific working conditions of that shop. This text cannot begin to cover all of the safety considerations that may arise. However, there are a few general practices which should be considered in every situation.

It should be policy to orient every worker to the safety rules and procedures of the shop. As part of this orientation, each technician should be certified to operate the tools and equipment she is expected to use in the shop. As stated earlier, all technicians should be required to use blade guards and other safety features where present. No one should be permitted or encouraged to operate any equipment that is unfamiliar to them. Along with this certification procedure, tool maintenance policies and procedures should be expressed.

Work clothes should be considered for their impact on the safety of the shop, and guidelines set out for all workers. In general, no loose garments or hair should be allowed. Proper footwear for the work conditions should be required at all times. Personal safety equipment such as safety glasses, goggles or full-face shields, dust masks or respirators, ear protection and gloves as required should be mandatory and, in some cases, supplied by the shop.

Everyone in the shop should be cautioned against conduct that may cause distractions. Unusual movements such as running or loud noises can distract a technician long enough to cause a problem. Never speak to anyone who is operating a tool or engaged in work. Wait for people to complete their tasks before you approach them.

Emergency information and procedures should be explained to each worker and posted in appropriate locations in the shop. This should include telephone numbers for the fire department, ambulance service, hospital emergency room, police department and poison control center. Evacuation plans and exit maps should also be a part of the orientation. If possible, it is a good idea to provide basic training in emergency first aid and the use of the first aid equipment and supplies the shop stocks.

A clean, well-organized shop is also an aid to safety. Develop shop policies that promote and encourage workers to maintain the shop in an orderly condition. A part of this policy must be proper material disposal. Follow all local ordinances for the disposal of hazardous materials. For all other materials, consider the environmental impact of the waste. Follow or develop waste disposal programs that minimize any negative impact on the environment. Proper waste disposal begins with the acquisition of materials. Use nontoxic and recyclable materials whenever possible.

The Shop Environment

Adequate lighting should be available at all times. Lighting standards have been established for most industries, and meeting these standards not only enhances the safety of the shop, but also its quality and efficiency. These lighting standards are often overlooked when the work shifts from the shop to the stage. Too often carpenters find themselves working in the subdued light of an inadequately illuminated stage—or in the dark while electricians are focusing lights. Make arrangements to provide sufficient light whenever the carpenters are working onstage.

All known and potential hazards should be identified and clearly marked. This includes moving machine parts, hazardous material storage areas and containers, demarcation around operational areas of certain tools, cautionary signage for physical hazards such as overhead work, and posting of load ratings or capacities. Safety equipment and supplies, including first aid kits and fire extinguishers, should also be well marked.

STAFF ORGANIZATION

The staffing and organization of scene shop personnel depends on the type of shop or parent organization being discussed. The first distinction pertains to the shop's status as a commercial (for profit) venture or a nonprofit (not-for-profit) organization. A commercial shop is in business to generate a profit for its owners or is part of a larger organization that is looking to turn a profit. Nonprofit status typically describes a larger (or parent) organization of which the scene shop is a component. Examples of such organizations would include professional nonprofit companies found in many of the nation's larger cities, university theater programs and community theater groups. While nonprofit organizations are not prohibited from making a profit, the primary purpose of the organization is something other than making money.

Commercial Shops

The organizational structure of a commercial shop is defined largely by the fact that business conditions can and do change. The amount of work coming into the shop may be affected by the general state of the economy, seasonal variations in demand for scenic services from producers, and competition from other shops. Under these conditions, a considerable amount of flexibility to adjust personnel to meet current demands is desirable. The chart in Figure

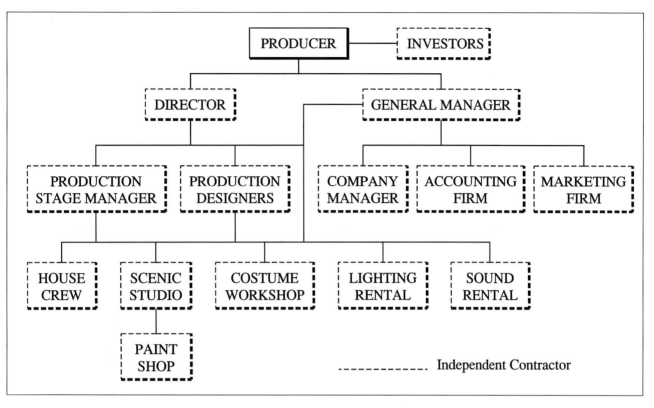

PRODUCER — INVESTORS

DIRECTOR   GENERAL MANAGER

PRODUCTION STAGE MANAGER   PRODUCTION DESIGNERS   COMPANY MANAGER   ACCOUNTING FIRM   MARKETING FIRM

HOUSE CREW   SCENIC STUDIO   COSTUME WORKSHOP   LIGHTING RENTAL   SOUND RENTAL

PAINT SHOP   ------------ Independent Contractor

FIGURE 3-77
A general organizational chart for a commercial theater

3-77 represents the organizational structure of a commercial theater-producing entity. In this structure, scenic services and the other entities responsible for furnishing the physical elements of the production are separate and distinct businesses. They exist independent of any one producing organization and typically must enter into working relationships with several producers in order to sustain a viable business.

To achieve the flexibility required to meet the demands of a fluid business climate, permanent staffing in a commercial shop focuses on management, personnel who develop business and generate construction bids, key craftspeople or technicians who might provide the shop with a competitive edge because of their particular skills and experience, and staff for general business functions. In very small shops, as few as one or two people must fulfill all these functions; in large operations, there may be two or more people in each of these areas. The basic effort in a commercial shop is to keep the overhead costs at a minimum. Permanent staff repre-sents a significant portion of these overhead costs. The chart in Figure 3-78, page 64, represents the organizational structure of an independent commercial scene shop. Note that the majority of the technicians are not full-time permanent employees of the scene shop, but temporary employees hired based on the quantity of work or the specific skills required by the project.

There are some commercial shops that exist as part of a larger organization such as a film or television studio. In the short term, these shops are somewhat isolated from the economic forces of business, but over time they too will have to justify their costs and illustrate their benefit to the company.

Nonprofit Shops

The organizational structures of scene shops that are part of a nonprofit organization come in many shapes and sizes. At the community level, the entire shop may be staffed by volunteers. The university scene shop, or a shop associated with an educational program, is typically a mixture of

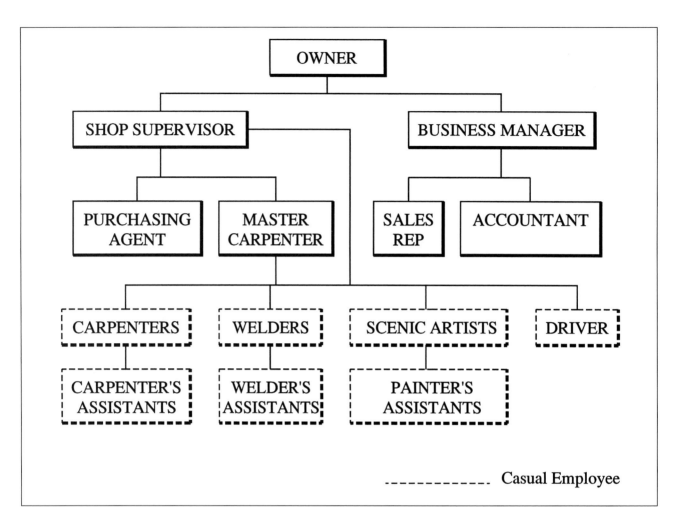

OWNER

SHOP SUPERVISOR

BUSINESS MANAGER

PURCHASING AGENT

MASTER CARPENTER

SALES REP

ACCOUNTANT

CARPENTERS

WELDERS

SCENIC ARTISTS

DRIVER

CARPENTER'S ASSISTANTS

WELDER'S ASSISTANTS

PAINTER'S ASSISTANTS

------------- Casual Employee

FIGURE 3-78
A general organizational chart for a independent commercial shop

professionals and students. Some nonprofit professional companies, facing harder economic conditions and less government funding, are structuring their shops in a fashion that closely resembles a commercial shop. Others have established structures that depend on a mixture of professionals, volunteers and interns (or apprentices). However, one thing should be kept in mind when considering the staffing options of a nonprofit scene shop: All of these shops and their parent organizations are in business for some reason other than making a profit. The university shop exists to support the academic pursuits of students in theater, film, television, music and dance programs. The staffing of these shops should reflect this purpose and address the unique nature of this situation. Community theaters come into existence for a variety of social and cultural reasons.

The staffing of a community theater shop must be influenced by these factors. A resident professional company often strives to develop a community of artists and craftspeople in pursuit of specific artistic goals. These goals should be a factor in the organizational structure of the shop. Figure 3-79 illustrates the organizational chart for a large university shop, and Figure 3-80, page 70, the chart for a resident professional theater shop.

Job Descriptions
Shop Supervisor
The shop supervisor has overall responsibility for the operation of the shop. The supervisor sets quality standards and establishes the specific construction techniques and operational procedures used in the shop. Maintenance, safety and security rules and procedures are also developed,

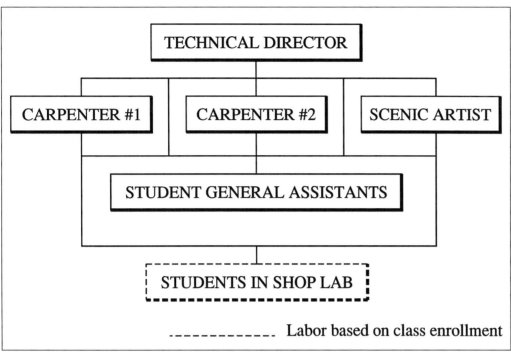

FIGURE 3-79
A general organizational chart for a university shop

implemented and monitored by the shop supervisor. The shop supervisor also is responsible for estimating time and material costs for each project, establishing construction schedules and budgets, and ensuring these guidelines are met. In some organizations this position is occupied by the technical director.

Purchasing Agent
The purchasing agent is primarily responsible for material acquisition. This entails calculating quantities, sourcing material and supplies, pricing, ordering, receiving and inventory control. This work is done in accordance with any material specifications, estimates and deadlines pertinent to the project. A good purchasing agent will keep an inventory of common items in stock at all times. He will also maintain a database for vendors and suppliers of the materials used in the shop. Often the purchasing agent is called upon to literally go out and shop for certain items—and is called a shopper or buyer in some organizations.

Draftsperson
This individual drafts any construction drawings required by the shop, as well as the installation drawings and "as builts" that might go out with the show. She also manages the construction documents that come into the shop from the designer (chapter four defines these documents and their uses).

Master Carpenter/Layout Carpenter
This is the chief carpenter working on the construction floor and managing the routine operation of the shop. The master carpenter is responsible for distributing the work among the available craftspeople, coordinating the various steps in the fabrication process, and ensuring that construction is proceeding according to time and material estimates. In many situations, master carpenters, because of their superior skill and experience, are responsible for the layout of intricate scenic units.

Carpenter
The carpenter is responsible for the basic wood construction of all scenic units.

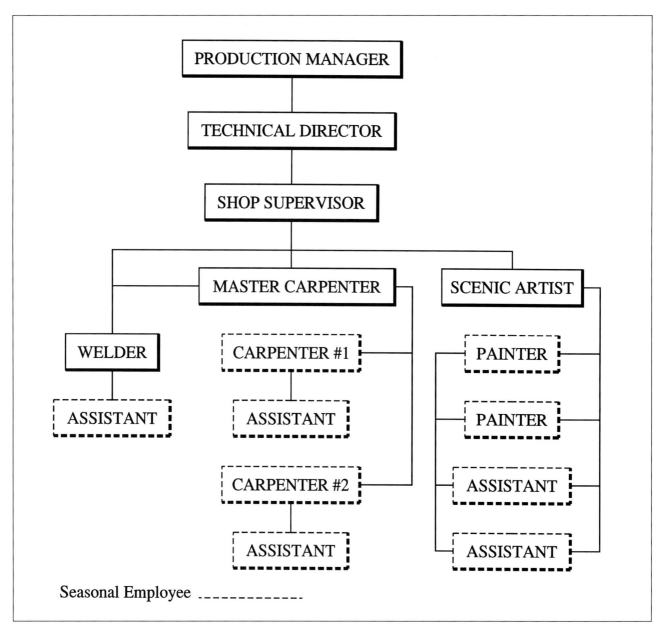

FIGURE 3-80
A general organizational chart for a resident theater shop

Some have specialized as framing carpenters and finish carpenters.

Apprentice
Carpenter's apprentice is an entry-level position designed to assist the carpenter with basic manual tasks of construction.

Welder
A scenic carpenter is often a jack-of-all-trades, and many are competent welders. However, when serious metalwork is required, a certified welder is recommended—and often required. The welder is responsible for the layout and assembly

of steelwork. An assistant or apprentice is often employed for cutting material to size and preparing the material for welding under the direction of the welder.

Scenic Artist
The scenic artist paints the scenery. The charge person is the supervising scenic artist and has responsibilities similar to those of the master carpenter. Apprentice scenic artists are often employed for paint preparation, applying base coats and assisting the scenic artists. Some scenic artists also have skills as sculptors.

CHAPTER 4

CONSTRUCTION DOCUMENTS

The communication tools used to express the designer's concepts to the technicians who will construct the set come in a variety of forms. Sketches, scale drawings, models, photographs, computer images, full-scale samples and written descriptions are among the most common forms of communication. No method should be overlooked in the effort to describe the designer's vision: The principal undertaking of stagecraft is to bring this vision to life. This chapter will cover the most common documents or tools used in communicating this vision and how they are used.

SCALE DRAWINGS

As the saying goes, a picture is worth a thousand words—particularly to describe the physical appearance of a set. Scale drawings are the single most useful communication device for scenery construction. All scenery that is to be constructed should be defined by a scale drawing that includes essential information about the look of the scenery, its size, construction materials and assembly information. To represent a three-dimensional object such as a piece of scenery in a two-dimensional drawing, at least two and often three different but related views are required to provide information on all three dimensions. Ordinarily, a piece of scenery can be most fully described by a series of related drawings that illustrate the top, front and side views of the unit.

A scale drawing is one in which a fraction of a measured foot is used to represent one foot in actual size, thus maintaining the proportions of the object at a greatly reduced size. Since most scenery is too large to be drawn at full size, this is a very useful tool. This technique allows for a 30'-wide by 24'-deep set to be graphically defined on a 3' by 2½' piece of paper. As an example, a ½" scale drawing (½" = 1'0") would represent one foot (12 inches) at full scale (actual size) as ½" on the drawing: Every ½" on the drawing is equal to 1' at full scale. In Figure 4-1, a wall that will be six feet wide when constructed is represented by a drawing that is only 3" wide (6 × ½") on the page. The same wall in ¼" scale would be represented by a drawing only 1½" wide (6 × ¼") on the page. In the ¼" scale drawing ¼" = 1'0".

To read and understand scale drawings, a carpenter must have and know how to use a scale rule. Generally, there are three different types of scale rules. An architect's scale subdivides a foot into twelve inches, much like a normal ruler. An engineer's scale subdivides a foot into tenths of a foot. Metric scales are available to work in meters and centimeters. Theater designers and technicians in the United States use an architect's scale.

The scale comes in a variety of forms. The most common and useful is the triangle scale. This scale, as illustrated in Figure 4-2, page 68, has eleven different scales in addition to a full-size ruler. Each scale is simply a miniature of the full-size ruler extended over the length of the scale rule. Figure 4-3 shows one face of the scale marked for ⅛″, ¼″, ½″, and 1″ scale. Look closely at the ½″ scale on the upper left edge of the ruler in Figure 4-4. The area of the scale from the 0 to the left is ½″ of actual size subdivided into twelve inches in scale. To the right of the 0, the scale is marked at ½″ increments, each mark representing one foot in scale. With this scale you can measure feet and inches at ½″ scale. It should become second nature for all technicians to read a scale.

Drafting Conventions and Symbols

A number of drafting conventions exist to aid in the understanding of scale drawings. These conventions have their roots in architectural and mechanical drawing, but the theater has made some adaptations to these conventions and has added a few of its own.

Lines are the basic element of any drawing. Line variations—thick or thin, straight or curved, solid or dashed—have specific meanings in theatrical drafting. Line weights are assigned in a manner that helps focus the eye of the reader on the most important objects and enhances the readability of the drawing. The following is a list of common line types and their application, accompanied by one or more examples.

• *Outline* or *object lines* are medium-weight solid lines that define the shape, or outline, of an object. The outline of a wall or a platform is drawn using this type of line.

• *Hidden lines* are medium-weight dashed lines that define the shape of an object that is hidden in the current view.

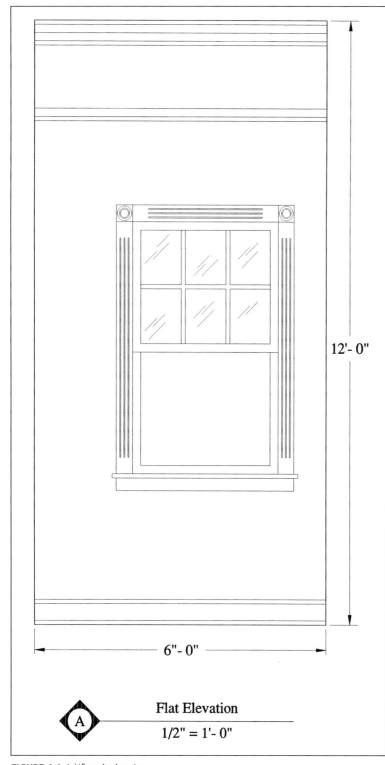

12'- 0"

6"- 0"

Ⓐ   Flat Elevation
             1/2" = 1'- 0"

FIGURE 4-1 *A ½″ scale drawing*

FIGURE 4-2 *Architect's triangle scale*

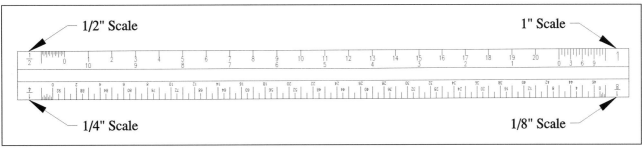

FIGURE 4-3
One face of an architect's triangle scale

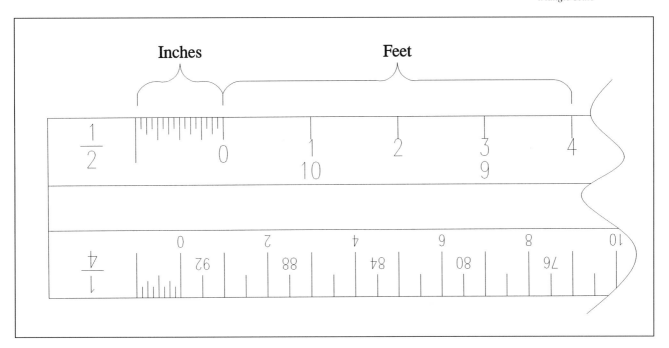

FIGURE 4-4
Detail of the ½" scale on an architect's scale rule

• *Dimension lines* are lightweight solid lines used to indicate the surface or edge of an object being measured. They typically terminate with arrowheads, or some other termination mark, at each end. Dimension lines are accompanied by the text of the dimension.

• *Extension lines* are lightweight lines that are used in conjunction with dimension lines to extend the outline of an object to the dimension line. This convention is used to keep the outline of the object as clear and clutter-free as possible. Note the extension line does not touch the object.

• *Vertical dimensions* on a plan view are indicated by placing a circle around the dimension text. The text is preceded by a plus or minus sign (+ or −) to indicate the direction from the stage floor, which serves as the baseline for all vertical dimensions. A plus sign indicates a height above the stage floor, while a minus sign indicates the distance below the stage floor.

• *Leader lines* are lightweight solid lines used to indicate the object, or *reference point*, of a note or dimension. They terminate on one end with an arrowhead or similar termination mark. Like extension lines, they are used to organize the information on the drawing.

• *Alternate position lines* or *phantom lines* are lightweight dashed lines that indicate an alternate position for a piece of scenery, such as its storage position, an alternate position as the result of a scene change or an item that has been removed from a particular view for the sake of clarity.

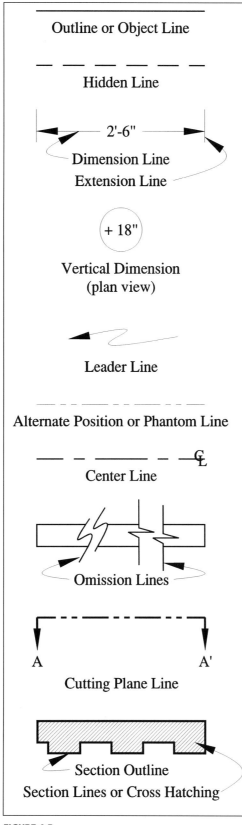

FIGURE 4-5
Drafting line types

• *Center lines* are medium-weight lines made up of alternate long and short dashes. Center lines define the centerline of the theater, a piece of scenery, a drawing or the center of a circle. Center lines are labeled with the initials *CL* superimposed over each other and the line, as illustrated in the example.

• *Omission lines* are medium-weight solid curved or angular lines that interrupt an object line to indicate that part of a drawing or object has been omitted. This is a space-saving technique used when a scenic item is larger then the space available for the drawing and no pertinent information is lost as a result of the omission. Omission lines are also used to cut away the outer surface of an item to reveal the inner structure.

• *Cutting-plane lines* are heavyweight lines alternating between a long dash and two short dashes, and terminating at both ends with arrows. These lines define the location of the imaginary slice of the cutting plane for a section drawing. The arrows denote the direction of view of the section drawing.

• *Section outlines* are heavyweight solid lines that define the edges of an object that are cut by the cutting plane.

• *Section lines* or *cross-hatching* are regularly spaced, lightweight solid lines used to indicate surfaces or planes that have been cut by the cutting plane.

The small scale of some drawings requires the use of symbols and other conventions to enable the incorporation of all applicable information and enhance the readability of the drawing. A number of symbols have been established for use in scale drawings for the theater. These symbols are primarily utilized on plan views. Figure 4-6 illustrates the most common ground-plan symbols used in the theater. The symbols are drawn to the desired size of the scenic component. Whenever possible, the drawing should depict the actual shape of the object.

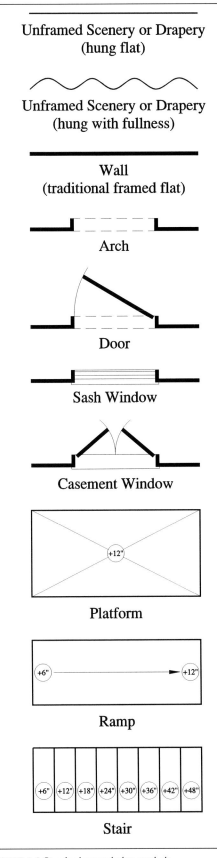

FIGURE 4-6 *Standard ground plan symbols*

SHOW TITLE		
Drawing Title		
Director:		Sheet #:
Designer:		
Venue:		
Drawn By:		Of:
Date:	Revision #:	Scale:

FIGURE 4-7
A typical drawing title block

Designer's Drawings

The designer's drawings are an organized set of scaled two-dimensional illustrations that portray everything about the set, from its overall position onstage to the smallest finish detail. Each drawing should have a title block that includes identifying information about the production, the title of the drawing, the names of the director, designer and draftsperson, the date the original drawing was made, date and revision number for any revisions, the sheet number (page number) of the drawing and the scale (see Figure 4-7). In addition to the picture and dimensions on the drawing, material specifications and explanatory notes for construction and assembly should be included on each drawing.

Ground Plans

The ground plan (or floor plan) is an illustration of the assembled set in its position onstage. This drawing is the foundation and reference sheet for most of the other drawings in the set. It is an essential drawing for all members of the production team—particularly the director, stage manager, technical director, lighting designer and carpenters. Figure 4-8, page 72, illustrates a ground plan for a simple set. Many people think of the ground plan as simply an overhead, or "bird's-eye," view of the set. This is not true.

Imagine drawing a horizontal line around the entire set and stage approximately four feet above the stage floor, as illustrated in Figure 4-9, page 73. Now

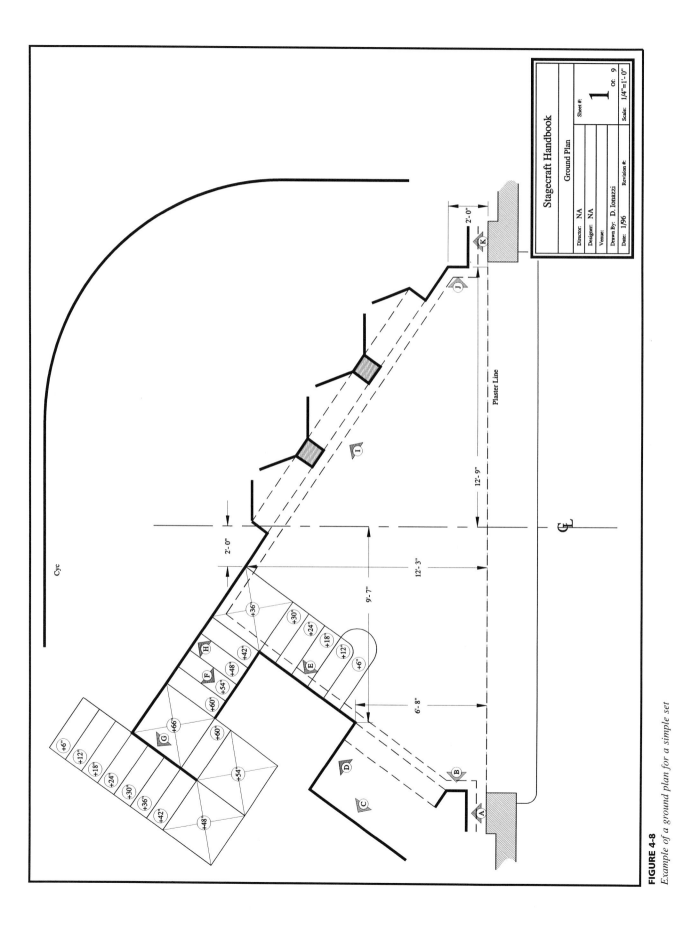

FIGURE 4-8
Example of a ground plan for a simple set

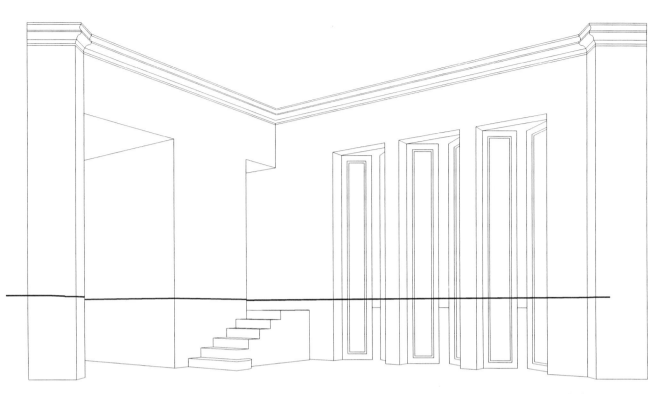

FIGURE 4-9

Elevation of the set represented in Figure 4-8

imagine removing everything above that line, as in Figure 4-10, page 74. A ground plan is actually an overhead view of the stage and set under these imaginary conditions. Figure 4-8 is an overhead view of the remains of the set in Figure 4-10. The reason for slicing through the set and stage in this fashion is to reveal as much information about the set, and such things as its door and window openings, as possible. If you were to draw only what you saw from a vantage point above the set, you would draw only the top of the ceiling or tops of walls, as in Figure 4-11, page 75. If you think about this in terms of a single-story house, a viewpoint some distance above the house would reveal only the roof and the items that project up from the roof. If you remove the roof, the placement of all the walls is revealed. Taking this a step further, as in the imaginary condition described above, slicing through the walls at an appropriate height and removing the upper section reveals the door and window openings and other details that do not project through the top of the walls. This imaginary view provides a much clearer picture of the physical arrangement of a house—or the set in our example.

To make this discussion just a little bit more complicated, there are a few rules you must know about this process of cutting through the set and drafting a ground plan. The level at which you cut through the set is not predetermined to be four feet, as in the example above. The cut should actually be made at a level that provides the most illustrative view of the shape of the set. In many cases, this means that the level of the cut varies at different locations around the set in order to reveal all of the door and window openings, no matter at what height they occur. The cutting plane should never cut through a platform, stair or ramp; these items should always be drawn in view on the ground plan. Items below the cutting-plane line, such as platforms and stairs, are drawn with outlines. Items above the cutting plane, such as cornice moulding or flying units, are drawn with hidden lines. For those items that are cut by the cutting plane, such as a wall, use a section outline. A ground plan is actually a horizontal section (more about section drawings later in this chapter). The ground plan serves four primary purposes:

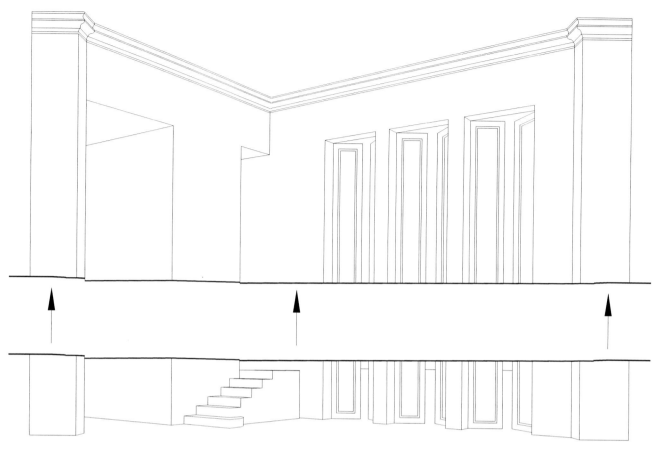

FIGURE 4-10
Elevation of the set with top removed

1. To locate the set on the stage. Typically, this is done using two reference lines, which must be included on every ground plan. The theater's centerline is an imaginary line that bisects the proscenium or the playing area from downstage to upstage into two equal parts, left and right. The *plaster line* is an imaginary line drawn across stage at the upstage edge of the proscenium (see Figure 4-12, page 76). In other physical configurations of the theater, such as a thrust theater or an arena, the reference lines may be in slightly different positions or simply two centerlines that divide the space, as illustrated in Figures 4-13 and 4-14, page 76 and page 77. The positions of key elements of the set are measured from these two reference lines and the dimensions included on the ground plan. Any point onstage may be defined by its distance up- or downstage from the plaster line and left or right from the centerline.

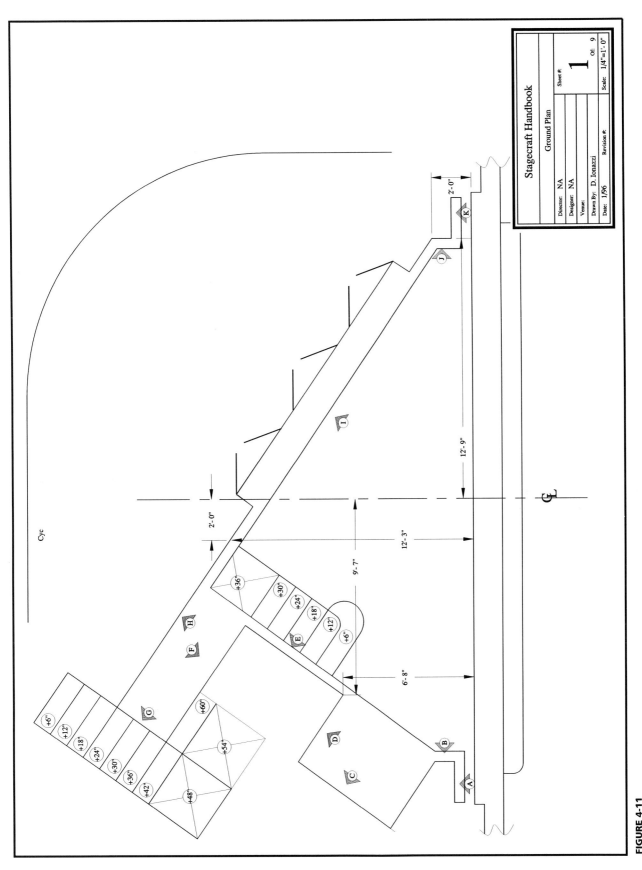

FIGURE 4-11
Overhead view of set without the convention of removing the upper portions of the set

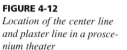

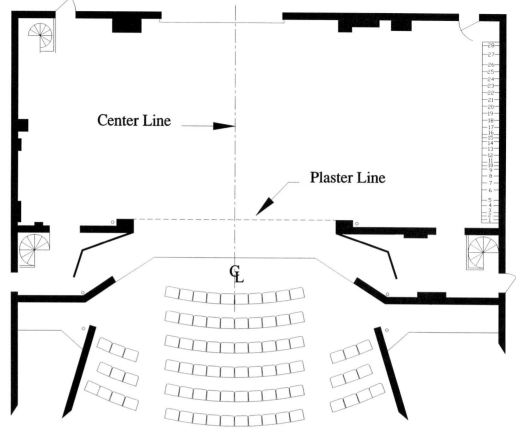

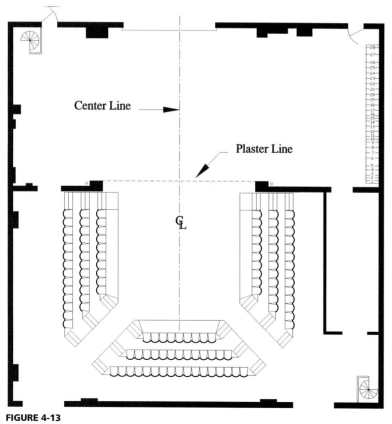

FIGURE 4-13
Location of the center line and plaster line in a thrust theater

2. To show the physical relationship of the various parts of the set. All scenic units, masking and production equipment should be included on the ground plan. The dimensions of individual scenic units are typically not included on the ground plan for reasons of clarity. The complete dimensions of these units will appear on the elevations (discussed later in this section). However, because the ground plan is a scale drawing, you can measure these items with a scale rule with some degree of accuracy. Vertical dimensions are often given for stairs, platforms and ramps. These dimensions are typically referenced from the stage floor as plus or minus the appropriate number of inches (see Figure 4-15 for a detail of this drafting convention).

3. To determine the audience's horizontal sightlines. This is accomplished by drawing a line from the "worst seat" to each edge of the proscenium. The area between the two lines is in the audience's

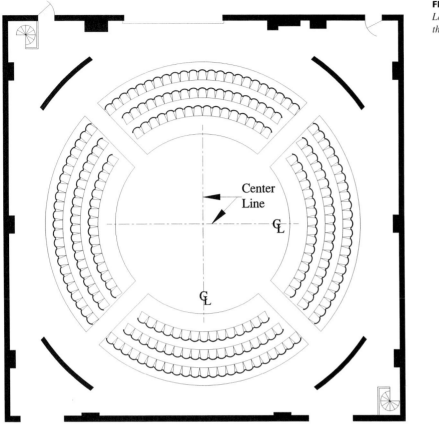

field of view, or sightlines (see Figure 4-16, page 78).

4. To act as a reference, or table of contents, to the complete set of drawings. Examine Figure 4-8 once again: Notice the labels which identify the walls of the set. These labels identify the scenic unit for reference on the designer's elevations. Very little construction can actually take place from a ground plan alone: Elevations and detail drawings are required to provide the information needed for fabrication.

The designer's drawings should include a ground plan for each set or physical change to the basic set. Multi-set productions require a ground plan for each set. Additionally, specific plan views should be included for platforms and floor treatments. A platform plan for the set in Figure 4-8 is illustrated in Figure 4-17, page 79. This plan shows the size and shape of the platforms and steps being used in the set in more detail. In this type of plan, no

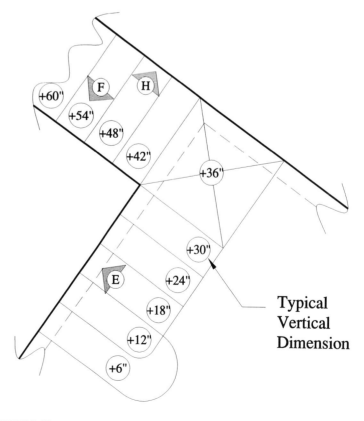

FIGURE 4-15
Vertical dimensions on a ground plan

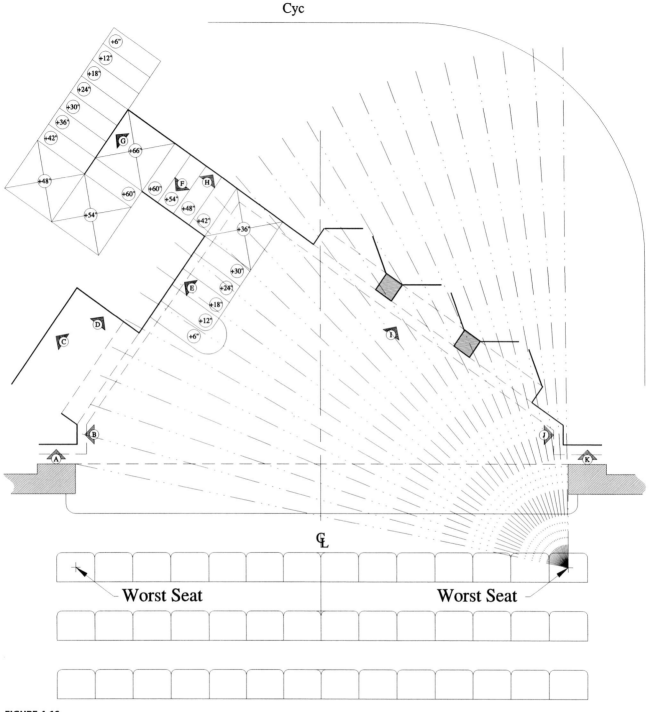

FIGURE 4-16
Establishing the sightlines in a proscenium theater

imaginary cut is made as in the ground plan. The view is truly overhead, revealing the "footprint" of the platforms and steps. This drawing is used to construct the various working levels of the set and must include all dimensions, material specifications and explanatory construction and assembly notes. Notice also the inclusion of positioning dimensions referenced to the centerline and plaster line.

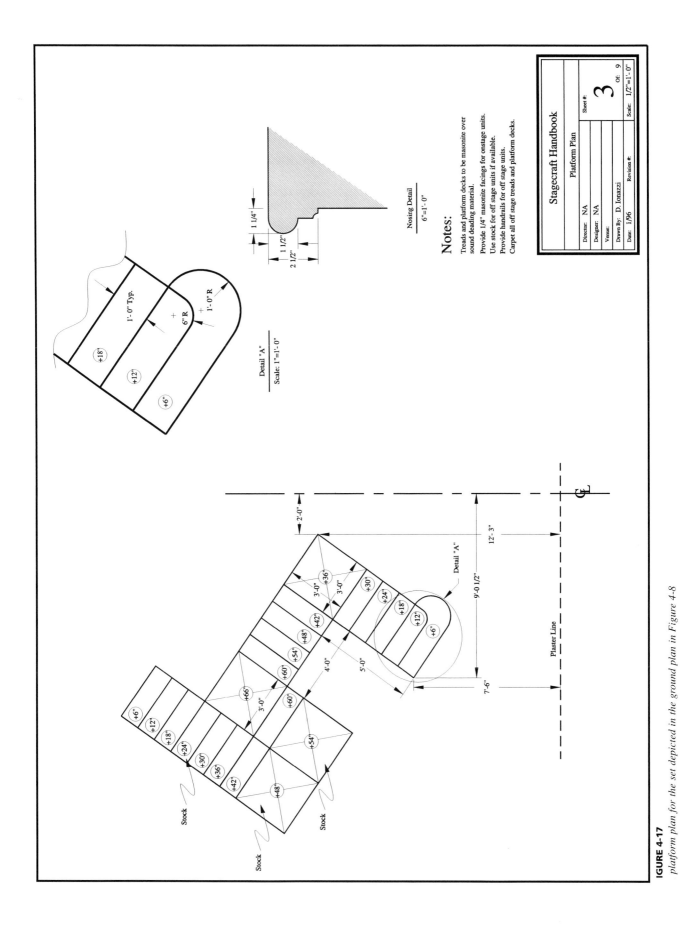

Nosing Detail
6"=1'-0"

1 1/4"
1 1/2"
2 1/2"

Notes:

Treads and platform decks to be masonite over
sound deading material.
Provide 1/4" masonite facings for onstage units.
Use stock for off stage units if available.
Provide handrails for off stage units.
Carpet all off stage treads and platform decks.

Stagecraft Handbook

Platform Plan

Sheet #:

3

Director: NA
Designer: NA
Venue:
Drawn By: D. Ionazzi
Date: 1/96   Revision #:
Scale: 1/2"=1'-0"   Of: 9

Detail "A"
Scale: 1"=1'-0"

1'-0" Typ.

6" R

1'-0" R

+18"
+12"
+6"

+36"
+42"
+48"
+54"
+60"
+66"
+6"
+12"
+18"
+24"
+30"
+36"
+42"
+48"
+54"
+60"
+54"

+30"
+24"
+18"
+12"
+6"

3'-0"
3'-0"
4'-0"
5'-0"
3'-0"

2'-0"

12'-3"

9'-0 1/2"

7'-6"

Detail "A"

Plaster Line

Stock
Stock
Stock

IGURE 4-17

platform plan for the set depicted in the ground plan in Figure 4-8

Sections

Sections, an entire class of drawings illustrating views that are not visible, provide valuable information for the purpose of construction. As stated previously, the ground plan, with its imaginary horizontal slice through the stage and set, is an example of a section. Sections frequently cut open three-dimensional scenic units to reveal the exact shape of the unit or its inner structure. Often this drawing is more useful and replaces a simple side view.

The centerline section is a drawing, similar in use to the ground plan, that reveals the vertical dimension not available in the ground plan. The centerline section takes an imaginary vertical slice through the theater and the set at the centerline. The left or right half of the theater and set are removed, and a drawing is made of the view that remains. Figure 4-18 is a centerline section of our example set. If the left and right halves of the set are very different, a centerline section is developed for each side of the set. The centerline section is used to establish the vertical dimensions and placement of the scenery, masking and other theatrical equipment, and to determine the vertical sightlines. As with the ground plan, this drawing is very useful to the entire production team.

Elevations

Elevations are drawings that view an object horizontally. They are typically drawn in ½″ scale and can be front, rear or side views of a scenic item, providing all pertinent dimensions and applied detail such as window and door openings, trim and mouldings. Designer's elevations are front views of the scenery and are normally positioned on the page from stage right to stage left in order, as illustrated in Figure 4-19, pages 82-83. You can think of these drawings as dismantled and flattened-out views of the set that are organized so that the individual scenic units maintain their relative positions to one another. Notice that the elevations are labeled with the reference letter used on the ground plan. The designer's elevations are the detailed drawings used for construction purposes. These drawings must be fully dimensioned and must include material specifications and all appropriate explanatory construction and assembly notes.

Elevations are often accompanied by sections and detail drawings. As discussed previously, sections are cutaway views of a scenic item revealing a view of the object that helps to define its shape and size in three dimensions. Sections accompanying elevations often come in one of two ways. The *revolved section* (Figure 4-20, page 84) is superimposed on top of the elevation. The location is chosen for its ability to reveal important details about the scenic element. The *removed section* (Figure 4-21, page 85) is simply a sectional drawing placed to the side of the elevation. The cutting-plane line used to indicate the location of the section is drawn on the elevation and labeled to reference the section.

Detail Drawings

Detail drawings are just that: A portion of a scenic unit is enlarged to reveal the specific detail required for construction. Details are referenced from the source drawing by a number. They can be drawn adjacent to the source drawing or collected on a separate page of detail drawings. As a rule of thumb, a detail drawing should be drawn in as large a scale as possible. In some cases, as in mouldings, the drawing should be done in full scale (i.e., actual size). Because the scales of detail drawings can vary, it is very important to include the scale as part of the label for each detail. A full-scale drawing is labeled *F.S.D.*

Pictorials

A variety of drawings known as *pictorials* are also available to help communicate the shape of intricate or complex objects. These drawings attempt to represent all three dimensions in a single view. The perspective drawing foreshortens the lines

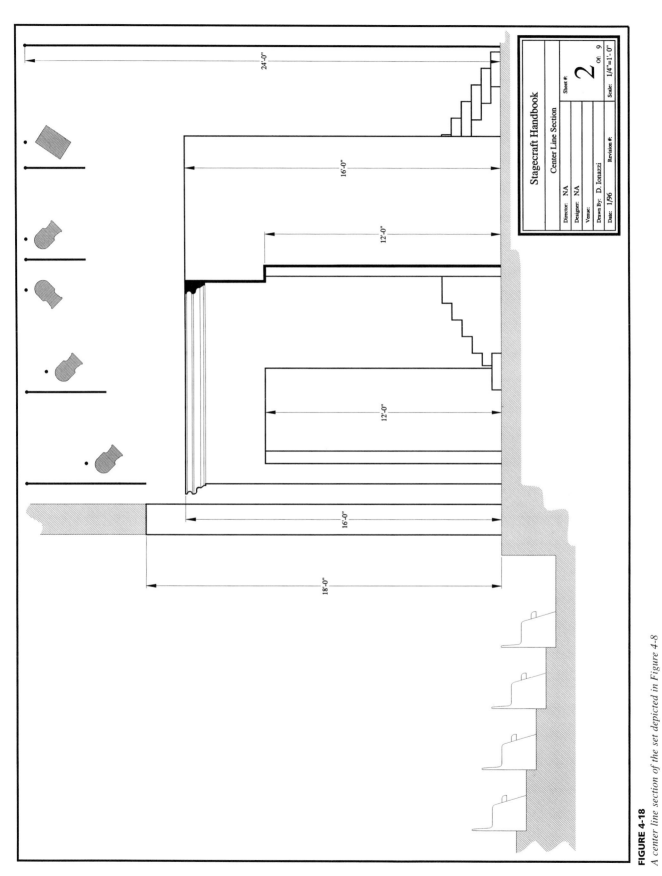

FIGURE 4-18

A center line section of the set depicted in Figure 4-8

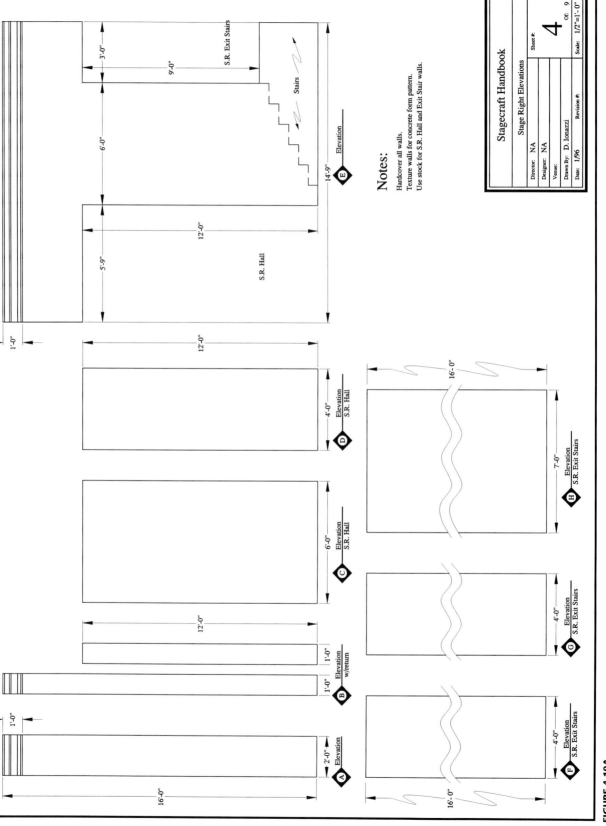

FIGURE 4-19A
Elevations of the set in Figure 4-8

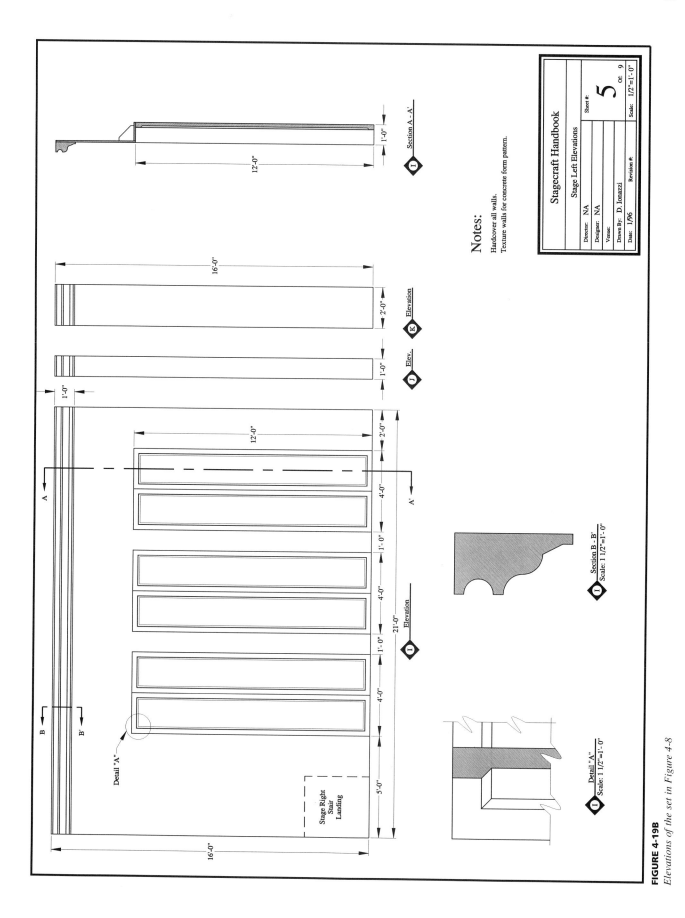

FIGURE 4-19B

Elevations of the set in Figure 4-8

FIGURE 4-20
Example of a revolved section

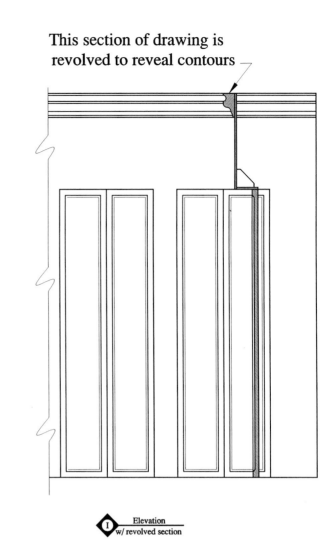

This section of drawing is
revolved to reveal contours

Elevation
w/ revolved section

that recede from the viewing plane to give the illusion of three dimensions. These drawings may be very loose freehand sketches or precise mechanical drawings. Because of the foreshortening technique used to create the illusion of three dimensions, perspective drawings are not scale drawings and are not suitable for construction purposes. However, they are very informative as to the overall look of the set. Often these drawings are rendered in full color to evoke the mood and atmosphere of a particular scene. Three types of pictorials are scale drawings.

• The *isometric drawing* takes a view that rotates the object 45° to the left or right to reveal a side view and tilts the object up or down to reveal the top or the bottom.

This angle permits viewing of three adjacent sides or faces at the same time (see Figure 4-22, at lower right).

• *Oblique drawings* start with a front elevation of the most complicated face. The draftsperson then selects one side or the other and the top or bottom and projects these surfaces back from the front elevation at a 30° or 40° angle, as in Figure 4-23, page 86. Again, the drawing is made to scale.

• *Cabinet drawings* attempt to reduce the distortion of an oblique drawing by proportionally reducing the projected length of the side and top or bottom surfaces. Figure 4-24, page 86, is a cabinet version of Figure 4-23. The reduction can range from 25 to 50 percent, based on the depth of the object being drawn.

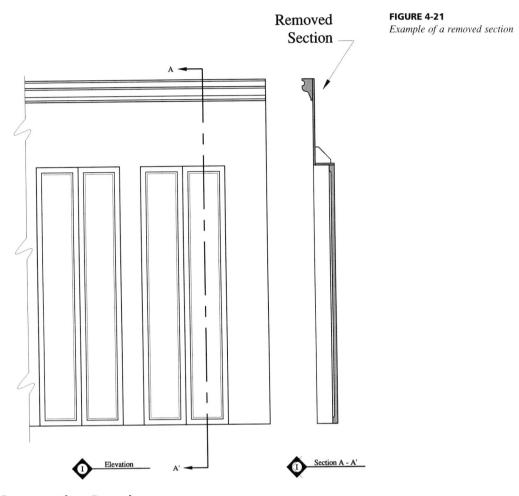

Removed Section

FIGURE 4-21
Example of a removed section

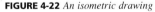

I Elevation   A'

I Section A - A'

Construction Drawings

Construction drawings are made when particularly complex and intricate scenery is to be built. These drawings are generally produced by the shop responsible for the actual fabrication of the set, and not by the designer. The focus of these drawings is the construction methods and components to be used to achieve the finished results required by the designer. A construction drawing is often a rear elevation of a wall or flat. In this view, the framing members can be clearly illustrated. Some construction drawings omit the finished surface to reveal the inner skeleton of the scenic unit. The same drafting conventions and rules discussed previously in this chapter apply to construction drawings. Examples are provided in chapter six.

To convert designer drawings to construction drawings, many technicians trace the outlines of the designer's drawings or

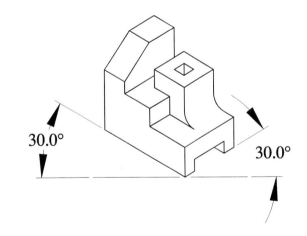

30.0°   30.0°

FIGURE 4-22 *An isometric drawing*

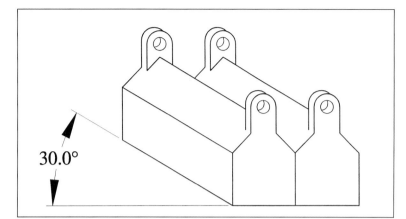

FIGURE 4-23 *An oblique drawing*

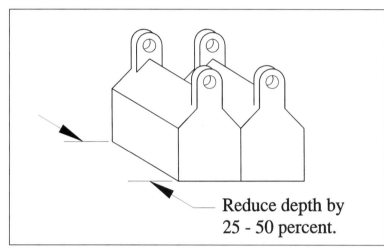

Reduce depth by
25 - 50 percent.

FIGURE 4-24 *A cabinet drawing*

superimpose their drawing over the top of a copy of the designer's drawing.

PAINT ELEVATIONS

The designer's vision of the painted set is communicated through the use of a painted model, paint elevations, full-scale samples, pictures or a combination of these techniques. Paint elevations are customarily ½″ scale front elevations of each scenic element painted without the effects of stage lighting. The precise colors and painting techniques are depicted. Color swatches or samples and full-size details, along with notes specifying procedures to be followed or techniques to be used, can and should be included.

For particularly elaborate or freehand-rendered scenic units such as a drop painted with a landscape scene, a 1′- to 2′-scale grid is placed over the painter's elevation to aid in the process of enlarging the painting to full scale. This grid is typically drawn on a clear sheet of acetate, which is then positioned over the painter's elevation. A full-scale version of the grid is also chalked onto the scenic unit. The painter can use the grids as a reference to sketch in the painted scene.

MODELS

Many designers choose to build three-dimensional scale models of their sets. Models are very effective in illustrating all three dimensions of a set and the spatial relationships among the elements of the set and the stage. They are also extremely useful in illustrating the scene changes that will take place during the production. The level of detail in a scale model is dependent on the skill and patience of the model maker. I have seen models that are works of art in and of themselves. However, as intricate and accurate as some models may be, they are not a substitute for scale drawings.

A very simple model known as a *white model* can be easily constructed without the time and expense of a fully detailed model. This facsimile provides the three-dimensional benefits of a model that are so useful in understanding how a set fits together and moves. A white model is generally constructed of foam-core or mat board. The basic scenic units are cut out and assembled without applied detail, color or texture.

One method for quickly creating a white model with a bit more information is to adhere a copy of the designer's elevations to foam-core or mat board, and then simply cut out the scenic units, following the lines of the elevations. Fasten a copy of the ground plan to a piece of plywood or framed Masonite as a guide to assembly. Secure the cutout elevations in their respective locations on the ground plan and you have a white model with the added information supplied by the elevations.

FIGURE 4-25A *A model created by Melissa Anderson*

FIGURE 4-25B *A model created by Ellen Files*

FIGURE 4-25C *A model created by Jennie Humphrey*

CHAPTER 5

SCENIC MATERIALS

The materials used in building scenery are generally easy to acquire, relatively inexpensive and easy to work with. In most smaller operations, wood, wood by-products and fabric are the principal construction materials. Steel has become a significant building material in larger shops due to the engineering requirements of much of today's scenery and environmental considerations. The rest is hardware, fasteners and adhesives that, with few exceptions these days, are no longer specific to the theater industry.

WOOD

There are only a few types of wood that have all the characteristics required for scenery construction. Fortunately, they are not hard to find in most parts of the country. In choosing wood, look for straight grain and even texture; this will ensure a wood that will machine well and is generally easy to work. The need for scenery to be easily shifted and transported demands a wood that is of medium weight, strong and rigid. It should also be straight and not prone to warping. Well-seasoned lumber is desirable to maintain this characteristic. Finally, the wood should be inexpensive and available in sufficient quantities to meet the needs of your project. While hardwoods such as oak, walnut and cherry are beautiful and strong, they are also heavy, hard to work and very expensive. Softwoods such as pine, hemlock and fir have characteristics more suitable to constructing scenery.

Board Lumber

The most desirable woods for general scenery construction are Northern (Eastern) white pine and Idaho white pine. These particular species are in short supply and not available everywhere in the country. Slightly less desirable but still very usable are Western white pine and Ponderosa pine, which are more commonly available but weigh slightly more. Western red cedar, white wood and redwood can be used for framing, but do have their drawbacks. For weight-bearing structures, a stronger and stiffer wood is desirable. Douglas fir and Southern pine are good choices under these conditions.

All board lumber is quality graded for appearance and structural integrity. The best lumber falls in the category of *select* and is rated from A to D. A select is very rare in any quantity and is considered for all practical purposes as hypothetical. B select is difficult to acquire and expensive. In practice, the top grade for use in the construction of scenery is referred to as *C and Better*. This grade of lumber has a limited amount of small blemishes or defects that do not detract from its appearance or structural integrity. D select allows more surface blemishes, but none so great as to detract from a painted finish or in any way significantly affect the structural properties of the material.

After the select grades come the common grades. These grades are rated *1* through *5*, with *1* being the best of the category. Grades *1* and *2* are generally considered structurally sound and can be used for scenery framing or where appearance is not a factor. Grades *3* through *5* are increasingly difficult to use without a considerable amount of waste, due to the large number of knotholes and other defects that must be avoided.

Sizing

Board lumber is referenced by its thickness and width and is sold by the board foot. A board that is 1″ thick and 12″ wide is known as a 1 by 12 (written 1 × 12). Board feet are calculated using the thickness, width and length of a piece of lumber. A board foot is 12″ × 12″ × 1″ thick. A piece of 1 × 12 that is 12″ long is one board foot. The same 1 × 12 stock at 16′ long would be 16 board feet. Pricing is generally quoted per one thousand board feet. The 1 × 12 reference is a nominal size. The actual size of the lumber is the mill size, or dressed size, which is smaller. A 1 × 12 will actually be ¾″ thick and 11¼″ wide. A 2 × 4 is actually 1½″ thick by 3½″ wide. Mill sizing is standard for all board lumber. You can special-order lumber at its full size but it is very expensive.

Board lumber can be purchased in the following standard sizes and generally comes in maximum 16′ lengths (without special order).

1 × 2—Used for small framing members.

1 × 3—Used for standard framing.

1 × 4—Used for battens or large framed units.

1 × 6 and 8—Used for door and window casings and framing, and architectural trim.

1 × 10 and 12—Used for properties, furniture and architectural trim.

⁵⁄₄″ × 3 and 4—Used for light-platform framing and large framed units.

2 × 4, 6, 8, 10 and 12—Used for weight-bearing structures and trusses.

Larger size lumber such as 1 × 12 can be ripped down to any smaller width as

1 X 2
1 X 3
1 X 4
1 X 6
1 X 8
1 X 10
1 X 12

5/4 X 3
5/4 X 4

2 X 4
2 X 6
2 X 8
2 X 10
2 X 12

FIGURE 5-1 *Useful board sizes*

required. Four pieces of 1×3 can be cut from a single piece of 1×12.

Sheet Goods

Sheet goods, or paneling, are manufactured products created from the by-products of wood. A variety of different products are available, and many have uses in the construction of scenery. All these products come in $4' \times 8'$ sheets and in varying thicknesses. They are sold by the sheet or by the square foot. New and improved products are developed often in this category.

Plywood

Plywood is commonly used in scenery construction for flooring surfaces, including false floors, platform lids, step risers and treads, profile cutouts and some forms of framing. It is manufactured by bonding several thin layers of wood together, with the grain of adjacent layers placed at 90° to each other. An odd number of layers is used to ensure the grain runs in the same direction on both faces of the panel. It is rated for interior or exterior use, which is reflective of the adhesive used in bonding the layers of wood together. Standard thicknesses of ¼", ⅜", ½", ⅝", ¾" and 1" are commonly used in scenery construction. Plywood is typically manufactured using several species of wood and graded for the appearance of its two faces. There are five grades, which are specified *A*, *B*, *C*, *C* plugged, and *D*, with *A* being the best. Plywood can be purchased with almost any combination of face grades and glue type.

Lauan

This hardwood plywood, made of Philippine mahogany, is used predominantly as the covering for hard-covered flats. It is also used for facings and other profile uses. It comes in ⅛"- and ¼"-thick 4×8 sheets, and can also be purchased in 4×10 sheets in the ¼" thickness. This material is lighter, easier to work and less expensive than ¼" plywood. However, there are some environmental concerns in using this product and the industry is trying to find an acceptable alternative.

Particle Board

Particle board is manufactured from small wood chips, sawdust and glue. This material costs considerably less than plywood, but is also considerably weaker and a good deal heavier. Particle board is very hard and brittle, making it tough on tools and difficult to work. Nails are hard to drive into particle board, and the material crumbles easily around the edges or when screws are used. Particle board is often used for cabinets and countertops. This material is not a substitute for plywood used for platform lids.

MDF (Medium-Density Fiberpine)

MDF is a very fine-grain version of particle board. Because of this fine grain, the edge of a panel machines very well during operations such as routing.

OSB (Oriented Strand Board)

OSB is composed of compressed strands arranged in layers (usually three to five) oriented at right angles to one another. The orientation of layers achieves the same advantages of the cross-laminated layers in plywood. These panels can be used in the same applications as plywood when the finish is not important. OSB is often referred to as waferboard.

Masonite

Masonite is the brand name for a sheet material made of wood pulp. It is also known as *hardboard* or *pressboard*. In scenery construction it is typically used in either ⅛" or ¼" thickness for nonstructural flooring and facing. Masonite comes tempered (a very hard surface) or untempered. It can also be purchased smooth one side or smooth two sides and in lengths of 8, 10, 12 and 16 feet.

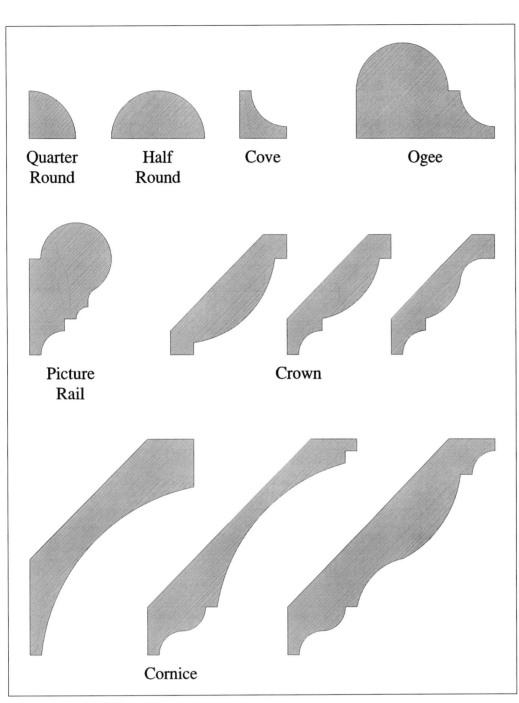

FIGURE 5-2 *Standard molding shapes*

Homosote

Homosote is also a brand name for a sheet material manufactured from compressed fibers. This is not a structural material, but works well for sound deadening as part of the decking of a floor or platform. It can also be used as the top surface of a deck for a sculpted or heavily textured finish.

Celotex

Another brand name for fiberboard, this product is less expensive and more readily available than Homosote. It is softer and requires greater care to prevent compression when used in flooring applications.

It is softer and requires greater care to prevent compression when used in flooring applications.

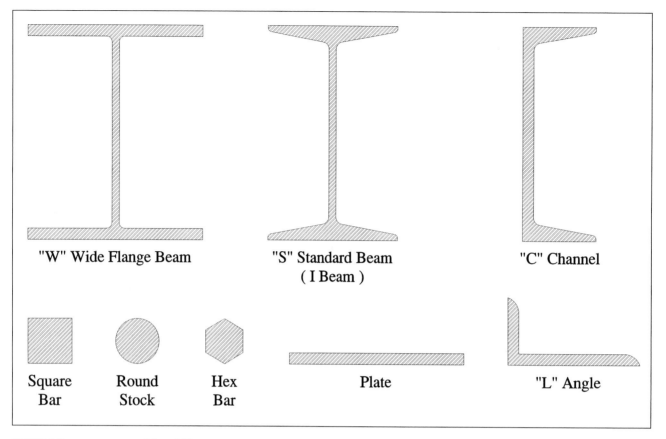

FIGURE 5-3
Standard structural steel shapes

Moulding

Moulding is sold by the running foot or linear foot. It can be purchased in a number of standard patterns and sizes. Some of the most common patterns used in the theater are half round, quarter round, cove and crown. A variety of other shapes for door and window casings, baseboards, chair rails, picture rails and cornice mouldings are also available. Note that it may be less expensive to mill your own moulding with the right tools. In chapter six, you will learn how a few shapes can be used to build up an elaborate cornice moulding.

METAL

The costs, availability, quality and environmental considerations of using lumber have made steel a desirable alternative to traditional wood construction. In addition, the structural characteristics of steel meet many of the demands of modern scenic-design practices. A wide variety of steel shapes and sizes are now commonly avail-

able, and the material is easily recyclable. The costs are very competitive and often superior to wood when cost to strength is considered.

Structural Steel

The steel used in scenery applications is mild steel, or structural steel (A7 or A36) with a plain oxide finish. For machine parts, choose low-carbon machinery steel. A variety of cross-sectional shapes are available, as illustrated above.

Tubing

Round, rectangular and square steel tubing is perhaps the most useful steel construction material for scenery. Tubing is a great alternative for board lumber, and in many cases is superior. Steel tubing comes in 20' lengths and is sized by its outside dimensions and wall thickness. The table in Figure 5-4 provides information on the most useful shapes and sizes.

Pipe

Pipe is sized by its inside diameter and is available in three wall thicknesses. The standard wall thickness is schedule 40, extra strong (XS) is schedule 80, and double extra strong (XXS) has no schedule number. Numerous threaded fittings are available, such as 45° and 90° elbows, tees, crosses, couplings, caps and flanges. Other joining systems such as scaffolding clamps and roto-locks are also available and are very useful in erecting scaffolding, grids and railings from ordinary pipe.

PLASTICS

Plastics are synthetic or organic materials that may be shaped when soft and then hardened. A more general definition of plastic is material capable of being moulded, or of receiving form. Perhaps because of the often intimidating chemical names or the enormous number of these materials, plastics have not made their way easily into some theater shops. Commercial shops and larger institutions have embraced many types of plastics, but smaller operations have only isolated experiences with these materials.

Styrofoam

The most prevalent form of plastic in general use is Styrofoam. This is actually a trade name for rigid expanded polystyrene foam (RPF). Styrofoam is available in a variety of densities. The craft grade of Styrofoam is white and its resistance to compression is a comparatively low 15 to 25 pounds per square inch (psi). It is commonly available in 4 × 8 sheets and comes in ¾", 1" or 2" thicknesses. Blue Styrofoam, which is actually designed as insulation, comes in compressive strengths of 40, 60 and 115 psi. Styrofoam is also available in blocks 6" to 10" thick. When using this material, read all the safety literature concerning fire ratings, health hazards and proper disposal.

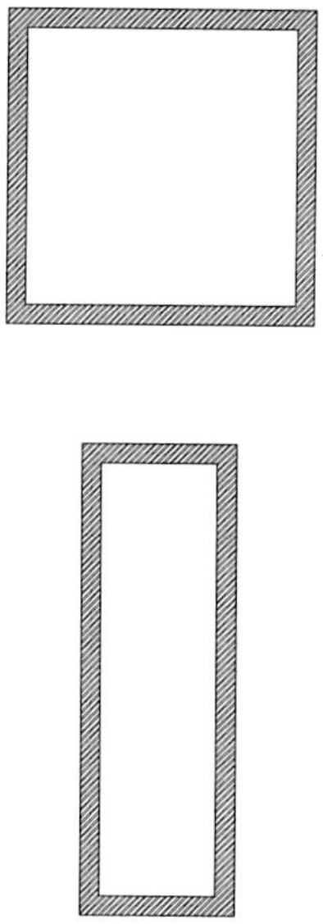

Gauge Wall Thickness	16 .06"	14 .075"	11 .12"
1"	.77	.94	1.44
1 1/2"	1.18	1.45	2.25
2"	1.58	1.96	3.07
3"	2.40	2.98	4.70
4"	3.22	4.00	6.33
1" X 2"	1.18	1.45	2.25
1" X 3"	1.58	1.96	3.07
1" X 4"	1.99	2.47	3.88
2" X 3"	1.99	2.47	3.88
2" X 4"	2.40	2.98	4.70

Pounds / Linear Foot

FIGURE 5-4
Square steel tubing sizes and weights chart

Beadboard

Beadboard is manufactured from expandable polystyrene beads and is often mistakenly called Styrofoam. It is most often found formed into sheets for use by the building trades as insulation. Some companies can manufacture expanded polystyrene into almost any size blocks per your specifications.

Acrylic

Another relatively popular plastic is acrylic. This material is most commonly known in its sheet form by the trade name Plexiglas. Acrylic comes in sheets, rods and bars, as well as some extruded shapes. It is also available in a variety of textures and colors, including clear and frosted.

Lexan

Lexan, a trade name for polycarbonate, is highly resistant to impact. Similar to acrylic, it is ideally suited for transparent weight-bearing surfaces.

Ethafoam

Ethafoam is low-density polyethylene. It is a flexible material available in sheets and rods. The rods can be purchased in sizes from ¼" to 6" with the smaller sizes available in 1,000' rolls. Because of its flexibility, the rods are particularly useful for a number of moulding and trim applications on curved surfaces.

Polyurethane Foam

Polyurethane foam is a two-part liquid that, when mixed together, expands and hardens into a rigid polystyrene-like material. Once hard, the material can be carved very easily. The liquid can also be mixed in a mold to form an unlimited variety of shapes, or sprayed onto a form to provide the texture and look of rock and other natural materials. This material is available under some trade names and is often referred to as A-B Foam.

PVC

PVC, polyvinyl chloride, is used to manufacture a wide variety of products. It is most commonly used in the theater as pipe, but is also available in rods and sheets. As pipe it is most commonly available in diameters of ⅛" to over 12". A large assortment of PVC pipe fittings are available.

FABRIC

The fabrics used in theatrical-scenery construction and general stage use fall into three basic categories: scenery fabrics, stage draperies and specialty fabrics. Each of these is discussed in detail below.

Scenery Fabrics

Scenery fabrics are used in scenic construction with the goal of representing something else. These fabrics are typically meant to be painted.

Muslin

Muslin, a plain-weave cotton fabric, is the most common material in this category and is used primarily for drops and soft-covered flats, and to provide a quality painting surface on hard-covered scenic units. Muslin is typically available in widths ranging from 40" to 197" and in a limited assortment of colors, including natural (or unbleached), sky blue, night blue, light gray, bleached white and black. It can also be purchased as a flame-retardant fabric and in light, medium or heavy weights. The number of threads per square inch determines the weight of the fabric. A heavy-weight muslin will have a higher thread count than a lightweight muslin, and consequently will be stronger and more opaque.

Wider widths of muslin are also available for large drops. Seamless muslin from one supplier is available in widths of 14'5", 20'4" and 32'9". It comes in natural, bleached white, sky blue and gray.

Canvas

Canvas is a very strong and durable, closely woven cotton fabric used primarily for ground cloths and to provide a quality paint surface for false floors and platforms. Canvas is also used as a covering for scenic units that are very large or expected to withstand heavy use or rough treatment. It is available in widths of 68" to 144" and typically in natural and black. Additional colors are available through larger suppliers. Canvas is also classified by weight, with 7 to 18 ounces being fairly common.

Sharkstooth Scrim

Sharkstooth scrim is used extensively for theatrical applications requiring a bleed-through effect. When front-lit at an extremely steep angle and in the absence of any light behind the scrim, the fabric and any scene or decor painted on it appear to be opaque. When the front light is removed and the scene behind the scrim is lit, the scrim and its painting appear to dissolve, revealing the scene behind. Sharkstooth scrim is a very open-weave fabric. It comes in black, white, sky blue and gray, in widths of 15'6" to 35'.

Leno-Filled Scrim

Leno-filled scrim is an opaque, densely knit fabric. Unlike sharkstooth scrim, leno will not render a bleed-through effect. Leno is very elastic, making it virtually wrinkle-free and an excellent choice for cycloramas or full-stage backings. It is available in white, gray or sky blue, and can be painted. It comes in 31' widths.

Cotton Scrim

Cotton scrim is an open-weave fabric made of very fine threads. It can be used like sharkstooth scrim in smaller and less demanding applications. It is available in a natural finish in widths of 36" or 58".

Theatrical Gauze

Theatrical Gauze is coarser and a larger weave than cotton scrim. It comes in natural and white, and in 72" widths.

Bobbinet

Bobbinet has a larger open weave than sharkstooth and cannot be lit to appear opaque. It comes in white and black, and can be painted. The 97" width has slightly smaller openings than the 31' width.

Scenic Netting

Scenic netting is used to support cut-out drops, borders and legs. The fabric is 1" open netting which tends to disappear onstage. It is available in 24-yard pieces 30' wide. Scenic netting is available in black and white, and in cotton or nylon; the cotton fabric can be dyed.

Opera Netting

Opera netting is similar to sharkstooth but with a more open weave. It comes in 29' widths in white and black.

Cheesecloth

Cheesecloth is commonly used to cover foam and plastic. It is similar to gauze and comes 36" wide. It comes in white and can be painted.

Burlap

Burlap is a very coarse, heavy, plain-weave fabric made of cotton jute or hemp. It is most commonly used to provide a textured surface. It comes in a natural color and is available in a variety of widths and weights. Erosion cloth is a form of burlap that is used very often in scenic applications. This material looks like coarse netting but does not have the strength to be used for lifting.

Stage Draperies

These fabrics are used primarily for stage curtains such as front drapes, travelers, masking legs, borders and backdrops. They are also used to cover constructed pieces such as portals and hard legs, and as general-purpose masking fabric.

Velour

Velour is the first choice for stage draperies. It has a long, thick nap, which gives the fabric a rich texture and absorbs light well, making it an excellent fabric for masking drapes. It comes in a wide variety of colors, though black is standard for masking. The standard width for cotton velour is 54", and it is available in 12 to 32 oz. weights. For permanent or stock draperies, a heavyweight velour such as 25 oz. is most desirable. For scenic pieces, 16 to 19 oz. velour is recommended. Velour can and should be flame-retardant.

Velveteen

Velveteen is a lightweight velour available in 45" to 48" widths and in a wide variety of colors. It, too, can and should be flame-retardant.

Wool Serge

Wool serge is used in England in place of velour for stage draperies. It is an extremely dense, brushed-weave fabric with excellent light-absorption properties. It comes in black in a 59" width.

Duvetyn

Duvetyn is a soft felted fabric used extensively for masking and blackout drapes. It is an inexpensive substitute for velour, but does not come close to the richness or depth of velour. It comes in black and is available in 54″ widths.

Commando Cloth

Commando cloth is another name for duvetyn. The name *duvetyn* is more commonly used on the West Coast. The name *commando cloth* sometimes refers to a heavyweight duvetyn. It also comes in white, gray and beige, and can be found in some additional colors.

Other Stage Draperies

There are a variety of other fabrics that are used for stage draperies. Some are textured, while others have patterns woven into the fabric. These fabrics are generally available in assorted colors, and all of them are available in black. They range in width from 48″ to 54″. They are sold as Nassau chevron repp (herringbone pattern), Atlas oxford repp (a heavy herringbone pattern with a homespun texture), ranger cloth, reno and vegas.

Specialty Fabrics

A huge array of other fabrics are often used in scenic applications of one kind or another: display fabrics, such as nylon, taffeta, and chintz, in an assortment of colors; a wonderful lightweight and flowing inexpensive silk known as China silk; felt in a huge assortment of colors; and an ever-growing array of metallic fabrics. Mylar rain curtains, Glamé, slit drapes, metallic scrims and shrink mirror are examples of popular metallic fabrics. Check with a theatrical supplier for a complete range of products and samples in this category.

FASTENERS

Basically, four types of mechanical fasteners are used in scenery construction. Each comes in a variety of shapes, sizes and adaptations. Some simple projects may allow you your choice of fastener. In other applications, you will need to rely on the unique characteristics of only one of these fasteners.

Nails

Nails are generally used in joining wood to wood in scenery construction. The most frequently used nails are common nails, box nails and finish nails. These nails can be purchased loose for use with a hammer or packaged for use in a pneumatic nailer. A busy or professional shop will want to take advantage of the efficiency of a pneumatic system.

Common Nails

Common nails have a flat head and range is size from 2D (1 inch) to 60D (6 inches). The length of a nail is expressed in *D* or pennyweight. A 2D nail may be called a two-penny nail. Just how this method of sizing came into being is not exactly clear. The two predominant theories associate the notation or terminology with either the original cost of a specific size nail or its weight. From 2D to 10D, the length of the nail is ½″ plus a ¼″ for each *D* (see the chart in Figure 5-5). Nails less than 2D are specified in inches. Those above 10D do not follow a pattern. Common nails can be purchased with a ring, or grooved, shank for extra holding power.

Box Nails

Box nails have a large flat head, and a thinner-diameter shank than common nails, and come in a smaller range of sizes. They can be purchased as coated nails or ring shank, which increases their holding power.

Finish Nails

Finish nails are used to secure moulding or in any application where exposed nail heads would be obtrusive. They have a very small head, which can be driven just below the surface of the wood so as not to

Pennyweight	2d	3d	4d	6d	8d	10d	12d	16d	20d	30d	40d	50d	60d
Length in inches	1	1.25	1.5	2	2.5	3	3.25	3.5	4	4.5	5	5.5	6

FIGURE 5-5 *Nail sizing chart*

be visible. In intimate settings, the hole can be filled with wood filler or spackle, depending on the type of finish being applied. A brad is a very small version of a finish nail.

Duplex Nails

Duplex nails are also known as double-head or scaffolding nails. They are used for temporary fastening. The first head rests against the material when set; the top head remains approximately ¼″ above the surface to enable the claw of a hammer to grip the nail for removal. Duplex nails are sized as common nails.

Roofing Nails

Roofing nails have wide, flat heads, which makes them useful in holding soft and easily compressible materials like Homosote or Celotex. These nails can also be purchased for use in a pneumatic nailer.

Clout Nails

Clout nails are unique to scenery construction, but are no longer used professionally. These nails are designed to penetrate through the wood, strike a metal plate placed under the material and curl back into the wood fibers. This technique creates a secure joint, but modern techniques and tools have left this fastener behind.

Corrugated Fasteners

Corrugated fasteners are somewhat odd items that can come in handy from time to time. They can be used to temporarily hold a corner joint together until a permanent fastening can be completed. They come ¼″ to ½″ deep and are available for use in pneumatic nailers.

Staples

In addition to staples for hand staplers and electric fabric staplers, a wide range of staples for pneumatic staple guns are available for use in scenery construction. They are sized by the width of the staple (known as the crown) the staple length and the gauge of the wire from which the staple is formed. Staples are commonly available with crowns from ³⁄₁₆″ to 1″, ⁵⁄₃₂″ to 3″ in length, and in fine-, medium- and heavy-gauge wire (22 to 15 gauge). Staples are an excellent choice for securing corner blocks, keystones and hard covers to flat frames.

Screws

Wood Screws

Wood screws are most useful when a joint needs to be taken apart at a later date, to fasten hardware to scenic units, and on occasions when the clamping force and holding power of a screw can be used to advantage. Screws are sized by length in ⅛″ increments and the diameter of the shaft at its widest point. The shape of the screw head is either flat, oval or round, and designed commonly for either a slotted or Phillips screwdriver. Phillips-head screws have gained in popularity with the increased use of screw guns or electric drills to drive them. The Phillips-head design enables the driving bit to be seated and hold its position on the screw better than the plain slot design.

Drywall Screws

Drywall screws have also increased in usage with the adoption of screw guns. These screws were originally designed to fasten drywall (gypsum board) to wood or metal framing studs. In the theater, they are replacing nails in many instances, and are very useful for certain applications. They have a bugle-shaped Phillips-head, a narrow shaft, a very sharp tip or a self-drilling tip, and coarse, sharp threads. A trim head is also available when appearance is a consideration. Drywall screws are tempered, which causes them to shatter under certain conditions. Because they are so easy and convenient to use, they are sometimes used in inappropriate situations. Drywall screws should not be used to fasten hardware or against metal of any kind.

Lag Screws
Lag screws are very large, heavy-duty wood screws. They come with a square or hex head and are sometimes called *lag bolts*.

Sheet-Metal Screws
Sheet-metal screws are designed to fasten metal to metal. The shaft is not tapered, as in wood screws, and is threaded all the way to the head. A hole equal in size to the diameter of the shaft is required for use.

Self-Drilling Screws
Self-drilling screws, sometimes known as *Tek screws*, combine a drill and screw into a single efficient unit to save time and labor costs. They are designed to drill their own pilot hole into light-gauge metal. This is a terrific fastener to use when applying wood coverings to steel frames.

Bolts
A bolt is a fastener that is inserted through a hole and secured with a nut. Their size is specified by diameter, length and number of threads per inch. Threads are classified by the Unified National Thread Series. The most common series in use in scenery construction is UNC (coarse). UNF (fine) is used primarily for tools and machinery, or in situations where higher strength and resistance to loosening as a result of vibrations are required.

Machine Bolts
Machine bolts have square or hexagonal heads and are threaded over approximately the first 1½″ of the shank.

Stove Bolts
Stove bolts have flat or round slotted heads and are threaded over the entire length of the bolt shank.

Machine Screws
Machine screws are like stove bolts, but with finer threads.

Carriage Bolts
Carriage bolts have a round head and a square portion of shank just below the head. The square portion is designed to prevent the bolt from turning when set into wood. It is threaded over the first 1½″ of the shank.

Other Bolts and Adaptations
There are some very useful bolt adaptations and some very exotic bolts that are used in scenery construction. Eye bolts, U-bolts, elevator bolts, threaded rod, J-bolts and, for rigging and other high-strength needs, graded bolts are some of the items you may want to investigate for future needs.

Nuts are typically hexagonal or square. Wing nuts are used in temporary situations and can be tightened and loosened by hand.

Washers are often required to spread the forces of compression over a larger area than that of the bolt head and nut. Plain washers or fender washers are used under normal conditions. Locking washers can be used to prevent the nut from loosening due to vibration.

A knife-thread insert or T-nut can be set into wood to provide receiving threads for a bolt instead of a nut.

Adhesives
Adhesives are another category of products that come in a dizzying variety of choices, many of which are applicable to

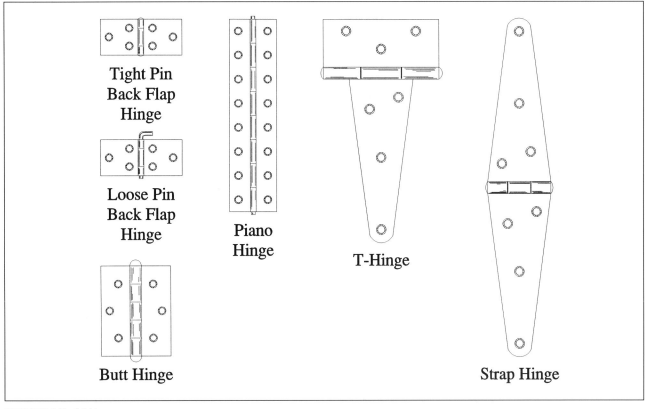

FIGURE 5-6 *Useful hinges*

very specific materials and circumstances. The scene shop requires only a few varieties under most circumstances. Do not hesitate to check with local suppliers if you have unusual requirements. There is probably some industry that has a similar set of circumstances for which an adhesive has been developed. Read all cautionary information before using these adhesives.

Yellow Glue
Yellow glue, or carpenter's glue, is used for most wood-on-wood applications. It can be purchased in 55-gallon drums or small squeeze bottles. It dries in one to two hours. Yellow glue should not be used to adhere muslin to flat frames because it discolors the fabric.

White Glue
White glue is more flexible, and is suitable for use with fabrics, wood and paper. It can be diluted and cleaned with water before it dries.

Construction Adhesives
A variety of construction adhesives have been developed for industrial applications. These products are formulated for porous or nonporous materials; some, such as mastic, are formulated specifically for foam. Many construction adhesives can be purchased in tubes for application with a caulking gun. Check with your local supplier for the brands available in your area.

Epoxy
Epoxy is used when a waterproof adhesive is required. It generally comes in two parts, which are mixed together for use. Epoxies are very strong and fast drying.

Contact Cement
Contact cement is most commonly used to adhere nonporous materials. Its advantage is that it holds on contact, which can be very useful for some theater applications. Latex-based contact cement works with foam.

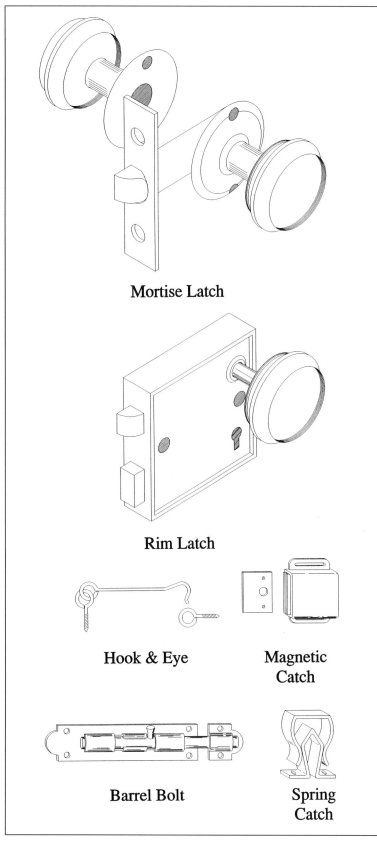

Mortise Latch

Rim Latch

Hook & Eye

Magnetic Catch

Barrel Bolt

Spring Catch

FIGURE 5-7 *Various latches*

Glue Sticks

Hot melt glue sticks are used with a glue gun for applications that do not require strength.

Hardware

The theater has developed an inventory of very specialized hardware over the years. However, changes in scenic styles and construction techniques, and improvements in tools, have made much of this theatrical hardware virtually obsolete. Some of the rigging hardware, which will be discussed later in this chapter, remains useful, but many items have been eliminated or replaced with more commonly available substitutes.

Hinges

Among the infinite variety of hinges manufactured for one purpose or another, there are four basic types (illustrated in Figure 5-6 on page 99) that are regularly used in theatrical applications. All of them are available in various sizes and an assortment of variations.

1. The *back-flap hinge* is the most theater-specific of the hinges. It is available with a tight pin or loose pin. The loose pin variety is typically used to temporarily join two scenic units together. The pin is easily inserted or removed to facilitate quick scene shifts. The tight-pin back-flap hinge is used for longer lasting unions.

2. The *butt hinge* is most commonly found on doors. It is designed to be mortised into the edge of the door and the door jamb.

3. The *piano hinge* is also known as a continuous hinge. It is usually available in 6' and 8' lengths and can be cut to any length required.

4. *Strap hinges* can also be either tight pin or loose pin and come in a useful *T* configuration.

Latches

Latches are used to secure doors, cupboards and windows, as well as for a vari-

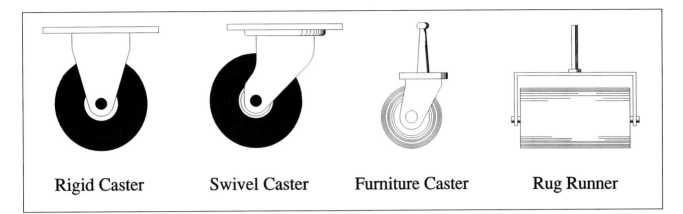

Rigid Caster   Swivel Caster   Furniture Caster   Rug Runner

ety of other creative uses. Figure 5-7 illustrates some of the latches commonly used in scenery construction.

FIGURE 5-8 *Common casters*

Casters

Casters used in theatrical scenery are classified as either swivel or rigid. Rigid casters are also referred to as fixed, straight or stationary casters. Rigid casters limit movement along a single line, while swivel casters allow for movement in any direction. Some swivel casters are equipped with a locking mechanism that turns them into rigid casters. Furniture casters may employ a ball or roller in place of the wheel.

When selecting a caster, consider the composition of the wheel, the load the caster can support and the overall size of the caster. The composition of the wheels will impact the capacity, rollability, noise level and level of floor protection. Polyurethane, neoprene and nylon wheels will provide good floor protection, a very low noise level while rolling and moderate rollability performance, but tend to have lower load capacities than similar-sized wheels composed of other materials. Metal, solid rubber, phenolic and polyolefin wheels will generally have greater capacities and superior rollability. They are also noisy and provide low to moderate floor protection.

Theater applications generally require a caster that is quiet and that will not damage the stage floor or painted show deck. Also, choose one rated to support a load greater

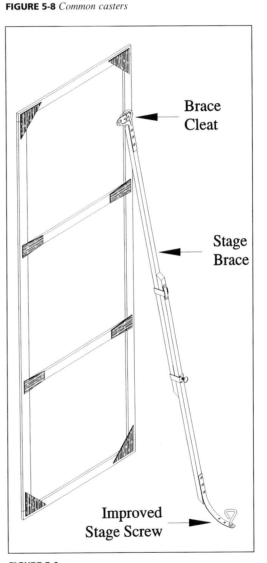

Brace Cleat

Stage Brace

Improved Stage Screw

FIGURE 5-9
A stage brace supporting a flat

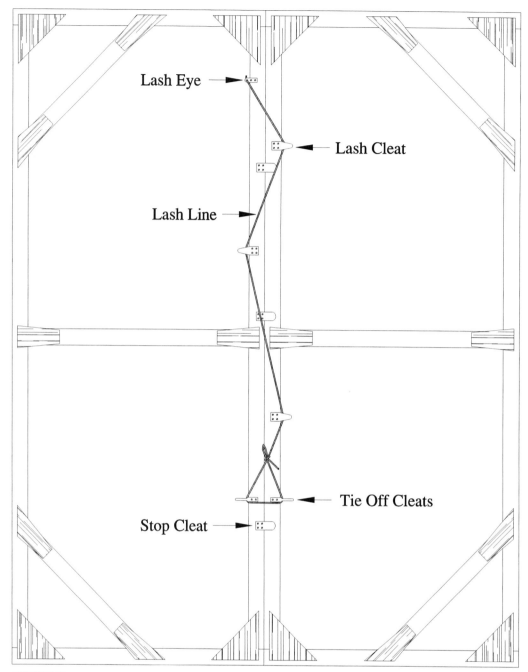

Lash Eye

Lash Cleat

Lash Line

Tie Off Cleats

Stop Cleat

FIGURE 5-10
Two flats joined together using traditional lashing technique

than the anticipated weight of the scenic unit. This will add a margin for error and ensure smooth operation.

Stage Hardware

Traditional stage hardware falls into three basic functions: bracing, joining and hanging. Stage braces were developed to facilitate quick, easy and repetitive changes in scenery without the use of any tools. A stage brace is used to hold a flat in a vertical position, as illustrated in Figure 5-9 on page 105. The length of the brace is adjustable. The top of the brace terminates in a pair of metal hooks that engage a stage-brace cleat attached near the top of the flat. The bottom of the brace terminates in a curved piece of strap steel through which a stage screw is inserted to fasten the brace to the deck.

A modification of the stage brace has been developed for use in the film and television industry. Both ends of the brace terminate in metal angle brackets. Drywall or standard screws are used to secure the brace to the flat and the deck. These modifications make for a more secure connection between the brace and both the flat and the deck, resulting in a more rigid structure. The length of the brace is fixed, since standard-height flats are normally used in this industry. This brace does not facilitate quick scenery changes.

Lashing hardware was developed to join traditional flat-construction scenery together quickly and easily without the use of tools. Lash cleats are alternately attached to the stiles of adjoining flats. A lash line is secured to the top of one of the flats and woven around the lash cleats to a set of tie-off cleats near the bottom of the flats. Stop cleats are installed to properly align the flats. When the hardware is properly positioned on the flats, an experienced stagehand can quickly lash the two flats together with a few flicks of the wrist. Figure 5-10 illustrates two flats joined together by lashing. This lashing technique is rarely used professionally in today's theater due to advances in technology and changes in design style. The stage brace still serves a limited function, but has been replaced with other bracing techniques in most professional operations.

Theatrical hanging hardware is still very common. This hardware is designed to hang scenic units on an overhead rigging system and to secure these units to the deck when they are in their playing position. The hanging iron illustrated in Figure 5-11 is the standard piece of hardware used to hang a flat. The iron is bolted to the bottom of the flat in line with one of the flat's stiles, with the ring at the top. The small bend in the iron is positioned under the bottom rail of the flat. This design lifts the weight of the unit from the bottom, eliminating tensile stress on the joints of the flat. Always bolt the hanging iron to the framing of the flat. A *keeper* is required to hold the top of the flat to the cable; this item

must also be bolted to the flat frame. Figure 5-12 illustrates two options available for use as a keeper. Ceiling plates are used when the scenic unit's playing position is horizontal rather than vertical.

When the scenic unit is brought into its playing position, it must often be secured to the deck to eliminate any movement. Two types of foot irons (illustrated in Figure 5-13, page 104) can be used for this purpose. A stage screw is used to fasten the foot iron to the deck.

Wire Rope and Accessories

Wire rope is a fairly complicated product that is manufactured for many different and very specific applications. Some of the most common properties of wire rope that bear consideration for theatrical applications are strength, flexibility, resistance to rotation and resistance to abrasion. The most common wire rope used in the theater is 6×19 extra-improved plow steel or 7×19 aircraft cable. The numbers indicate the number of strands and wires used to manufacture the wire rope. Figure 5-14 (page 104) depicts a cross-section view of the construction. The most common diameters range from $3/32''$ to $1/4''$, though many other sizes are available.

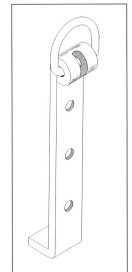
FIGURE 5-11
A bottom hanging iron

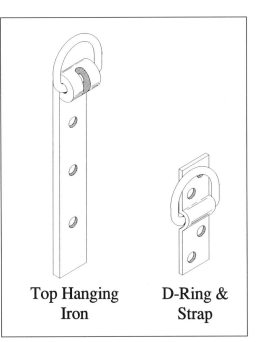
Top Hanging Iron   D-Ring & Strap

FIGURE 5-12
Two options for a keeper

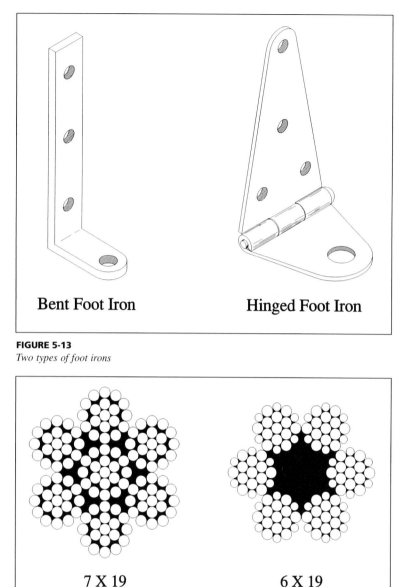

FIGURE 5-13
Two types of foot irons

FIGURE 5-14
Cross section of two common wire ropes
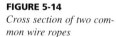

damage the wire rope and cause it to fail under loads well below its rated capacity. The thimble will bear no weight, but must be sized for the diameter of the wire rope in use.

Cable clips may also be used in wire-rope termination. These clips can be applied with commonly available tools; Figure 5-16 illustrates their application. A minimum of two clips must be used for wire-rope diameters up to ¼″. Notice in Figure 5-16 the orientation of the clip around the wire rope. The saddle of the clip must cradle the live end of the wire rope (the live end is the end which supports the load). The U-bolt goes over the portion that has been turned back, also called the dead end. The clip must be sized to match the diameter of the wire rope and should be purchased from a reputable manufacturer who has tested and rated the clips. Cable clips maintain only 80 percent of the wire rope's strength when they are applied correctly and the nuts are tightened to the manufacturer's recommended torque. Wire rope will stretch when a load is applied, causing a reduction in the diameter of the wire rope. Be sure to retighten the nuts on the cable clips to the recommended torque after the load has been applied. Follow the manufacturer's specifications for use.

Fist grips are similar to wire-rope clips, with one notable advantage. They are manufactured to provide a saddle for both the live end and the dead end of the wire rope (see Figure 5-17, page 106). With this construction, you need not be concerned with the orientation of the fist grips to the wire rope.

Turnbuckles are used to adjust trim or tension within the system in which they are installed. They are typically used in rigging to fine tune the trim height of a piece of flying scenery. The ends of the turnbuckle are supplied with one of four end fittings, or any combination of these fittings, as illustrated in Figure 5-18, page 106. The jaw or eye end fittings are the most useful for theatrical purposes.

Wire rope can be terminated or attached to an object with the use of nicopress sleeves or cable clips. Do not attempt to tie a knot to secure wire rope. When applied correctly, copper nicopress sleeves maintain 100 percent of the wire rope's strength. These sleeves require a special tool (chapter three) to crimp the sleeve around the wire rope. Figure 5-15 illustrates the termination of a wire rope around a pipe batten and around a thimble to form an eye. A thimble should always be used when forming an eye to prevent the wire rope from bending too sharply: A sharp bend will

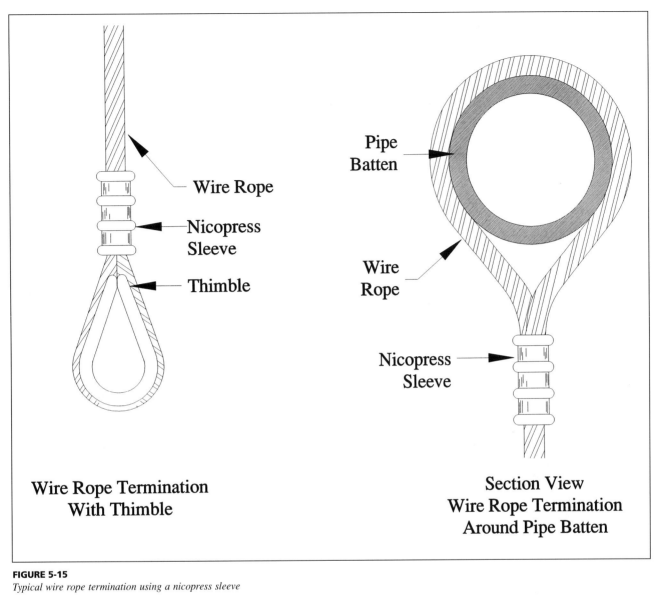

Wire Rope

Nicopress
Sleeve

Thimble

Wire Rope Termination
With Thimble

Pipe
Batten

Wire
Rope

Nicopress
Sleeve

Section View
Wire Rope Termination
Around Pipe Batten

FIGURE 5-15
Typical wire rope termination using a nicopress sleeve

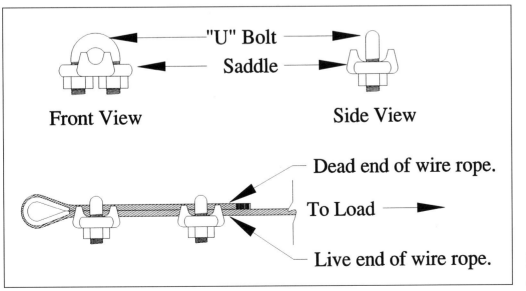

"U" Bolt

Saddle

Front View

Side View

Dead end of wire rope.

To Load

Live end of wire rope.

FIGURE 5-16
Wire rope clips and their application

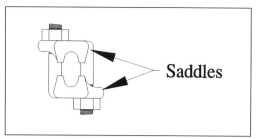

FIGURE 5-17 *A fist grip*

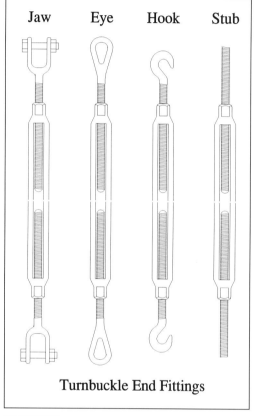

FIGURE 5-18
Turnbuckle end fittings

Purchase only rated turnbuckles of a capacity sufficient to meet your needs.

A safety measure must be taken when using turnbuckles to prevent them from loosening and ultimately coming apart while in use. They can be equipped with lock nuts or jam nuts tightened against the body of the turnbuckle as one solution. A cotter pin may also be inserted through the threaded rod at a point within the body of the turnbuckle.

Shackles are used as a method of providing a safe link between various rigging components. There are two basic types of shackles, as illustrated in Figure 5-19. The anchor shackle is the most common type used in theatrical rigging. Shackles are available with a screw pin, round pin or bolt to close the open end. Shackles are designed for maximum strength when the load is applied in line, as illustrated by the arrows in Figure 5-19. A reduction of up to 50 percent in the safe working load occurs as the load moves away from the in-line axis. As with all other components of a rigging system, these items should be sized and rated for the expected load.

Links and rings are useful when bringing several components together at one junction. They are available in three basic shapes (as illustrated in Figure 5-20) and a variety of sizes. The manufacturer's working-load limits should be observed at all times when working with these items.

Chapter seven will illustrate the methods and procedures for hanging scenery and the application of much of this hardware to accomplish this task easily and safely.

FIBER ROPE

Fiber rope is manufactured from organic or synthetic fibers. The standard for many years has been manila rope, an organic material derived from the abaca plant. Its set of characteristics has made it the most desirable organic fiber rope for rigging use. ¾" manila rope is commonly used as the hand line in counterweight rigging sys-

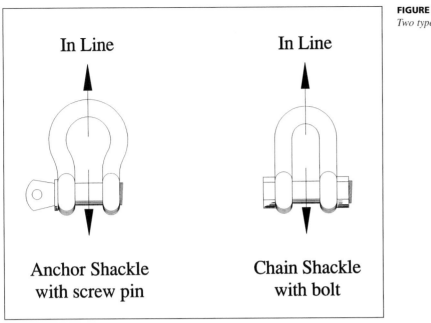

FIGURE 5-19
Two types of shackles

tems. Figure 5-21, page 108, indicates the breaking strength and safe working load for popular sizes of manila rope. Another common and useful organic fiber rope is cotton sash cord. This rope has many light-duty uses in the theater, but is not intended for overhead rigging applications.

A wide variety of synthetic fiber ropes have been developed in recent years, and some of them are finding their way into the theater. They have many advantages over organic fiber ropes, including better strength-to-weight ratios, absorption of little or no moisture and a superior ability to absorb shock loads, and are resistant to rot and mildew. Some synthetics are to be avoided because of unacceptable elongation and texture characteristics. These undesirable characteristics were common among synthetic fiber ropes when they were first introduced. The problem has since been addressed with some very good results.

While manila rope is most commonly constructed of yarns twisted into strands that are, in turn, twisted into the rope, the most interesting and successful synthetic-fiber ropes are braided or manufactured in

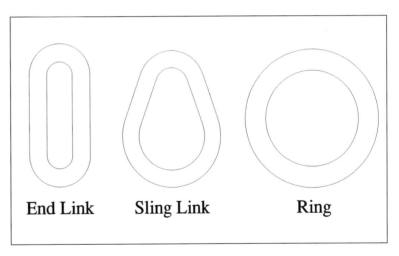

a variety of core and outer sheathing combinations that greatly improve the handling characteristics and strength of the rope. The breaking strength and safe working loads of some synthetic fiber ropes are listed in Figure 5-22 on page 108.

FIGURE 5-20 *Links and rings*

FIGURE 5-21
Safe working loads for manila rope

Rope Diameter	Breaking Strength	Safety Factor		
		5	8	10
1/4"	540 lbs.	108 lbs.	68 lbs.	54 lbs.
3/8"	1220 lbs.	244 lbs.	153 lbs.	120 lbs.
1/2"	2380 lbs.	476 lbs.	298 lbs.	238 lbs.
5/8"	3960 lbs.	792 lbs.	495 lbs.	396 lbs.
3/4"	4960 lbs.	992 lbs.	620 lbs.	496 lbs.
7/8"	6950 lbs.	1390 lbs.	869 lbs.	695 lbs.
1"	8100 lbs.	1620 lbs.	1013 lbs.	810 lbs.
1 1/8"	10800 lbs.	2160 lbs.	1350 lbs.	1080 lbs.
1 1/4"	12200 lbs.	2440 lbs.	1525 lbs.	1220 lbs.

Rope Diameter	Type Of Fiber	Breaking Strength	Safety Factor		
			5	8	10
1/4"	Sta-Set (polyester)	2000 lbs.	400 lbs.	250 lbs.	200 lbs.
	Polypropylene (twisted)	1130 lbs.	226 lbs.	141 lbs.	113 lbs.
	Nylon (twisted)	1490 lbs.	298 lbs.	186 lbs.	149 lbs.
1/2"	Sta-Set (polyester)	8000 lbs.	1600 lbs.	1000 lbs.	800 lbs.
	Polypropylene (twisted)	3600 lbs.	720 lbs.	450 lbs.	360 lbs.
	Nylon (twisted)	5750 lbs.	1150 lbs.	719 lbs.	575 lbs.
3/4"	Sta-Set (polyester)	15000 lbs.	3000 lbs.	1875 lbs.	1500 lbs.
	Polypropylene (twisted)	7600 lbs.	1520 lbs.	950 lbs.	760 lbs.
	Nylon (twisted)	12800 lbs.	2560 lbs.	1600 lbs.	1280 lbs.
1"	Sta-Set (polyester)	24600 lbs.	4920 lbs.	3075 lbs.	2460 lbs.
	Polypropylene (twisted)	12500 lbs.	2500 lbs.	1562 lbs.	1250 lbs.
	Nylon (twisted)	22600 lbs.	4520 lbs.	2825 lbs.	2260 lbs.

FIGURE 5-22
Safe working loads for synthetic ropes

CHAPTER 6

CONSTRUCTION TECHNIQUES

Throughout this chapter you will find instructions and suggestions for building several standard scenic units. Alternative methods based on available material, equipment and skills are common and are practiced by many theater technicians. After you have learned the basic techniques offered here, you may also discover alternative methods that fit the circumstances of your particular situation. Remember that good construction techniques are those that are simple, quick, safe and inexpensive. They must also produce quality scenery that meets the specific requirements of the production design and the fundamental requirements of all theatrical scenery.

To fully understand the techniques and methods suggested here, you will need to understand a few terms used to describe the physical aspects of the material and a limited number of joinery options. Figure 6-1 indicates the terms used to identify the surfaces of a board. The *front* and *rear faces* are the broadest surfaces of the material. The *edge* is the surface that defines the thickness of the material along the length of the board. The *end* also reflects the thickness of the material, but across the width of the board. These terms will be used to describe placement, position and orientation throughout the instructions in this chapter.

JOINERY

Joinery defines the method by which two pieces of material are joined together. The butt joint is the most common method used in the theater and can be utilized in a variety of orientations, as illustrated in Figure 6-2 on page 110. A butt joint is often reinforced with plywood, metal plates or wood blocks. The lap joint and half-lap joint are also common, useful techniques practiced in scenery construction. Biscuit or plate joints are relatively new and have replaced more time-consuming and difficult doweled joints and mortise-and-tenon joints.

UNFRAMED SCENERY

Drops, cut drops, legs and borders are perhaps some of the simplest and least expensive types of scenery. They are easy to construct and install, shift quickly and efficiently when used in conjunction with a fly system and require relatively little storage space, but provide a limited range

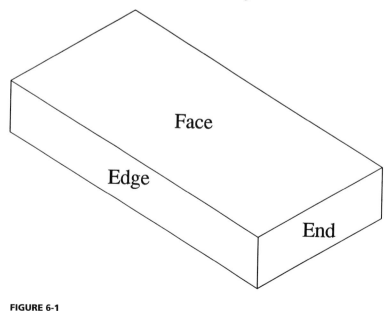

FIGURE 6-1
Identification of the various surfaces of boards or sheet goods

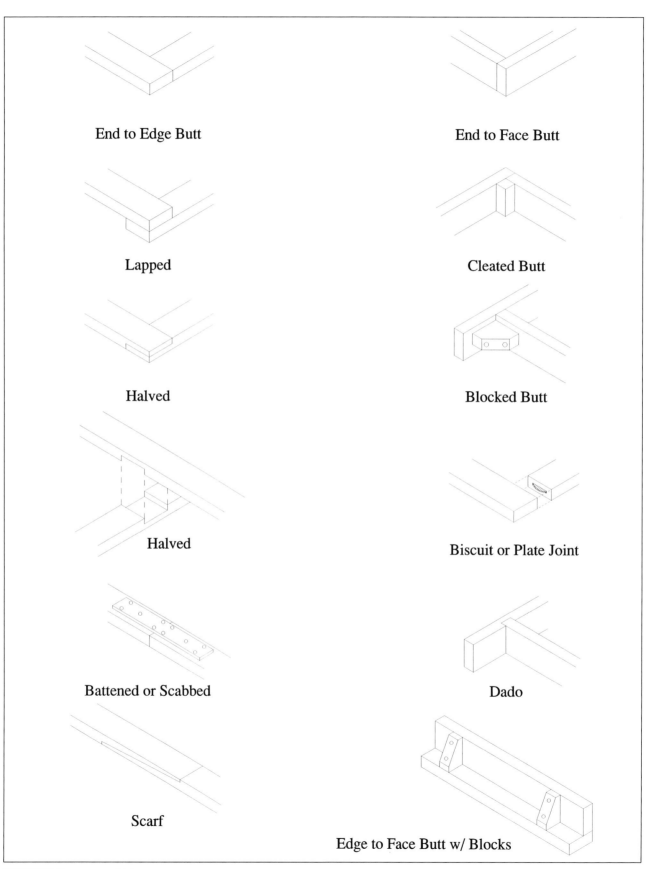

End to Edge Butt

End to Face Butt

Lapped

Cleated Butt

Halved

Blocked Butt

Halved

Biscuit or Plate Joint

Battened or Scabbed

Dado

Scarf

Edge to Face Butt w/ Blocks

FIGURE 6-2 *Common wood joints*

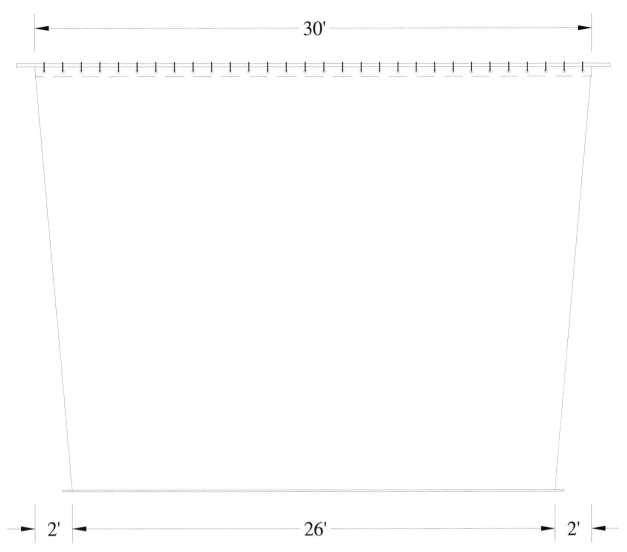

30'

2'   26'   2'

FIGURE 6-3
A typical muslin drop

of design opportunities. There are a number of suppliers who will manufacture these goods to your specifications quickly and at a cost which may be comparative with the labor and materials costs of your organization.

Drops, Legs and Borders

A *drop* is an unframed expanse of material, usually muslin or scrim, which provides the designer with an unbroken painting surface of almost any dimension. Drops are typically used as the back piece of a set, backgrounds such as the sky or some distant vista for exterior scenes, and backings for window and door openings of interior sets. Drops are normally constructed with horizontal seams and a simple 1″ hem on the vertical edges. Seamless drops can be

constructed from wide widths of muslin when backlighting is required. The vertical edge should be cut at an angle, forming a trapezoid; the top of the drop should be approximately two feet wider on each side than the bottom of the drop. This technique helps eliminate the bow-shaped sag that occurs at the ends of rectangular drops (see Figure 6-3, above).

The top and bottom edges of the drop can be finished with or without permanent battens. To install permanent battens, the top edge of the drop is stapled, glued and sandwiched between two pieces of 1×4 pine. The 1×4 batten serves to stretch the drop horizontally and support the drop when installed. The batten is assembled using long lengths of 1×4 pine placed end to end until the batten is approximately one

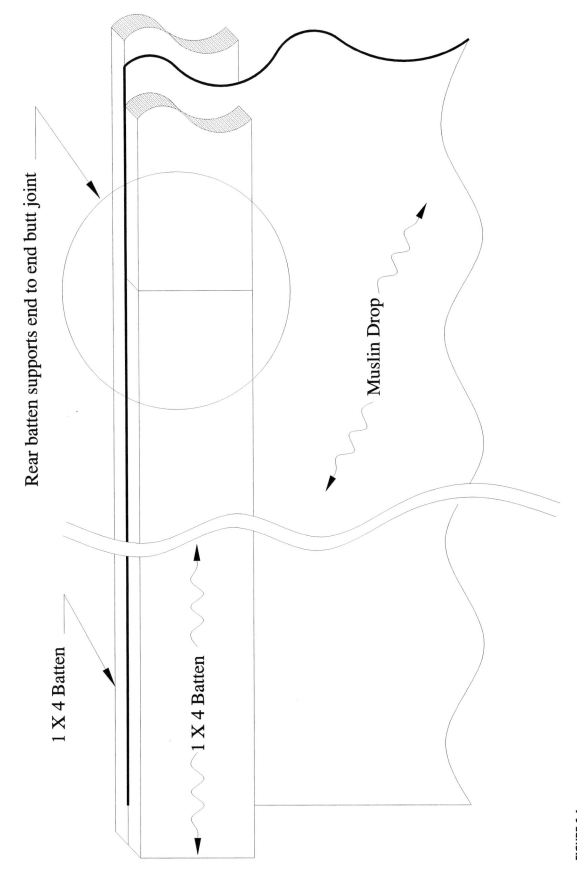

Rear batten supports end to end butt joint

1 X 4 Batten

1 X 4 Batten

Muslin Drop

FIGURE 6-4
Detail of a wood batten for a drop

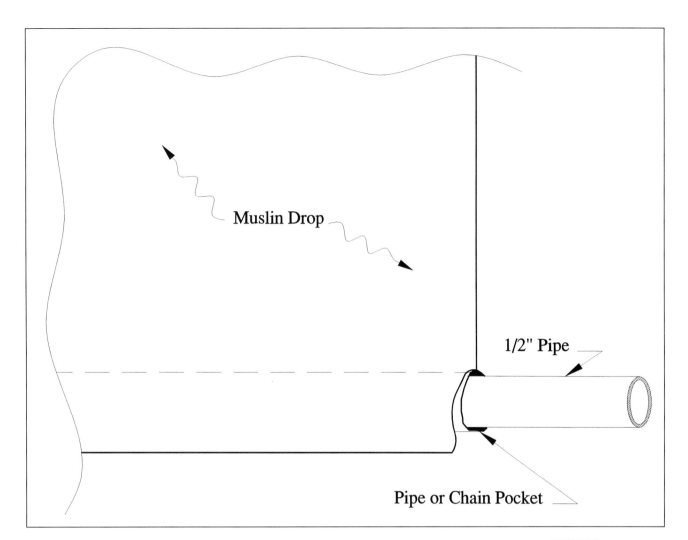

Muslin Drop

1/2" Pipe

Pipe or Chain Pocket

FIGURE 6-5
*Detail of a pipe or chain
pocket for a drop*

foot longer than the width of the drop. Stagger the seams in the front and back members of the batten to reinforce the joints, as illustrated in Figure 6-4.

The bottom edge of the drop is similarly attached between two pieces of 1″ stock that are just wide enough to provide enough weight for a suitable vertical stretch to the drop. The outer corners of the 1 × 2 are rounded to avoid creasing the drop when it is rolled for transportation or storage.

The top of the drop can alternatively be finished with webbing, grommets and ties. The fabric is sewn to a heavy-duty jute webbing, approximately 3½″ wide, along the entire top edge. No. 2 brass grommets are set through the fabric and webbing every 12 inches. The grommets are positioned ¾″ from the top edge of the drop.

The ties are made of twill tape cut to a length of 18 inches and secured through the grommet with a half hitch. With this method, the twill-tape tie lines are used to fasten the drop directly to the permanent batten of the fly system.

The bottom edge of the drop may be constructed with a pipe pocket, as illustrated in Figure 6-5, instead of a permanent batten. The pipe, inserted into the pocket once the drop is hung in position, provides the necessary weight to stretch the drop vertically. The pipe may be 10′ lengths of ½″ schedule 40, threaded on both ends and supplied with a coupler on one end. These shorter lengths of pipe make installation more manageable. After the first section of pipe is inserted into the pipe pocket, the next section is threaded onto the first and the two are then eased further into the

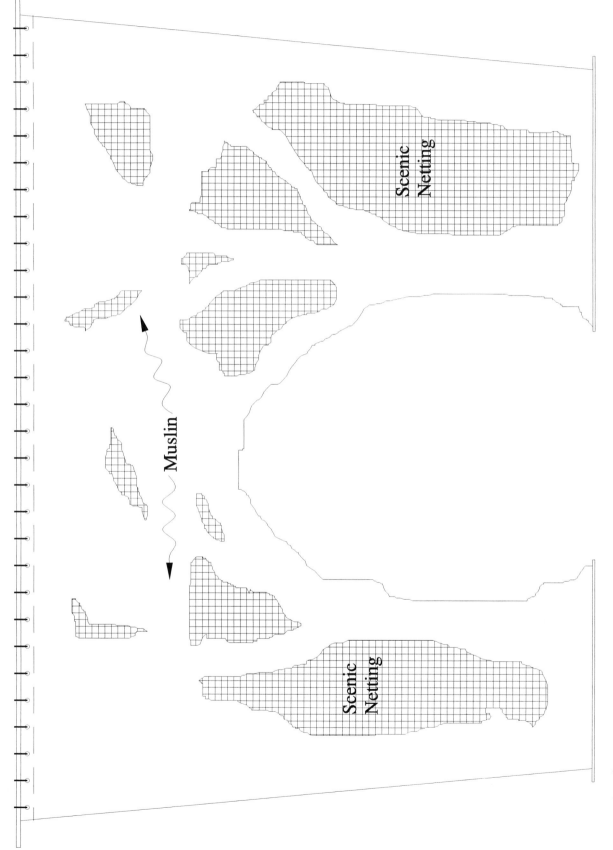

FIGURE 6-6 *A cut drop*

pocket. Additional sections of pipe are coupled to the preceding sections until the other end of the drop is reached.

I prefer the use of a pipe pocket on the bottom of the drop. Pipe has a better weight-to-size ratio than wood, and a pipe pocket is visually unobtrusive. In the event you choose to use a wooden batten at the top of your drop and a pipe pocket on the bottom, the drop will be rolled on the top batten, requiring the outer corners of the 1×4 batten to be rounded to prevent creasing the drop (as suggested previously for the bottom batten). Legs and borders are constructed in the same manner as drops.

Cut Drops

A three-dimensional effect can be achieved with the use of a series of properly designed and executed cut drops. The technique calls for portions of the drops to be cut and removed after the drops have been painted. This allows the audience to see through the layers of drops, imparting a sense of depth to the scene. The construction of these drops is the same as that of a conventional drop, with one exception: scenic netting must be applied to those portions of the drop that, as a result of cutting, are no longer supported by the natural hang of the drop. This includes those portions that have been cut free from the main body of the drop (see Figure 6-6). Legs and borders can also be designed and manufactured as part of a series of cut drops.

FRAMED SCENERY

Theater technicians have developed a simple, inexpensive and efficient framing system over the years that continues to be the basis for most two-dimensional scenery. A few improvements have been made in the tools and fasteners used in constructing these items, but the basic technique remains the same.

Flats

Figure 6-7 illustrates a rear view of the frame for a standard flat typical of those used in theaters for many years. The basic framing components of a flat are the top and bottom rails, stiles, toggles, diagonal braces, cornerblocks and keystones. It gets only slightly more complicated than this with larger units or with the addition of door and window openings. The techniques used to construct a flat frame are relatively simple. The two most important factors in any construction are the precision with which the components are cut and the strength and accuracy of the joints.

The Cut List

Examine the dimensioned rear elevation illustrated in Figure 6-8 on page 118. Based on this construction drawing, a cut list for a 4′ wide by 10′ tall flat can be prepared. This cut list is shown on page 119.

The Flat Joint

The joint used to assemble a flat is a basic end-to-edge butt joint reinforced with a piece of ¼″ plywood. This plywood reinforcement can be of any shape and size, as required by the project. Some standards have been established in the theater that have proven to combine strength and efficiency. The cornerblock is generally used on outside corners of the flat frame. It is cut in the shape of a triangle to the typical dimensions illustrated in Figure 6-10 on page 120. An added touch that will enhance the quality of your work is to sand or bevel the edges of the cornerblock, or any reinforcing plate, to remove any splinters or sharp edges created while cutting the plywood to size. Some carpenters refer to this process as "taking down the edge" or "knocking off the edge." Other sizes may and can be used as the project requires, but a standard size should be established for typical construction purposes.

The cornerblock is positioned across the joint (as illustrated in Figure 6-11 on page 121) and secured with a pneumatic stapler using wire staples and glue. If a pneumatic stapler is not available, other fasteners can be used, including screws and clout nails.

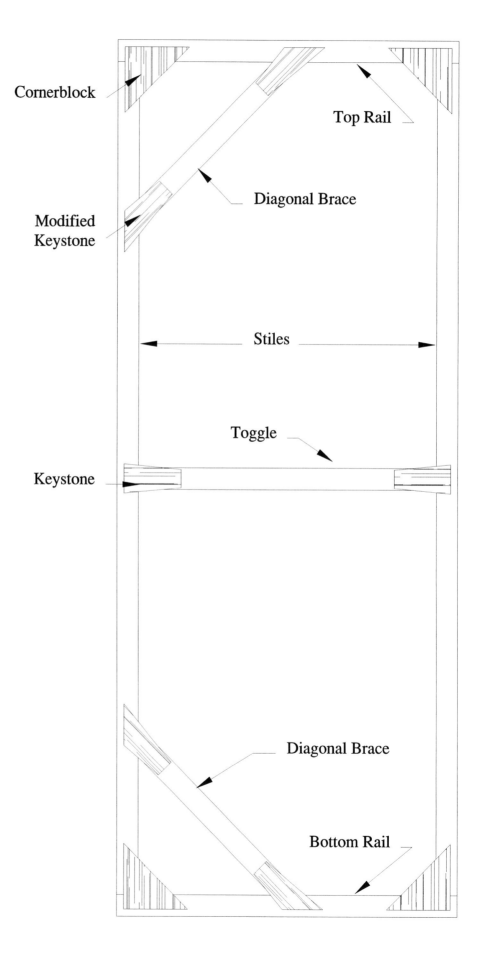

Cornerblock

Top Rail

Diagonal Brace

Modified
Keystone

Stiles

Toggle

Keystone

Diagonal Brace

Bottom Rail

FIGURE 6-7
*Standard components
of a flat frame*

Please note the position of the fasteners in the illustration. While not a significant problem when using wire staples, due to the thin gauge of the wire, this pattern limits the tendency of the wood frame to split as a result of the fasteners being placed in the same grain line of the 1×3 frame.

In most cases you will want to inset the cornerblock 1″ in from the outside edges of the frame. This setback will keep the cornerblocks out of the way when joining two flats together at a 90° angle (as illustrated in Figure 6-12 on page 122). This setback may not be required in all instances, but it is a good standard practice to maintain, particularly if you intend to establish an inventory of flats for stock.

There are two important provisions that must be met in assembling this joint to ensure strength. First, it is important for maximum strength to position the cornerblock so that the visible grain of the cornerblock runs perpendicular to the line of the butt joint (see Figure 6-11 on page 121). If the grain runs parallel to the joint, the joint is considerably weaker. Second, there should be no gap between the two framing members of the flat.

The keystone is used like the cornerblock to reinforce the internal joints of a flat. The shape and dimensions are illustrated in Figure 6-10 on page 120. Take note of the direction of the grain. As with the cornerblock, the keystone should be held back 1″ at any location where another flat or other scenic element may join the frame.

Using the general criteria described above, a variety of other shapes and sizes can be used to create custom joining plates. This construction method illustrates the benefits of an economical, simple and adaptable system.

Flat Assembly

To begin assembly of the flat, you must have, or create, the framing stock. You can purchase 1×3 pine direct from the lumberyard, which is often the most economical choice and frequently results in less waste and better quality lumber. Alternatively, you can purchase 1×12 pine and rip the material to the appropriate width. (See Step 1, Figure 6-13A on page 123.) In either event, once you have the 1×3 you are ready to cut the required framing members to length. With each new stick of 1×3 you must square and clean one end before cutting it to length. (See Step 2, Figure 6-13B on page 123.) This ensures that both ends of the piece are cut at precisely 90° to the length of the board and that any splits in the ends of the board have been removed. Check the measurement of each cut board to ensure it has been cut to the proper length. If you are using a stop gauge on the saw for multiple cuts (see Step 3, Figure 6-13C on page 123), you will only need to check the accuracy of your cuts after each new position is set.

Once you have cut all the material per the cut list, lay out the pieces in their proper positions on the framing table or the shop floor. Use the guides on the framing table or a 24″ steel framing square to establish true 90° corners (see Step 4, Figure 6-13D on page 124). Secure the frame to the table or floor using double-headed nails (scaffold nails) or finish nails. I prefer finish nails for lighter weight and less bulk in my nail apron. They are also less destructive to the framing material, more economical and very easy to remove. When using finish nails, leave the head of the nail at least ¼″ above the frame. If you should drive the head into the framing member, it is very easy to pull the frame up over the head of a finish nail.

Check the accuracy of your overall dimensions. If there are any discrepancies, now is the time to find them and make corrections before you have assembled the joints. It is a good idea to check for square by comparing the measurements diagonally from corner to corner (see Step 5, Figure 6-13E on page 124). If the measurements are the same, the unit is square. This step is particularly important if you are not using a framing table.

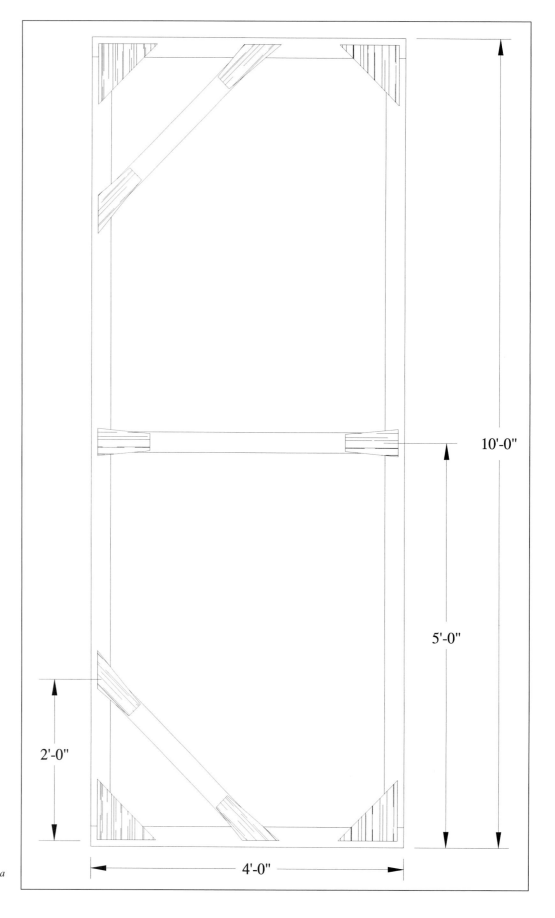

FIGURE 6-8

*Construction drawing for a
typical flat frame*

CUT LIST FOR FIGURE 6-8

TOP AND BOTTOM RAILS

2 pieces 1 × 3 pine 4'0" long
The 4'0" dimension equals the width of the flat and comes straight off the drawing.

LEFT AND RIGHT STILES

2 pieces 1 × 3 pine 10'0" minus 2 widths of 1 × 3
Note in Figure 6-8 that standard construction practice places the stiles between the top and bottom rail. Flats are constructed in this fashion to form a skid of sorts to reduce the tendency of splitting the frame or weakening the joint when the flat is slid along the stage floor during shifts. The actual length of the stiles is determined by the height of the flat, per the drawing's dimensions, minus the combined widths of the top and bottom rails. Two examples follow:
Example 1: If your framing stock is actually 2¾" wide, then the stiles are cut to 10'0" minus 2 times 2¾", or 10'0" minus 5½", or 9'6½".
Example 2: If your framing stock is 2⅝" wide, then the stiles are cut to 10'0" minus 2 times 2⅝", or 10'0" minus 5¼", or 9'6¾".

Remember the term *1 × 3* reflects the nominal size of the lumber. The actual size is ¾" thick and a width ranging any-where from 2½" to 2¾". It is good practice to actually measure the width of the framing stock you are using for the unit you are building, as widths can vary from piece to piece.

TOGGLE

1 piece 1 × 3 pine 4'0" minus 2 widths of 1 × 3
The length of the toggle in this case is the width of the flat, per the drawing, minus the combined widths of the two stiles. Using the stock sizes indicated in the two examples above, the toggle would be 3'6½" long if the stock is 2¾" wide or 3'6¾" long if the stock is 2⅝" wide.

DIAGONAL BRACES

l2 pieces 1 × 3 pine approximately 3'0" long, mitered at 45° on both ends
The dimension of the diagonal brace is usually not critical. Under ideal circumstances, it should be of a length sufficient to reach the midway point of the top or bottom rail; in this case, approximately 3'0".

Additionally, 4 cornerblocks, 2 keystones and 4 modified keystones will be required to assemble the flat. The entire cut list is represented in Figure 6-9.

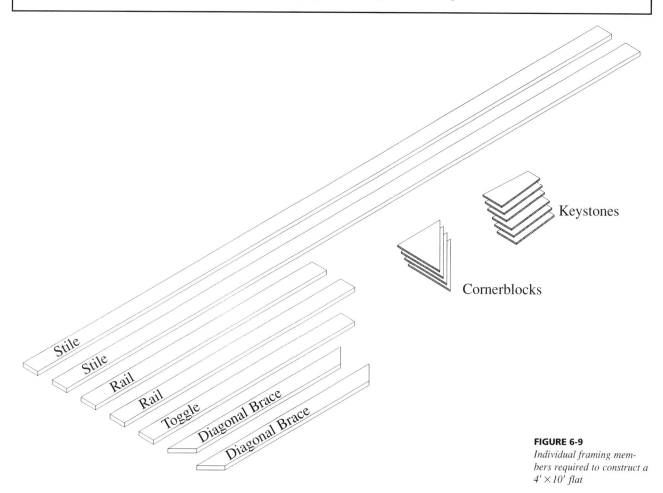

Keystones

Cornerblocks

Stile
Stile
Rail
Rail
Toggle
Diagonal Brace
Diagonal Brace

FIGURE 6-9
Individual framing members required to construct a 4' × 10' flat

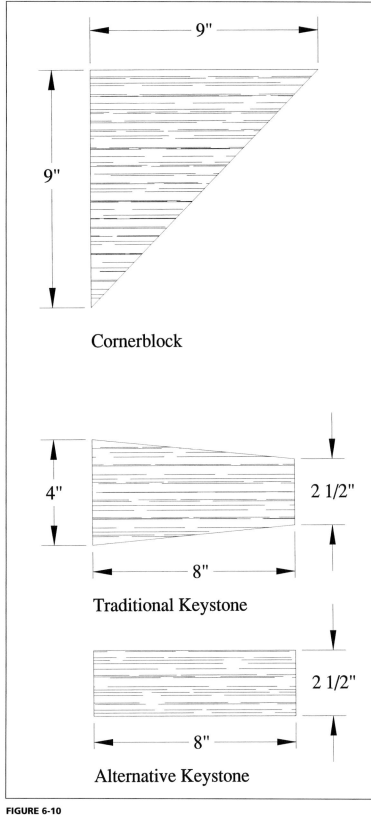

9"

9"

Cornerblock

4"

2 1/2"

8"

Traditional Keystone

2 1/2"

8"

Alternative Keystone

FIGURE 6-10
Standard cornerblock and keystone detail

If all is well, scribe a line 1″ from the outside edge of the flat wherever you anticipate the use of a cornerblock or keystone. This line is your guide to ensure the 1″ setback required to enable flats to be joined together at right angles, as discussed previously. Now pick any corner to begin assembly. Position the cornerblock using the lines you scribed, and remember to orient the grain of the cornerblock across the seam of the joint (see Step 6, Figure 6-13F on page 123.). Glue and staple the cornerblock to the rail and stile using the pattern illustrated in Figure 6-11.

Following the same procedure described above, continue around the flat, assembling the remaining outside corners. Next, install the toggle. The toggle is centered at five feet (see Step 7, Figure 6-13G on page 123). The toggle is cut to the width of the flat minus the width of the two stiles. Set a keystone across the joint (see Step 8, Figure 6-13H on page 123). If your keystones were cut correctly, the grain will be oriented in the proper direction. Be sure the toggle and the stile form a 90° angle and attach the keystone. Follow the pattern illustrated in Figure 6-11. Use the same procedure to join the other end of the toggle to the opposite stile. Any warp in the stiles may cause the toggle to appear too long or too short. If you are sure the toggle is cut to the appropriate length, you can pull apart or push together the stiles of the flat to fit the toggle.

Finally, set the diagonal braces in place and secure with the modified keystones. Standard keystones may be trimmed for this application, or custom plates can be fabricated.

Remove the nails holding the frame to the table or floor and you are finished with the frame assembly (see Step 9, Figure 6-13I on page 123). If all is well, you can proceed with covering the flat.

I often add an additional step to aid scenic artists in their work. When a paintbrush comes in contact with the inner corners of a flat frame, the image of the frame is

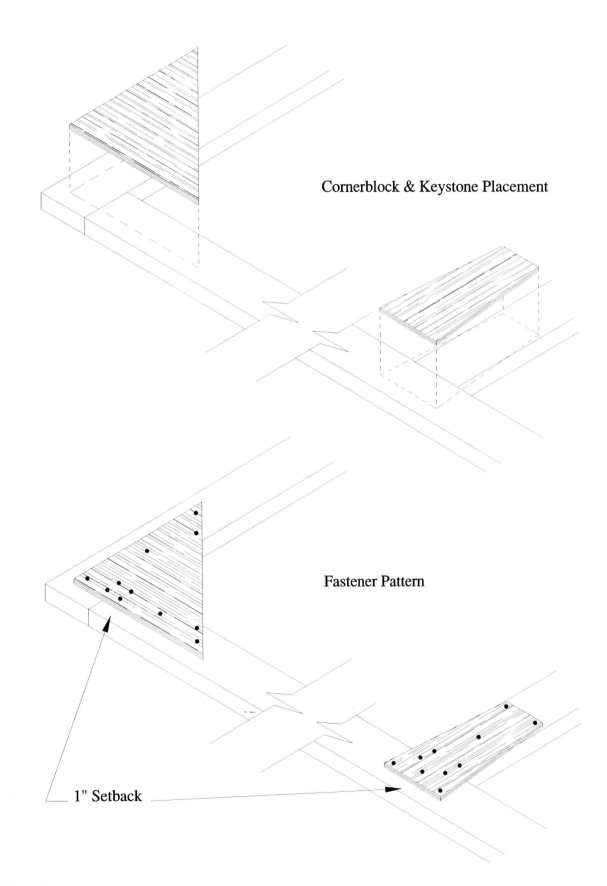

Cornerblock & Keystone Placement

Fastener Pattern

1" Setback

FIGURE 6-11
Standard position and orientation of cornerblocks and keystones including fastener placement

Cornerblock setback
to allow flats to join.

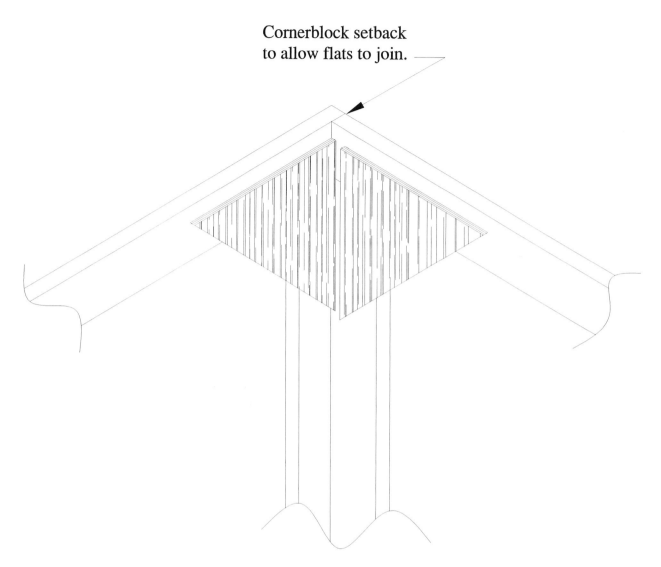

FIGURE 6-12
Cornerblocks and keystones are held back from the edge to permit a flush joint between two flats

sometimes revealed as a result of the contact through the fabric covering. By routing the inside corner on the face of all the framing members with a roundover bit, you can remove the corner of the frame that causes this effect.

Typically, the only variation in construction when building standard flats is the number and position of internal framing members. Figure 6-14, on page 125, illustrates the framing for a flat 5′ wide by 16′ tall. You can see that the framing is very similar to the first example, with two exceptions: The framing members are longer to accommodate the larger size of the flat, and two additional toggles are required. For general use, there should be a framing member every four to five feet. If you fol-

low this rule of thumb, you will be able to determine the amount and placement of internal framing for any size flat. The cut list for this flat is shown on page 125.

The maximum width of a flat is traditionally 5′9″, the standard dimension of the loading door of the railroad cars that were used to transport the scenery of a touring production. Though wider flats are possible, 5′9″ is still a good maximum width unless some other criteria are present. This is the largest size which is reasonably maneuverable and useful in stock. Also, 72″ wide fabric can still be comfortably used to cover these flats. The maximum height should be determined by your space limitations, available lengths of lumber (or your skill and ability to splice lumber together) and general usefulness. Larger units can easily be created by joining one or more flats together, which will be discussed in chapter seven.

Door and Window Flats

The techniques described above are also used to build the many variations of door and window flats. Some of these variations are illustrated in Figure 6-15 on page 126. Standard framing is altered only to accommodate the placement and dimensions of the specified door or window opening. The window flat in Figure 6-16 on page 127 illustrates the typical approach to framing a window opening. The toggles are positioned to frame the top and bottom of the window opening. Two additional framing members are positioned to frame the sides of the opening. Note the use of modified cornerblocks to reinforce the joints of the window opening. One leg of the cornerblock has been trimmed to fit within the available space. The cut list for this window flat is shown on page 126.

To assemble this window flat, follow the same steps described previously for the standard flat. Position the toggles to correspond to the dimensions of the top and bottom of the window opening. The bottom toggle is positioned so that the top edge of the toggle is 2'8" from the bottom of the flat. This dimension is shown on the drawing. The position of the top toggle is such that there is five feet between the two toggles, as indicated by the dimensioned height of the window opening on the drawing. If your cut list is correct, you can use the window stiles, which are cut to length at this dimension, to position the top toggle. The window stiles are positioned to create a 2'6" opening in the center of the flat, per the drawing. Once all the framing members are in place and nailed to the work table or shop floor, check all the critical dimensions. The overall flat and the window opening must also be checked for square. Assemble the joints as described

FIGURE 6-13A
Step 1—rip the framing material to the desired width

FIGURE 6-13B
Step 2—clean and square one end of the framing material

FIGURE 6-13C
Step 3—cut each framing member to length

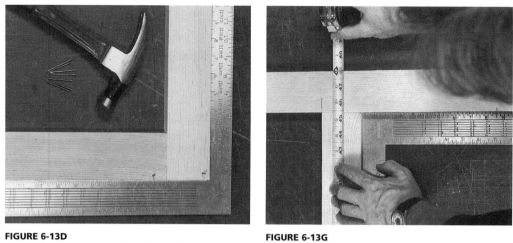

FIGURE 6-13D
Step 4—layout frame on workbench, template table or shop floor, and secure to work surface

FIGURE 6-13E
Step 5—check the diagonal measurement to ensure a square frame

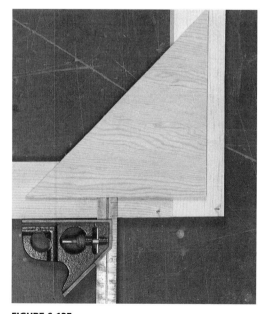

FIGURE 6-13F
Step 6—position and fasten each cornerblock to the framing members

FIGURE 6-13G
Step 7—check for proper width at the position of the toggle

FIGURE 6-13H
Step 8—position and fasten each keystone

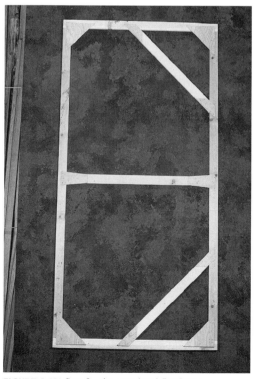

FIGURE 6-13I *Step 9—the completed flat frame*

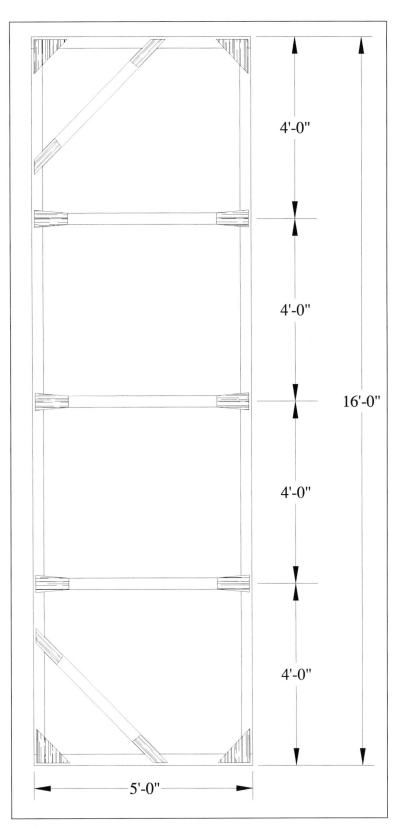

CUT LIST FOR FIGURE 6-14

TOP AND BOTTOM RAILS
2 pieces 1 × 3 pine 5′0″ long
The 5′0″ dimension is equal to the width of the flat.

LEFT AND RIGHT STILES
2 pieces 1 × 3 pine 16′0″ minus 2 widths of 1 × 3
Determined by the height of the flat, per the drawing's dimensions, minus the combined widths of the top and bottom rails.

TOGGLES
3 pieces 1 × 3 pine 5′0″ minus 2 widths of 1 × 3
The width of the flat minus the combined widths of the two stiles.

DIAGONAL BRACES
2 pieces 1 × 3 pine approximately 3′6″ long mitered at 45° on both ends

Additionally, 4 cornerblocks, 6 keystones and 4 modified keystones will be required to assemble the flat.

for a standard flat, beginning with the outside corners.

The door flat in Figure 6-17 on page 129 is also framed in the same manner as all the previous examples. The door opening in this case is 3′0″ wide and 7′0″ high. Only one toggle the full width of the flat is used. This toggle is positioned as the header for the door. The door stiles frame the sides of the door opening. Two short toggles are used between the flat stiles and the door stiles and positioned at about the middle of the door opening. Custom reinforcing plates are used in places where several joints are in close proximity to each other. The seams of the joints of the header toggle are perpendicular to each other, making it impossible for the grain of a single reinforcing plate to run across both joints. Two solutions are acceptable: (1) The reinforcing plate can be cut so the grain is at 45° to all the joints, which provides equal support to all the joints; or (2) the reinforcing plate is positioned so the grain is across the

FIGURE 6-14
A larger version of a typical flat frame

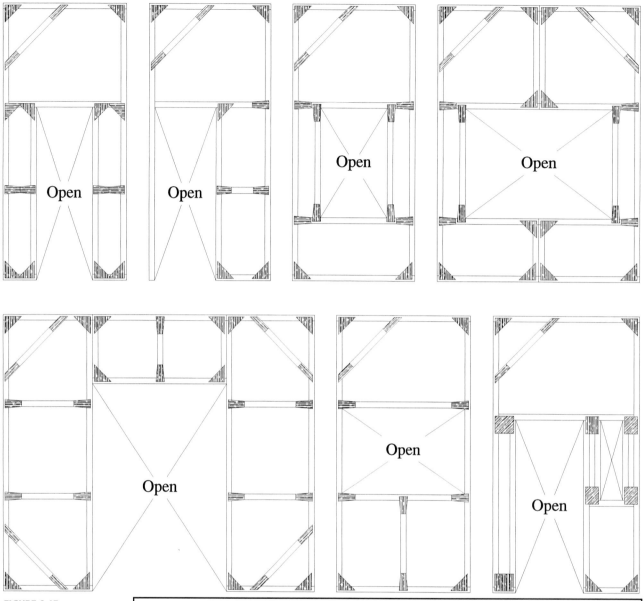

FIGURE 6-15
A variety of framing techniques to accommodate door and window openings

CUT LIST FOR FIGURE 6-16

TOP AND BOTTOM RAILS
2 pieces 1 × 3 pine 5'0" long

LEFT AND RIGHT STILES
2 pieces 1 × 3 pine 10'0" minus 2 widths of 1 × 3

TOGGLES
2 pieces 1 × 3 pine 5'0" minus 2 widths of 1 × 3

WINDOW STILES
2 pieces 1 × 3 pine 5'0"

DIAGONAL BRACES
2 pieces 1 × 3 pine cut to fit

ADDITIONAL PARTS
4 cornerblocks, 4 modified cornerblocks, 4 keystones and 4 modified keystones

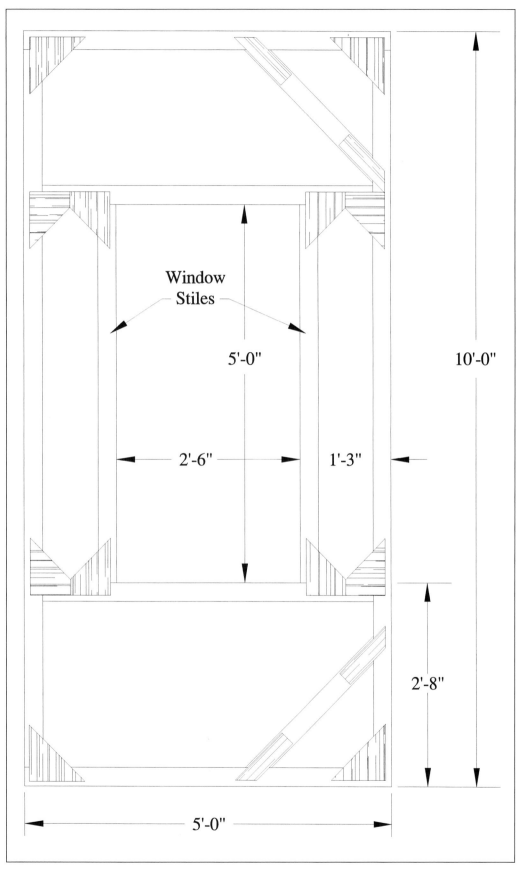

FIGURE 6-16 *Construction drawing of a typical window flat*

joint that is under the greatest stress. In this case, the door stile to header toggle is the most critical joint. The cut list for this door flat is shown at right.

Position and secure the frame to the work surface. Assemble the top corners of the flat first; then, using the custom corner-blocks, connect the bottom rails to their respective flat stiles and the door stiles. The header toggle is attached next to the top of the door stiles and the flat stiles using the remaining custom cornerblocks. Finally, the short toggles and diagonal brace can be secured. It is critical that the door opening be square, since it will most likely need to accommodate a working door at some future time. A sill iron can be installed to help ensure the opening is square. This is recommended if the flat is going into stock. The sill iron is made from $\frac{3}{16}''$ thick, $\frac{3}{4}''$ wide strap metal. Countersunk holes are drilled in the sill iron to accept flathead wood screws. The sill is screwed to the bottom edge of the bottom rails and spans the door opening (see Figure 6-18 on page 130). When a sill iron is used, the dimensions of the frame must be adjusted for the $\frac{3}{16}''$ added thickness of the sill iron.

A door or window opening can be turned into an arched opening with a small addition, as illustrated in Figure 6-19 on page 131. The desired shape is cut from a piece of $\frac{3}{4}''$ plywood or a suitable width of $1''$ pine. The curved sweep is then set into the normal door or window opening and secured using $\frac{1}{4}''$ plywood plates. Any irregular shape can be produced in this manner and attached to the standard framing members of a flat. Figure 6-20 on page 132 illustrates some profile possibilities.

Soft-Covering Flats

To begin, place the assembled frame face-up on a set of sawhorses so that you have access to all sides of the flat. Tear a piece of canvas or muslin a few inches longer than the length of the flat. (The weave used in the manufacture of these fabrics makes tearing an accurate technique for cutting

---

CUT LIST FOR FIGURE 6-17

TOP RAIL
1 piece 1 × 3 pine 5'0" long

BOTTOM RAILS
2 pieces 1 × 3 pine 1'0" long

LEFT AND RIGHT STILES
2 pieces 1 × 3 pine 10'0" minus 2 widths of 1 × 3

DOOR STILES
2 pieces 1 × 3 pine 7'0" minus the width of the bottom rail

TOGGLES
1 piece 1 × 3 pine 5'0" minus 2 widths of 1 × 3
2 pieces 1 × 3 pine 1'0" minus 2 widths of 1 × 3

DIAGONAL BRACE
1 piece 1 × 3 pine cut to fit

ADDITIONAL PARTS
2 cornerblocks, 4 custom cornerblocks and 6 modified keystones

---

the material to length. Scissors or other cutting tools can cut across the threads in both directions. Tearing the fabric follows a single thread across the width of the fabric, resulting in a square and even cut.)

At this point, all technicians have their own personal methods for covering a flat. Here are two common methods. Once you have gone through this process a few times, you will find a technique that works for you.

Method One
Position the fabric over the flat frame with the selvage (factory edge) aligned along the outer edge of one of the stiles. Staple the fabric on the face of the stile along the inside edge (see Figure 6-21A, page 133). Begin at the midpoint of the stile and work toward the rails. Set the staples every 12 inches and be sure the fabric lays flat and is free of wrinkles or puckers. These staples will be removed once the glue is dry, so do not set them flush the frame.

Proceed to the opposite stile and follow

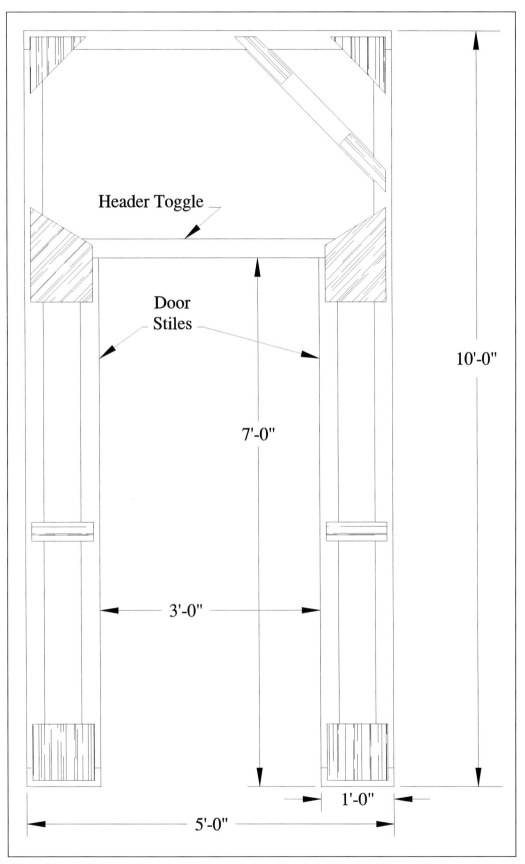

Header Toggle

Door
Stiles

10'-0"

7'-0"

3'-0"

1'-0"

5'-0"

FIGURE 6-17
Construction drawing of a typical door flat

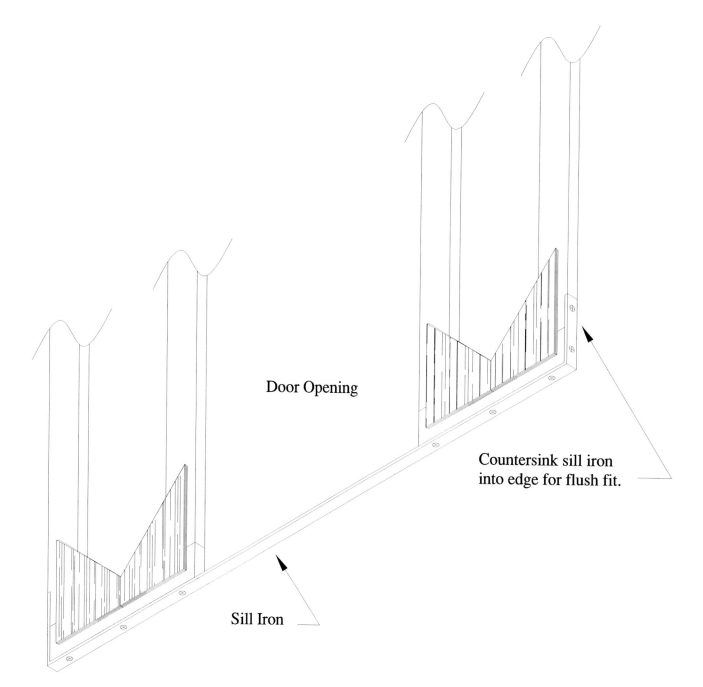

Door Opening

Countersink sill iron
into edge for flush fit.

Sill Iron

FIGURE 6-18
*The use or a sill iron across
a door opening*

the same technique in securing the fabric to the face of this stile (see Figure 6-21B, page 133). As before, work from the midpoint of the stile toward the rails, stretching the fabric across the frame and at a slight angle toward the corner. You must acquire a sense of how much the fabric will shrink when sized and painted. Muslin will shrink considerably more than canvas. It will require some practice and experimentation on your part to get the proper tension in the fabric. Too little tension and the fabric

will droop and wiggle. This is not a good thing when the flat is to represent a solid wall. Too much tension and the fabric may warp the frame or pull loose from the frame once it is sized and painted.

Complete this phase by securing the fabric to the top and bottom rails in the same manner. Make any adjustments required to eliminate wrinkles from the fabric by removing staples and reattaching the fabric.

Now, turn back the loose fabric to reveal the frame. Apply an even coat of glue to

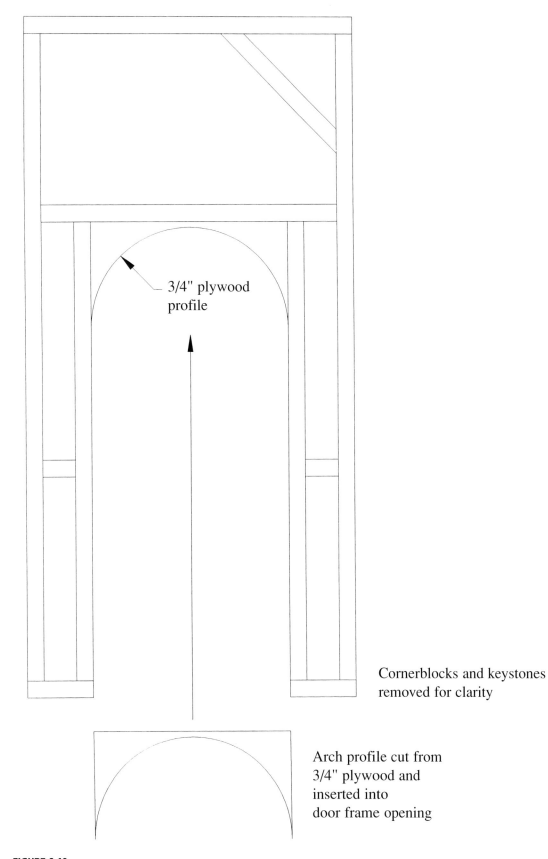

3/4" plywood
profile

Cornerblocks and keystones
removed for clarity

Arch profile cut from
3/4" plywood and
inserted into
door frame opening

FIGURE 6-19
Creating an arched opening

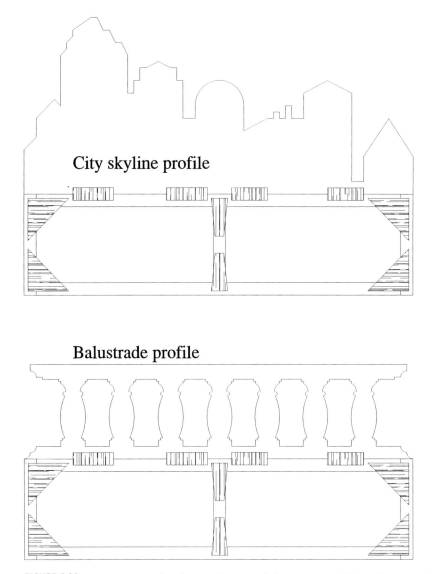

City skyline profile

Balustrade profile

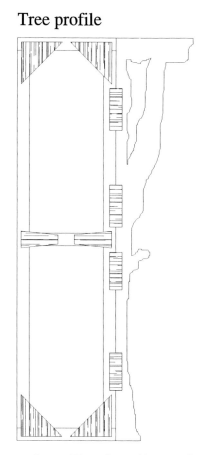

Tree profile

FIGURE 6-20
Adding profile pieces to standard flats

the face of one of the exposed framing members (see Figure 6-21C). I use a inexpensive 2″-wide paint-brush to apply the glue. White glue (plastic resin glue), thinned with water to aid in spreading, works well. Press the fabric firmly to the face along the entire length of the framing member. A small wooden block can be used like an iron to aid in this process (see Figure 6-21D, page 134). Hold the fabric in place by securing it to the outer edge of the frame with additional staples (see Figure 6-21E, page 134).

The fabric is glued to each of the remaining framing members in turn. Covering fabric is glued only to the outside framing members or those framing door and window openings. Toggles, diagonal braces and other internal framing parts are not glued to the covering fabric.

The glue must be completely dry before removing all the staples and trimming the fabric. Run a sharp utility knife along the face of the flat frame approximately ¼″ in from the outer edge of the flat to trim the excess fabric. Many people are tempted to run the utility knife along the outside edge, trimming the fabric right to this edge. The ¼″ setback helps prevent the edge of the fabric from coming in contact with other objects and peeling up.

Method Two

This method is faster but usually requires a second person, a little more experience and the ability to work quickly. Start as before, with the flat frame positioned face-up on a set of sawhorses and a piece of fabric with approximately two inches of excess material on each side. Apply a liberal and even coat of glue to all the appropriate framing members. Drape the fabric over the glued frame, pressing the fabric firmly into the glue, and wrap the selvage of the fabric around the outer edge of one of the stiles. Secure the fabric with staples to the edge of the stile beginning at its midpoint and working toward each corner. The staples should not be set flush to the frame since you will need to remove them once the glue is dry. As soon as the first few staples are set on the first stile, the second person can begin work on the opposite side, following the same procedure. There is less room for error using this method, since the fabric is being stretched and glued in one step. The two technicians must work together to achieve the proper degree of tautness in the covering material.

When both stiles are complete, move to the rails and follow the same basic procedures used on the stiles. Once the glue is dry, you can remove the staples and trim the excess fabric from the flat using the same technique described in the first method.

There are a number of variations to these two methods, and you will see that everyone has particular preferences. If the method you use achieves the desired results, it is the right method.

The same two covering methods can be used for covering door and window flats. In the first method, the fabric must be stapled to the face of the door or window framing as described above. The material is then carefully cut around the opening, and a small miter cut is made in the fabric at each corner of the opening to allow the material to fold back in order to glue the frame. The material is pressed into the glue and stapled as before. For the second method, the material is cut out of the opening, leaving enough excess material to

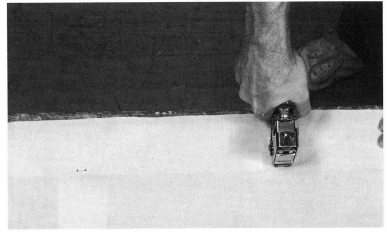

FIGURE 6-21A
Step 1—staple the muslin to the inside edge of one stile beginning at the center of the stile

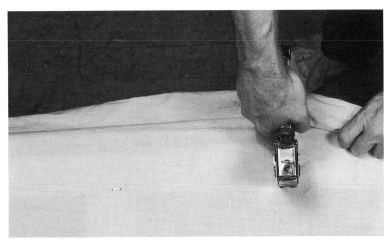

FIGURE 6-21B
Step 2—stretch the muslin across the frame to the opposite stile and staple along the inside edge again beginning at center. Complete this step by stapling the muslin to the inside edge of the top and bottom rails.

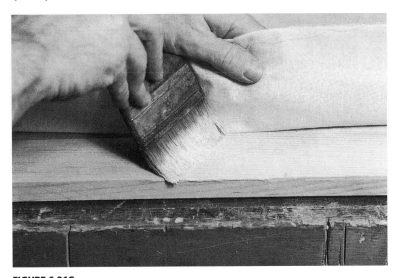

FIGURE 6-21C
Step 3—fold back the muslin and apply glue to the frame

FIGURE 6-21D
Step 4—press the fabric into the glue using a wooden block

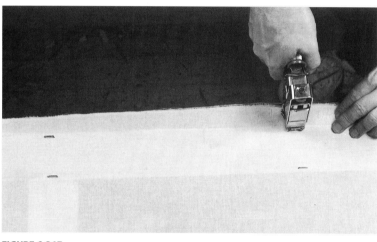

FIGURE 6-21E
Step 5—staple the muslin to the outer edge of the frame to secure the fabric until the glue dries

FIGURE 6-21F
Step 6—after glue has dried, remove staples and trim the excess muslin

wrap around the edge of the frame opening. The frame is then glued as before and the fabric is stapled to the edge of the flat frame and the door or window opening frame. When the glue is completely dry, the excess material is trimmed as before.

Hard-Covering Flats

In some situations, a fabric covering may not be adequate or desirable. On scenic units that sustain heavy usage, a hard covering may be necessary. Hard-covering flats is more costly, but it produces a much stronger and more durable scenic unit. Applying a hard cover is also much simpler and faster than stretching fabric, saving potentially costly labor. The material is simply glued and stapled to the frame. Lauan is the typical product used for this application, but other materials can be substituted. The hard cover material is not generally cut to size before attaching it to the frame. Instead, the material is secured to the flat frame and any excess is trimmed off using a router and a self-guiding trim bit. This produces an extremely accurate and clean-finished edge that is exactly the size of the flat frame. This trimming technique also works well for any internal openings in the flat frame.

Because hard cover material typically comes in 4×8 sheets, the framing of the flat must accommodate these dimensions to ensure a framing member will be available under each seam in the covering material. If you are using 4×8 sheets of Lauan, the 4×10 flat depicted in the earlier example would require one additional toggle centered on eight feet, as illustrated in Figure 6-22. Note that with the additional toggle in place, the position of the original toggle is adjusted down one foot for more even support. Also note that the diagonal braces used in the soft-cover flat are not necessary when a rigid cover material is used. The sheeting material may be covered with muslin or canvas to provide a consistent paint surface.

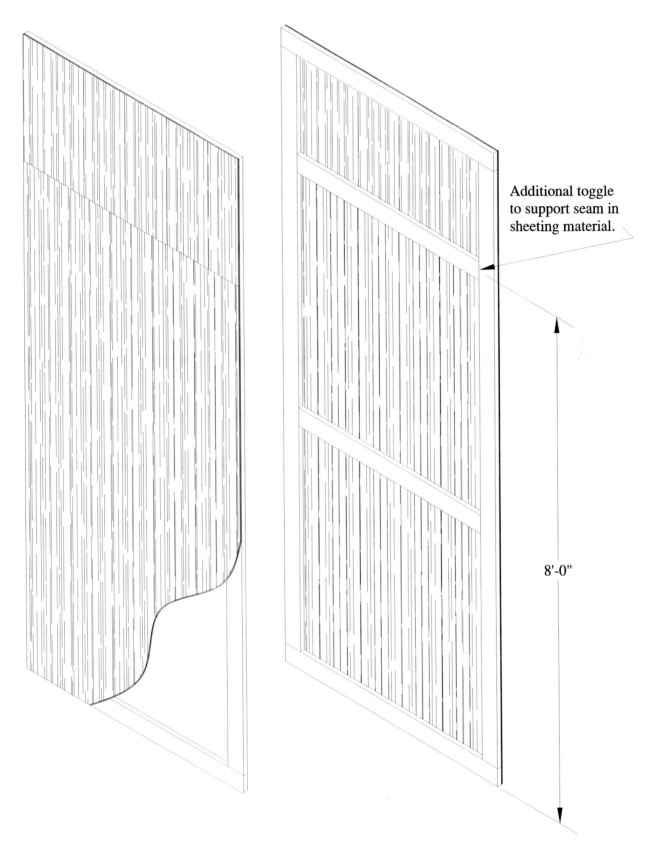

Additional toggle
to support seam in
sheeting material.

8'-0"

FIGURE 6-22
A typical hard covered flat

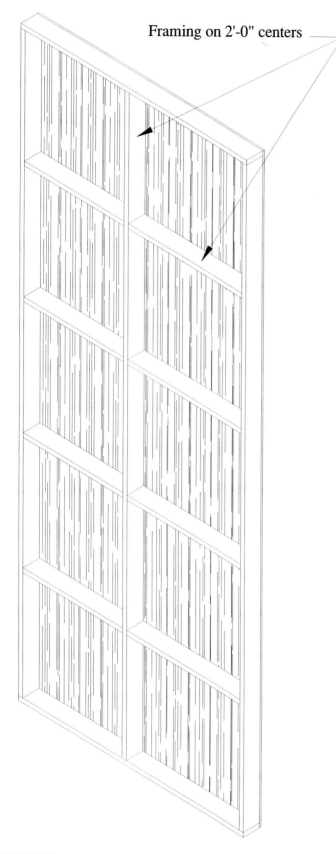

Framing on 2'-0" centers

FIGURE 6-23
A standard studio flat

Studio Flats

Studio flats, also known as TV flats or Hollywood flats, are a combination of traditional flat construction and residential framing techniques created for film and television production. They are stronger and more rigid than traditional flats. The principal differences are the orientation of the framing material and the joint. Figure 6-23 illustrates the framing of a standard 4×10 studio flat. The framing material is used on edge in this type of construction, and cornerblocks and keystones are not required. Note also that the framing is located on two-foot centers. This is not structurally necessary and, in fact, when constructed for theatrical use, framing is more typically on 4' centers (as in Figure 6-24).

To build a 4×10 studio flat, start with cleaning and squaring the 1×3 framing material. In principle, the cut list is calculated in the same manner as with the traditional flat. The top and bottom rails are cut to the width of the flat. The stiles are cut to the height of the flat minus twice the thickness of the framing stock. Because the orientation of the frame is on edge, the overall length of the flat must be reduced by the thickness of the top and bottom rails to find the true length of the stile. Likewise, the length of the toggles is the width of the flat minus the thickness of the two stiles. Remember that the terminology *1 × 3* refers to the nominal size of the material. The actual thickness of the 1×3 stock is ¾″. (See Figure 6-25 on page 138.)

The cut list is shown at right.

To assemble a studio flat, lay out the framing members in their proper positions on a framing table or the shop floor. Glue and nail or staple the outside corners. Then install the toggles. If you work quickly, it is not necessary to be too concerned about being in square at this time. Studio flats are hard-covered with Lauan or ¼″ plywood. If your sheet goods are square, you can square the frame when attaching the covering material, using the edges of the sheet

CUT LIST FOR FIGURE 6-24

TOP AND BOTTOM RAILS
2 pieces 1 × 3 pine 4'0" long

STILES
2 pieces 1 × 3 pine 9'10½" long

TOGGLES
2 pieces 1 × 3 pine 3'10½" long

as a large framing square. Attach the Lauan with glue and nails or staples. The rigidity of the covering material provides added strength to the joints and eliminates the need in most cases for diagonal bracing. You can trim any excess Lauan with a router and trim bit, as described previously. Remember that each seam in the covering material must be supported by a framing member. The narrow ¾" edge of the frame requires precise placement to catch both edges of the seam. If you have trouble with this, use two pieces of 1 × 3 together under the seam (as illustrated in Figure 6-26 on page 139).

Curved Walls

Curved walls are built using an adaptation of studio-flat construction techniques. The top and bottom rails and the toggles are made from ¾" plywood or appropriately sized and joined 1" stock. The radius of the curved wall is cut into these framing members (as illustrated in Figure 6-27). These horizontal sweeps are then joined together with 1 × 3 stiles on edge at each end of the curve. Additional stiles are notched into the back of the sweeps at two-foot intervals. Joints can be reinforced with blocks or ¼" plywood plates. A suitably flexible sheeting material is glued and stapled to the horizontal sweeps and the outside stiles. Be sure the framing is positioned to back any seams in the sheeting.

Curved walls require a significant amount of storage space and are difficult to handle. Two or more sections should be joined together to form large units in order

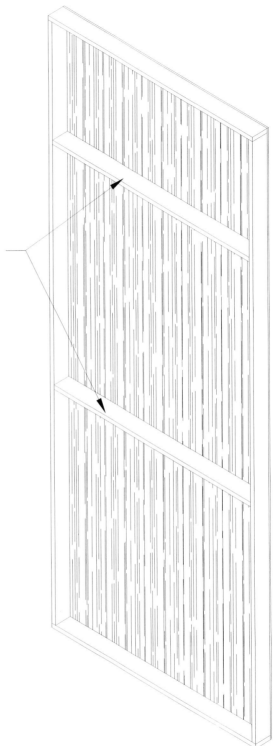

Framing on 4'-0" centers

FIGURE 6-24
A studio flat framed for the theater

FIGURE 6-25A
Step 1—complete cut list and fasten outside corners

FIGURE 6-25B
Step 2—fasten toggles and other internal framing

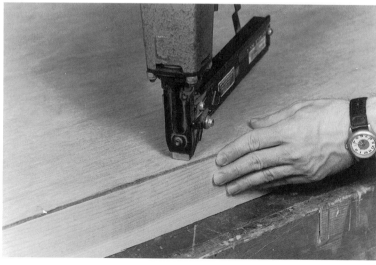

FIGURE 6-25C
Step 3—attach sheeting material squaring the frame as you go

to save space. The sections can be clamped, bolted or screwed together during installation.

Steel Flat Frames

Steel is rapidly becoming a serious alternative to wooden flat frames. Steel-tube frames are stronger for their weight than wood frames, longer lasting and more adaptable as stock scenery. Soft-covered flats are still best constructed with wood frames because of the difficulty of attaching fabric to steel. However, consider steel when a hard-covered flat is desired. Self-drilling screws make covering an easy one-step process. The same framing parameters described for wooden flat frames are used when fabricating in steel.

THREE-DIMENSIONAL CONSTRUCTION

Some three-dimensional units are only architectural or decorative in nature. Others are functional or weight-bearing structures that can present very complex design and fabrication problems despite the relatively simple techniques developed for their construction. To construct three-dimensional scenic units requires a little more planning, knowledge and skill. Like the basic framed units described in the last section, the methods and tools used to fabricate these items need not be very complicated. However, the quality and durability of three-dimensional scenic units can be greatly enhanced with more sophisticated milling and joining techniques. As a general note, any butt joint described in the following sections can be improved with the use of a biscuit or plate joint.

Doors and Windows

These are two of the most common three-dimensional scenic units you will encounter. They can be purely decorative or completely functional. They are designed in many shapes, materials and sizes (illustrated in Figure 6-28 on page 141), but all tend to have the same three basic components

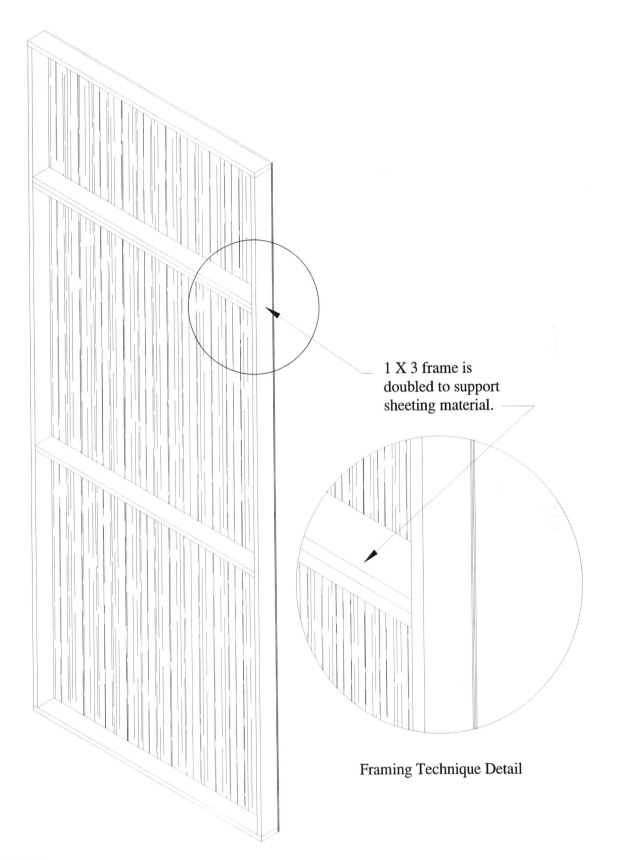

1 X 3 frame is
doubled to support
sheeting material.

Framing Technique Detail

FIGURE 6-26
Double toggle framing technique used to support sheeting material

FIGURE 6-27
Framing for a curved wall

(illustrated in Figure 6-29 on page 142). The *casing* is the visual frame of the door or window opening. This can be as simple or elaborate as the design demands. The *jamb*, or *reveal*, is that component that represents the thickness of the wall into which the door or window is set. The third component is the *shutter* for a door unit and the *sash* for a widow unit. These last components can be as varied as the designer's imagination allows.

The following construction examples illustrate only a few of the methods and techniques that can be used to construct door and window units. Several factors can influence the way these units are constructed. Before building a door or window unit, determine if the unit must actually operate or if it is purely decorative. Will it be an independent unit or one which is dependent on the underlying flat frame? How long does it have to last? Is it being built for stock? Does the unit have to shift during the course of the production? Answering these questions will tell you how to construct the scenic unit.

Windows

To construct the three-dimensional independent double-hung window unit with the finished dimensions of 2′6″ wide and 5′0″ tall (illustrated in Figure 6-30, on page 143), follow these steps:

1 Cut the pieces of the jamb to length from 1″ pine ripped to the width specified on the designer's drawing. The top (*lintel*) and bottom (*sill*) pieces of the jamb are each 2′7½″ long, the specified width of the window plus the combined thickness of the side pieces of the jamb (stiles). The stiles are cut 5′0″ long per the specified height of the window.

2 Assemble the jamb on edge into a box, lapping the lintel and sill over the stiles. Use glue and staples or nails to secure the face-to-end butt joints.

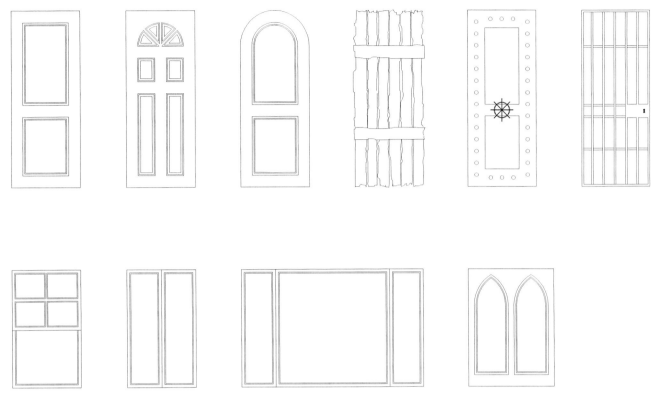

3 Cut the casing to length from 1″ pine ripped to the width specified on the designer's drawing. The top and bottom pieces are 2′6″ plus the combined width of the side pieces. The side pieces are 5′0″ long.

4 Glue and finish nail the individual casing pieces to the appropriate edges of the jamb. Countersink the nail heads.

5 Reinforce the seams of the casing with thin metal mending plates. This is another situation where a biscuit joint would eliminate the mending plate and make a cleaner and better joint.

If the sash does not need to be functional, it can be faked with little time and money. A simple plywood cutout that represents the design of the sash can be fabricated and installed in the jamb as illustrated in Figure 6-31 on page 144. A functional double-hung window requires separate upper and lower sashes. To construct a fully functional sash, continue with the following instructions.

6 An intricate window sash can be quickly cut from a sheet of ¾″ plywood as indicated in Step 5 and detailed with a router. For simpler sash frames, or for a higher quality product, fabricate from 1″ pine. The overall width of the sash frames should be slightly less than the width of the window opening to provide the clearance necessary to allow the sash to move. The height of each of the sash frames is typically one-half the height of the window opening plus half the width of the top or bottom member of the sash frame. When both frames are in their closed positions, the bottom member of the top sash frame should be directly behind the top member of the bottom sash frame, as illustrated in Figure 6-32 on page 145.

7 Assemble each frame using half-lap joints. The joints should be glued and clamped, ensuring that the frame is square.

Additional detail may be routed into the sash frame after the glue has dried.

8 After the glue has dried, attach the glazing material to the back of the sash frame. The glazing material can be anything from bobbinet to acrylic sheet, depending on the desired look and effect.

FIGURE 6-28
Various door and window styles

FIGURE 6-29
Basic components of doors and windows

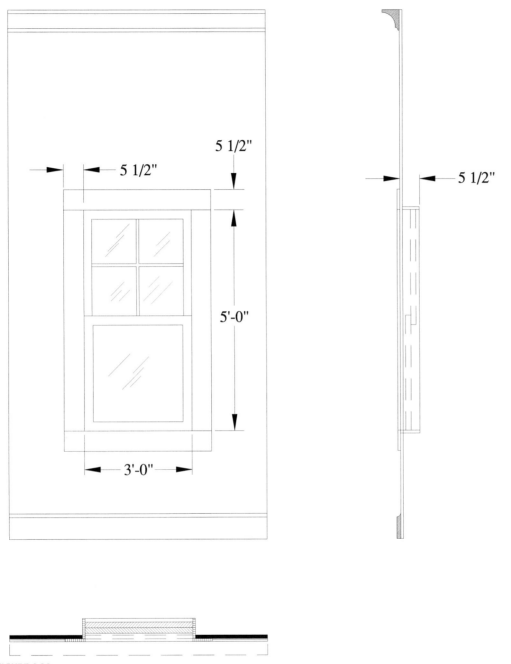

FIGURE 6-30
Typical window construction

9 Three narrow strips of wood on each of the jamb stiles are installed as tracks to guide the movement of the sash.

10 The window sash is held in its open position using one of the following methods:

A Line the track with felt sufficient to apply enough friction on the sash to hold it in place at any position in the track.

B Install spring catches on the sash frame that engage holes drilled into the window jamb.

C Purchase and install spring-loaded tracks. This product is available at local hardware or building supply stores and is designed to replace sash weights in residential applications. It is very economical and easy to use.

Window sash cut
from a single sheet
of 3/4" plywood

FIGURE 6-31
*A simple one piece plywood
window sash*

11 Insert the assembled window unit into the opening of the window flat from the front. Secure the window unit to the flat with 1¼″ screws from the rear through the flat frame into the casing.

Under certain conditions, the window unit may need to be removed quickly and easily. This is traditionally accomplished by installing strap hinges on the outer face of each vertical jamb. The hinge is positioned so that when the window is in place, the hinge is folded to wedge the window unit against the flat frame, holding it in place.

Please take special note that the designer's drawings will indicate the finished dimensions of the window. When constructing a flat with a window opening that will receive a three-dimensional window unit, the opening in the flat is made 2″ larger in each direction. This allows 1½″ for the combined thickness of the jamb in each direction and an extra ½″ of clearance for easy installation.

Doors

To construct the basic components of a three-dimensional door use many of the techniques described for the construction of a window unit. Two significant factors account for any differences in construction. First, a door unit is typically larger and heavier than a window. Second, the forces generated by opening and closing a door are considerably more destructive than those ordinarily encountered using a window. The following instructions include the adjustments for these factors.

To construct a three-dimensional independent door unit with the finished dimensions of 3′0″ wide and 7′0″ tall (per the drawings in Figure 6-33 on page 146), follow these steps:

1 Cut the lintel and stiles of the jamb to length from 1″ pine ripped to the width specified on the designer's drawing. The lintel is 3′1½″ long, the specified width of the door plus the combined thickness of the stiles. The stiles are cut 7'0" long per the specified height of the door.

2 The bottom member of the door jamb is known as the *threshold*. This piece is cut approximately 2" wider than the rest of the jamb. The extra width allows for the front and rear edges of the threshold to be beveled to reduce the risk of an actor tripping over the threshold. The length of the threshold is 3'0", the specified width of the door.

3 Bevel the front and rear edges of the threshold.

4 Assemble the jamb on edge into a rectangle, with the lintel overlapping the stiles and the threshold set between the stiles. Use glue and staples or nails to secure the face-to-end butt joints.

5 A 1" × 3/16" rabbet must be cut in the bottom of the threshold if a sill iron is used in the opening of the door flat.

6 Cut the casing to length from 1" pine ripped to the width specified on the designer's drawing. The top piece is 3'0" plus the combined width of the side pieces. The side pieces are 7'0" long.

7 Using blocked face-to-edge butt joints, glue and finish-nail the casing pieces to the appropriate edges of the jamb. Countersink the nail heads. The blocks should be screwed into the jamb and casing from the rear.

8 Reinforce the seams of the casing with thin metal mending plate. A biscuit joint would eliminate the need for the mending plate and make a cleaner and better joint.

Whenever possible, a stage door should be hinged on the offstage side of the door jamb. It should also be oriented to open off- and upstage for a few very practical time- and money-saving reasons. Under these conditions, only one side of the door need be finished, the open position of the door helps mask the view backstage, it does not require any valuable onstage

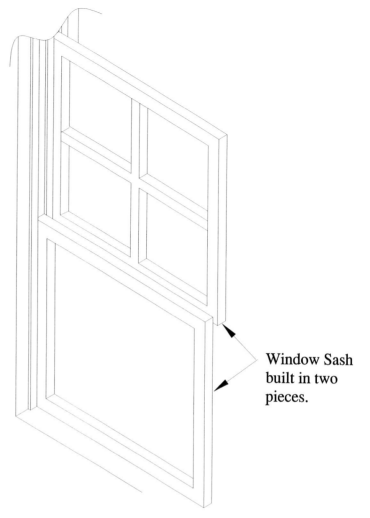

Window Sash built in two pieces.

FIGURE 6-32
A typical double hung window sash

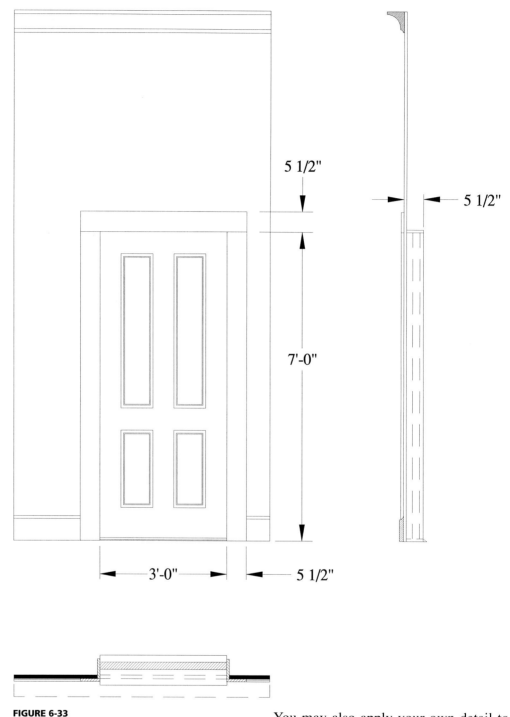

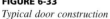

FIGURE 6-33
Typical door construction

space to operate, and it is simply much easier for actors to operate.

Inexpensive hollow-core flush doors are available from lumber suppliers. This can often be the most efficient solution to creating the shutter of a door unit. Hollow-core doors come in a variety of stock sizes and are available with some panel detail.

You may also apply your own detail to a plain door. If a hollow-core door is purchased, the dimensions of the door opening should be adjusted for sufficient clearance. I suggest adding ¼″ to ⅜″ to the width of the opening and ½″ to the height of the opening minus the threshold thickness.

You can build your own hollow-core flush door using the studio flat construction techniques described previously. Substitute $1'' \times 1\frac{1}{2}''$ pine for the framing material and cover both sides of the flat with hardboard or Lauan. If a mortise latch is used, additional wood reinforcement is required where the latch is installed.

Building a door shutter with recessed panels, as illustrated in Figure 6-33, is similar to building a hard-covered flat. The overall width of the shutter should be approximately $\frac{1}{4}''$ less than the width of the door opening to provide the clearance necessary to allow the shutter to open and close freely. The height of the shutter is approximately $\frac{1}{2}''$ less than the height of the door opening minus the thickness of the threshold.

1 Cut the rails, stiles and toggles of the shutter to length from $1''$ pine ripped to the widths specified on the designer's drawing. Note the width of the bottom rail, which is wider than the other pieces. The top and bottom rails are $2'11\frac{3}{4}''$ long, the stiles are $6'10\frac{3}{4}''$ long minus the combined widths of the top and bottom rails, and the toggles are $2'11\frac{3}{4}''$ long minus the combined widths of the stiles divided by two.

2 Cut a sheet of Lauan or $\frac{1}{4}''$ plywood $2'11\frac{3}{4}''$ wide by $6'10\frac{3}{4}''$ long. Under conditions where heavy use of the shutter is expected, you should consider $\frac{3}{8}''$ plywood.

3 Assemble the panel frame using biscuit joints. Half-lapped joints can be used, which requires longer overall length of the stiles and toggles to accommodate this joining technique. The joints should be glued and clamped, ensuring that the frame is square.

4 Attach the plywood sheet to the rear of the panel frame with glue and staples. I cannot emphasize enough how important it is to ensure the shutter is square at every step of this process.

5 Additional detail can be applied or routed into the edges of the panel frame as desired.

6 Hinge the shutter to the back of the jamb with strap hinges or large back-flap hinges. The back of the shutter should be flush with the back of the door jamb.

7 Attach a rim latch to the back of the door. The catch is mounted to the rear edge of the door jamb.

8 With the shutter closed, nail or staple stop moulding around the inside of the door jamb against the face of the shutter. The moulding prevents the door from swinging past its closed position, which will tear the hinges from the jamb, and prevents any light leaks around the door. Commercial weatherstripping can be used to block light from the bottom of the shutter.

9 Insert the assembled door unit into the door flat from the front. Secure the door unit to the flat with $1\frac{1}{4}''$ screws from the rear through the flat frame into the casing. If the door is heavily used or slammed, I suggest that the door unit not be attached to the flat. This will reduce the likelihood that the movement of the door will transfer to the wall, causing a very noticeable and unacceptable amount of movement in the wall. Separate jacks are installed to support the door unit in this situation.

A double-sided door is constructed by duplicating the panel framing and sandwiching the plywood sheet between the two frames. Standard butt hinges are used in place of strap or back-flap hinges, and a mortise latch replaces the rim latch when both sides of the door are visible to the audience.

Remember that the designer's drawings typically indicate the finished dimensions of the door. When constructing a door flat which will receive a three-dimensional door unit, the opening in the flat is made larger in each direction to allow room for the door jamb and the blocks reinforcing the joint between the door casing and jamb.

Moulding

Mouldings and other architectural details can be purchased from local suppliers or manufactured in your shop with a router, shaper and other carving tools. A variety of stock moulding shapes and sizes are available from lumber suppliers. These tend to be expensive, due in part to the superior grade of wood used to manufacture these products. A catalog illustrating the profiles and ordering information from the local supplier is a valuable resource for the shop and should be included in the shop library.

In many circumstances, mouldings for theatrical purposes can be manufactured in your shop from lesser grade lumber, making them less expensive than store-bought mouldings. Small, simple shapes such as half round, quarter round, crown, cove, ogee, chamfer, beading and veining can be milled with a router and the appropriate router bits. Larger and more complicated mouldings, such as cornices, can be assembled from many smaller shapes, as illustrated in Figure 6-34. A shaper and the appropriate cutting knives can provide more quality, speed and efficiency to your manufacturing operation.

Rigid foam should be considered as an alternative to wood for some moulding applications. Foam is much lighter, less expensive and carved more easily than wood. Large, ornate cornice mouldings that hang off the tops of flats are ideal candidates for foam fabrication. If the cornice were constructed of wood, the supporting flats would require significant additional framing to support the weight of the wooden cornice. The flats would also be top-heavy, making them difficult to shift.

A shaper for foam can be constructed using the shop drill press and custom-fabricated cutting knives manufactured from metal, aluminum or even Masonite. The blades are fastened to a shaft that is clamped in the chuck of the drill press. A fence is constructed and mounted to the drill-press table as a guide for the foam.

Alternatively, a hot-wire cutter can be constructed, with the wire bent into the shape of the desired profile or a straight wire guided by a cutout of the specified contour.

There are a number of companies that will manufacture foam moulding and other architectural items to your specifications. My experience with these products has been general satisfaction with quality, good delivery time and economically better or comparable to other solutions. The most significant drawback to foam is the inability to quickly join it to other materials. Mastic holds well but requires substantial setup time.

As with any use of foam, a covering material is required to harden the surface against dents and to provide a quality painting surface. Foam should be avoided underfoot or in areas of heavy traffic.

Columns

Traditionally, columns have been built using a wooden frame covered with a thin, pliable sheeting material and fabric. The construction method is similar to a studio flat, but in three dimensions. Figure 6-35 illustrates a column one foot in diameter. The cut list and assembly instructions for this column are shown on page 150.

1 The plywood circles should be gang cut if possible: Five squares of ¾″ plywood are cut slightly larger than the finished dimension indicated in the cut list. The pieces are then stacked, temporarily fastened together and cut to the specified diameter at one time. A moderate-size band saw should be capable of making this cut.

2 Mark the circle, dividing it into eight equal pie shapes. These lines mark the center lines of the eight stiles.

3 Strike another set of lines ⅜″ on each side of the centerlines. These lines indicate the thickness of the stiles.

4 The last layout line is scribed 2″ from the outside edge of the plywood circle and perpendicular to the centerlines. At this

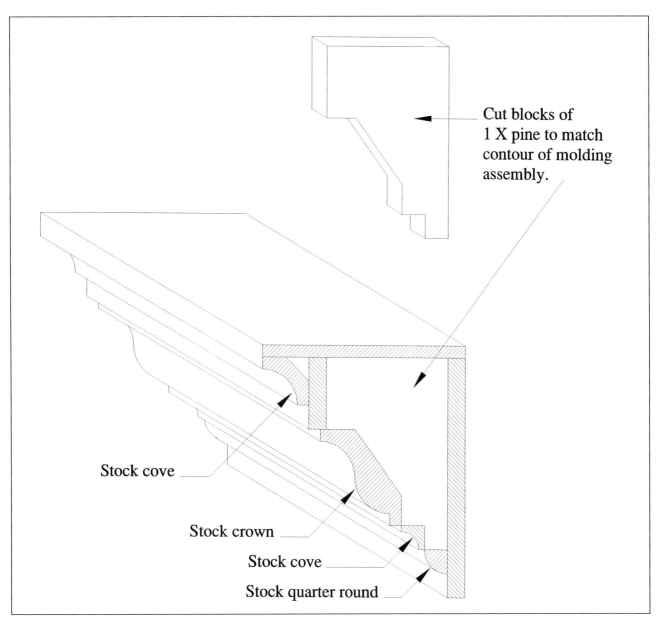

Cut blocks of
1 X pine to match
contour of molding
assembly.

Stock cove

Stock crown

Stock cove

Stock quarter round

FIGURE 6-34
*Creating a large cornice
from stock molding*

point, the positions of the eight stiles are completely outlined.

5 Notch the stack of plywood circles for each of the eight stiles.

6 You may choose to remove some material from the center of the circles to reduce the weight of the column. Leave at least 1″ of wood to maintain strength.

7 Separate the plywood circles.

8 Position the stiles into the notches of the plywood circles. The inner circles are spaced two feet apart.

9 Fasten with glue and either nails or staples. Be careful not to spilt the stiles; one fastener per notch is all that is required.

10 Choose one stile and glue and staple additional pieces of 1 × 2 along one side of the stile between the plywood circles. This extra thickness will back the seam of the covering material.

11 Glue and fasten the edge of the sheeting material to the double stile.

12 Apply glue to the other stiles and wrap the sheeting material around the frame, fastening the material to the stiles as you go.

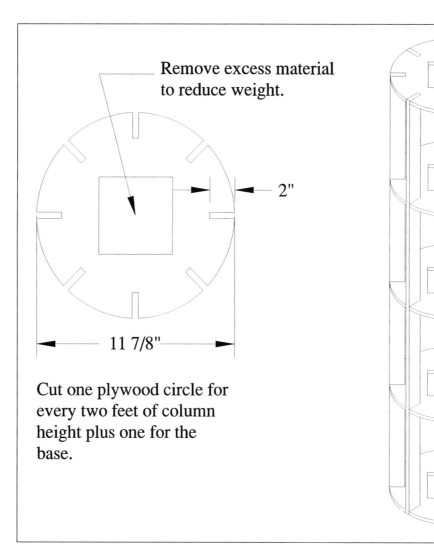

Remove excess material to reduce weight.

2"

11 7/8"

Cut one plywood circle for every two feet of column height plus one for the base.

FIGURE 6-35 *Framing for a column*

CUT LIST FOR FIGURE 6-35

8 pieces 1 × 2 pine 8′ long
These pieces act as the stiles of the column frame.

5 pieces ¾″ plywood 11⅞″ diameter
These circles act as the rails and toggles of the column frame.

1 piece ⅛″ easy curve or bender board 8′ tall, 3′1¹¹⁄₁₆″ wide

The circumference of the column is πD (3.14 × 12 = 3′1¹¹⁄₁₆″)

13 Trim the sheeting material if necessary and fasten the edge to the double stile.

14 The column may be covered with canvas or muslin for painting or painted as is.

15 Add a column base and a capital if desired.

Tapered columns use the same construction technique as outlined above with two exceptions. The plywood circles are not the same size. They typically reduce in size from bottom to top, although other shapes are possible. The outer skin also changes shape. In the example above, the skin was precut for the circumference of the circle. A tapered column requires additional calculations based on the design of the column. It may be easier to create a paper pattern off the frame than to calcu-

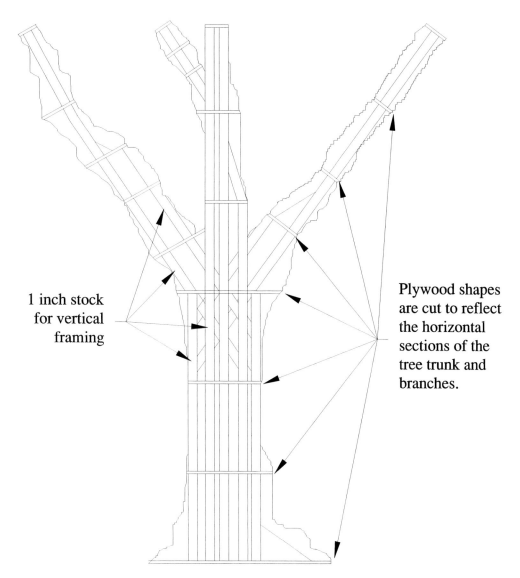

1 inch stock for vertical framing

Plywood shapes are cut to reflect the horizontal sections of the tree trunk and branches.

FIGURE 6-36 *Framing for a tree*

late the true shape of the skin.

An alternative to this framing technique uses a product known as Sonotube as the column shaft. Sonotube was designed as a form for concrete columns and is similar to cardboard tube used as the core for bolts of fabric or carpet rolls. To use Sonotube for a theatrical column, two ¾″ plywood circles are cut to the inside diameter of the Sonotube. Cut the Sonotube to the desired length and insert one plywood circle into each end. Nail or staple through the Sono-tube into the edge of the plywood. The ply-wood provides a foundation for the column base and capital. The Sonotube should be covered with fabric unless a heavy texture is to be applied.

A relatively successful tapered column can also be achieved using Sonotube. The Sonotube is slit lengthwise and a small wedge is removed from the back of the tube. The width of the wedge at the top is equal to the diameter of the tube minus the diameter of the top of the column specified in the drawings. The top plywood circle is cut to fit the smaller diameter of the top of the column. The bottom plywood circle is inserted and secured as before. The Sono-tube is compressed around the smaller top circle and secured as described above. If the design taper of the column is too great, this method will not work well.

Rigid foam columns are another very

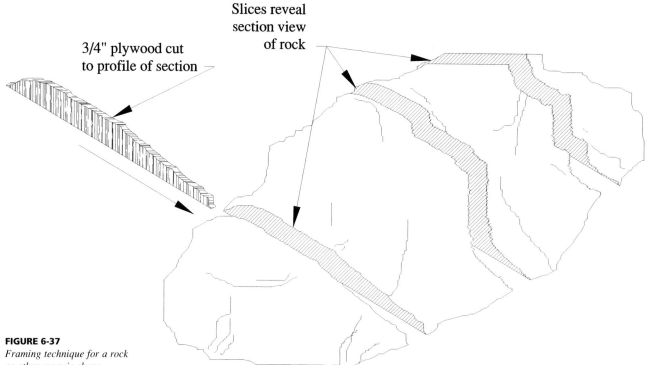

3/4" plywood cut
to profile of section

Slices reveal
section view
of rock

FIGURE 6-37
*Framing technique for a rock
or other organic shape*

reasonable alternative to wood-frame columns. As mentioned previously, several
companies have a variety of stock sizes and
shapes available or will carve foam columns to your specifications. I have found
these products to be very economical, extremely lightweight and, with the proper
coatings or coverings, they are reasonably
sturdy.

Trees

A tree can be fabricated with a simple adaptation of the technique used to construct
a column (as illustrated in Figure 6-36).
The basic framing technique is the same.
Plywood shapes are cut to reflect various
horizontal sections of the tree trunk and
branches. One-inch stock is used as the
vertical framing members linking the plywood pieces together. The specific contour, number and location of the plywood
shapes is determined by the overall shape
of the tree, but in no event is the plywood
spaced more than four feet apart. The vertical frame is positioned at the angles required by the design.

Hardware cloth or chicken wire is used

to cover the wooden frame and provide additional shape to the tree. These wire products will hold their shape reasonably well
and can be moulded to meet the contour
requirements of the design. Hardware cloth
is particularly suitable for this purpose.
The wire is covered with a thin batting material to disguise any pattern from the wire,
and finally covered with muslin or canvas.
Fiberglass can be used in situations where
a stronger and more rigid surface is
required.

Rocks

Rocks and other natural forms can be built
with similar methods. Imagine making a
number of slices through a rock (as illustrated in Figure 6-37). Each slice, or section
view, reveals the outline of the object at that
location. If a series of plywood plates are
cut to follow the outlines of the section
views, they can be assembled in the appropriate order to form a three-dimensional
frame of the rock. An appropriate covering
material such as hardware cloth is then applied and shaped to form the foundation for
the outer skin. For more detail, make an-

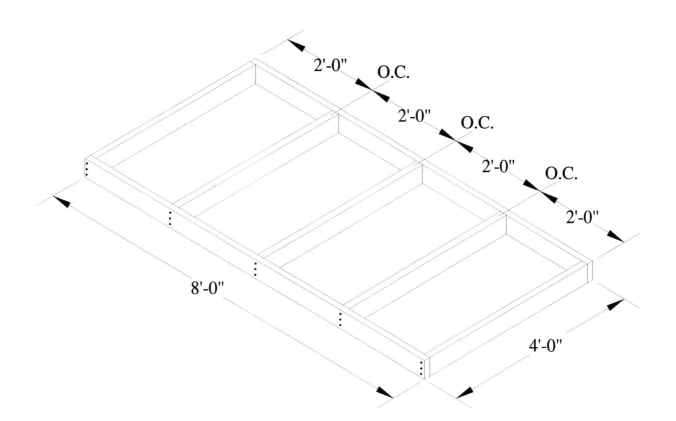

2'-0"   O.C.
2'-0"   O.C.
2'-0"   O.C.
2'-0"
8'-0"
4'-0"

FIGURE 6-38
Standard 2 × 4 framing for a platform

CUT LIST FOR FIGURE 6-38

2 pieces 2 × 4 fir 8'0"

4 pieces 2 × 4 fir 4'0" minus the thickness of two pieces of 2 × 4

The cross rails are cut to the width of the platform minus the thickness of the long rails.

---

other set of slices that are perpendicular to the first. The second set of plywood plates is joined with the first to more clearly define the contour of the object.

If the rock is simply decorative, the wooden framework does not need to be very strong and a simple muslin or canvas covering should be sufficient. However, if the rock is practical (that is, if it must bear the weight of an actor), the rock and its wooden frame must be designed to support the weight. Canvas or fiberglass should be used for the outer skin.

Foam may also be carved into natural shapes quite successfully. This is a faster method of creating such objects. With the proper-density material, foam will even support the weight of an actor. Care must be taken to protect the foam from chipping with use. A cheesecloth or fiberglass covering will protect the foam very well.

WEIGHT-BEARING SCENIC UNITS

This group of scenic units is constructed to support the weight of the actors and other scenic units. They include platforms, wagons, show decks, turntables, ramps, stairs and their various adaptations. The construction of these items requires materials and joints that can withstand the loads and forces of actors in motion. There are a wide variety of construction techniques that fulfill this requirement as well as the general theatrical requirement of being efficient and inexpensive to manufacture.

Platforms

Platforms are composed of three components: the deck or lid, the supporting frame, and the legs. The deck of a platform can

FIGURE 6-39
The configuration of a layered platform deck

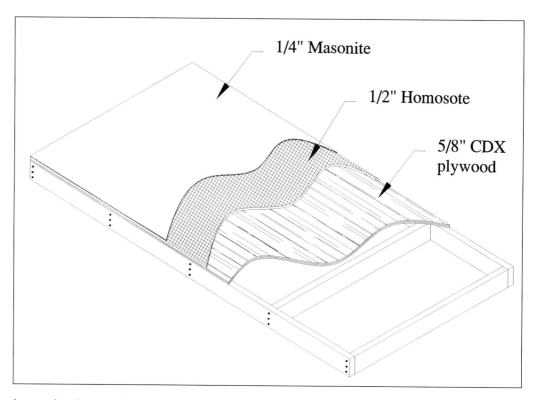

be as simple as a single sheet of plywood or several layers of material, each employed to fulfill a specific function. The supporting frame and legs can be made of wood or steel. Platforms are most commonly constructed in $4' \times 8'$ modules and bolted together to form larger units. You will recall that plywood, the principal decking material for platforms, comes in standard $4' \times 8'$ sheets. This is also a reasonable size unit to handle, store and transport. Larger, smaller and irregular-shaped platforms can also be fabricated using the construction methods described here.

A 2×4 fir supporting frame for a 4×8 platform is illustrated in Figure 6-38 on page 153. The most economical choice for the supporting frame is 2×4. In this design, the long rails are the main structural supports of the platform. The cross rails provide additional support for the decking and lateral support to the long rails. They are cut to fit inside the long rails; however, the actual arrangement of the joint can be altered to fit the specific engineering requirements of the project.

The cut list for the support frame is shown on page 153.

Arrange the framing members in their appropriate positions and assemble the frame using 12D nails. The frame is constructed on edge so that the strongest cross section of the wood supports the downward forces acting on the platform. The frame will be squared when the decking material is applied.

Figure 6-39 depicts a layered decking for this platform. The layer next to the supporting frame is the structural component of the deck that supports the weight of the actors, props or other scenic units. In this layered decking, the plywood is not visible and hence does not require an appearance-grade finish. The use of ⅝″ CDX plywood is typical under these conditions. The layer above the plywood is used to deaden the drumming noise caused by actors walking on the platform. This material is generally Homosote or Celotex. Homosote is the better choice, but it is also more costly than Celotex. This layer can be the finish layer if a textured surface such as carved stone is desired. For a smoother finish, the top layer is typically Masonite painted to represent the final look of the floor. Other sheet goods can be used to represent

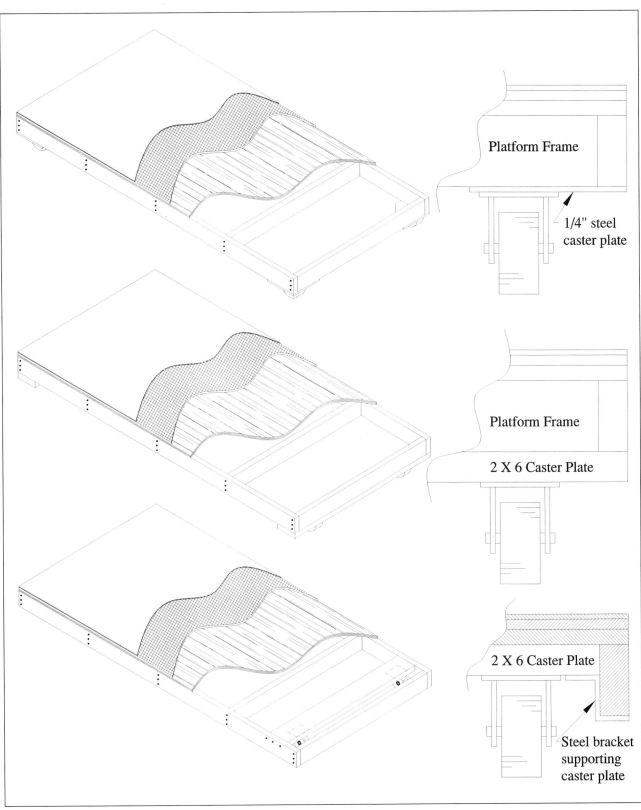

Platform Frame

1/4" steel caster plate

Platform Frame

2 X 6 Caster Plate

2 X 6 Caster Plate

Steel bracket supporting caster plate

FIGURE 6-40
Three methods of installing caster plates

various finishes. Lauan in routed sheets or cut strips works well for planked or parquet wood floors.

Screw the plywood lid to the frame with 2″ screws. Use the plywood sheet as a guide to ensure the frame is square. Screws are used to enable the platform to be disassembled and the material salvaged after the production. They also resist movement better than nails, resulting in fewer annoying squeaks at inopportune times during the play. The Homosote or Celotex layer is secured to the plywood sheet with wide-crown staples or roofing nails because the soft material is easily compressed. The final layer is secured with nails, staples or glue, depending on the desired look. Be sure the fasteners are long enough to go through the sound-deadening layer into the plywood.

If noise is not a consideration or if the final finish is carpeting or a rug, the plywood sheet may be the only layer required. An appearance-grade ¾″ plywood is recommended if the plywood is visible.

The same support frame configuration and decking can be used with 1×6 or $\frac{5}{4} \times 4$ pine stock. I recommend blocked butt joints, glued and either nailed or stapled, when using this stock. These materials are more expensive but have some advantages. The support frames are lighter and can be fabricated with higher grade material, which will enable more precise construction. They are also my choice for building stock platforms. One advantage of a 1×6 frame is that it provides a very usable one-step stock platform without legging. If the platform is being built for stock, I suggest glue and nails or staples be used to secure the plywood deck. Sound-deadening and finish layers are not considered part of the stock platform and should be removed after each use.

The legs for any wood-frame platform are most efficiently and economically constructed of 2×4 fir. The leg is cut to the specified height of the platform minus the combined thickness of each layer of the decking material. I like to make two small diagonal cuts at the foot end of the leg to help prevent the leg from splitting, which frequently occurs as a result of dragging the platform across the floor.

Two ⅜″ carriage bolts are typically used to fasten the leg to the frame. Remember, in the framing plan being illustrated, the main structural supports are the 8′-long members of the support frame. The legs should be bolted to these framing members. Bolts are used to ensure a sufficient compressive joint and to expedite disassembly. Note the position of the bolts. This placement reduces the potential for weakening the support frame or leg when both bolts are placed in the same grain line. Use a $\frac{7}{16}$″ drill bit to make insertion of the bolt a little easier. A $3\frac{1}{2}$″-long bolt is required when using a 2×4 supporting frame and legs. The head of the carriage bolt is set with a hammer, embedding the square portion of the shank into the support frame. A washer is used under the nut.

Two diagonal braces are installed between each leg and the support frame to establish a rigid triangular structure. The braces are oriented at 90° to each other to provide maximum strength and stability.

An alternative to a 2×4 leg uses two pieces of 1×3 joined together to form an L shape. This assembly is then fastened to the supporting frame as described above using bolts of the appropriate length.

Steel makes an excellent material for platform frames and legs. A steel support frame will often allow for a shallower platform profile than a wood-frame platform of equal load-bearing capacity. Rectangular or square steel tubing are the most practical choices because of their similarity in shape to wood framing members. Other steel shapes, such as angle, channel or even I beam, can be used for heavier loads. These shapes weigh much more than steel tubing and should only be used when their greater strength is required. The support frame and deck configurations described above apply to steel framing. Self-drilling

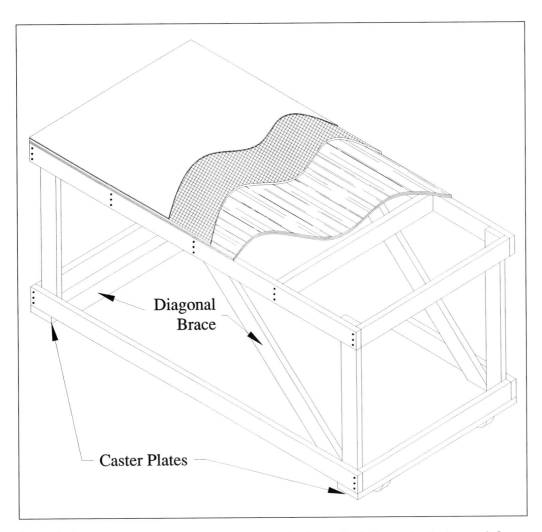

FIGURE 6-41
Using caster plates on elevated platforms

screws are used to secure the plywood deck to the steel frame. Additional deck layers are secured to the plywood layer as you would with a wood-frame platform.

A stress-skin platform is a slightly more sophisticated construction technique that adds considerable strength to a platform. The basic concept is to skin both the top and bottom of the support frame. The two skins work together to resist the tendency of the platform frame to flex under load. The top and bottom skins must be glued to the frame to achieve optimum strength. The bottom skin does not need to have the compressive strength or load-bearing ability of the top skin since it is not walked on. A variety of materials can be used for the internal support frame of the stress-skin platform, including standard wood framing, rigid foam, and honeycombed plastic and paper products.

Wagons

Wagons are, in their simplest form, platforms on wheels. The platform construction described above requires only a simple—but important—modification to create an ordinary wagon. Additional factors such as the type of caster, route of travel, guidance and propulsion increase the complexity of the engineering problems and associated construction techniques.

Think of the caster as a specialized platform leg or extension of a leg. Like a leg, the caster must be connected directly to the support frame to maintain the structural integrity of the platform. A caster plate is often used to satisfy this requirement. The

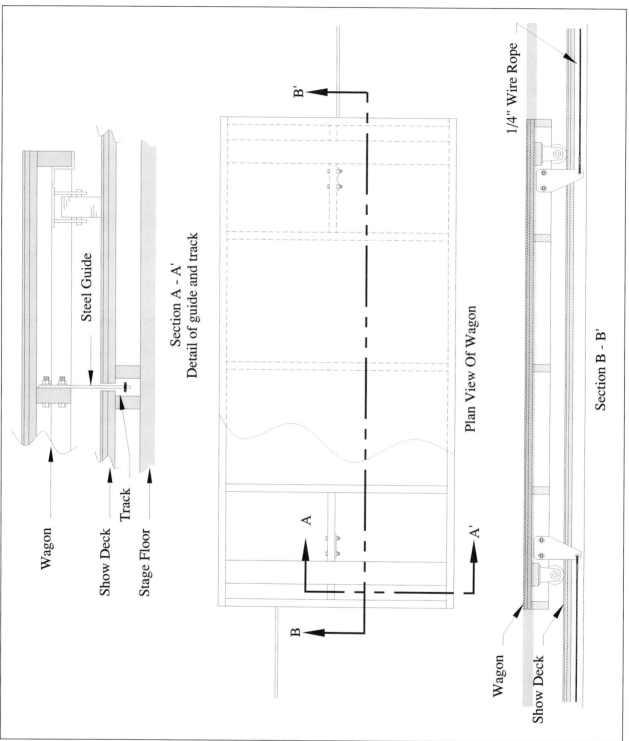

Wagon

Steel Guide

Show Deck

Track

Stage Floor

Section A - A'
Detail of guide and track

Plan View Of Wagon

A

A'

B

B'

1/4" Wire Rope

Section B - B'

Wagon

Show Deck

FIGURE 6-42 *A technique for tracking a platform*

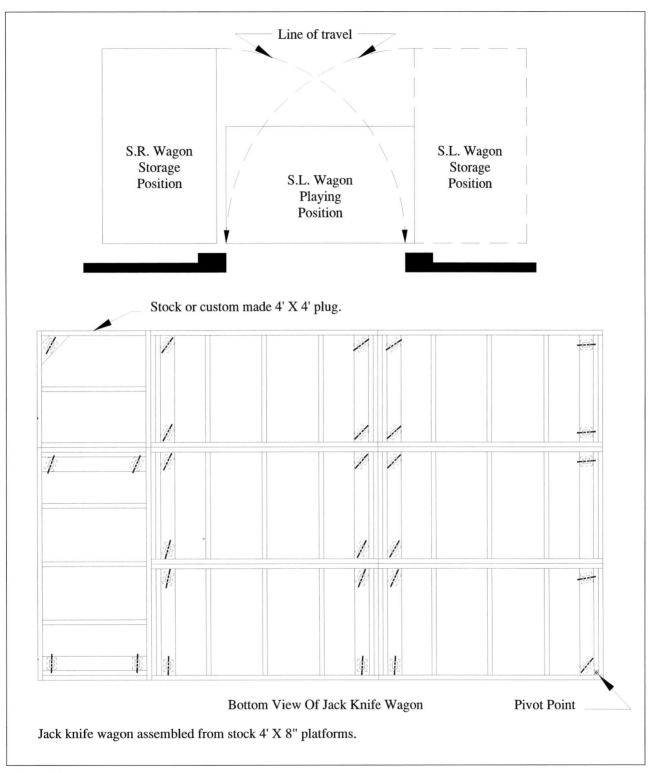

FIGURE 6-43
Orientation of casters for a jackknife wagon (the number and position of casters is based on the specific loading conditions of the wagon)

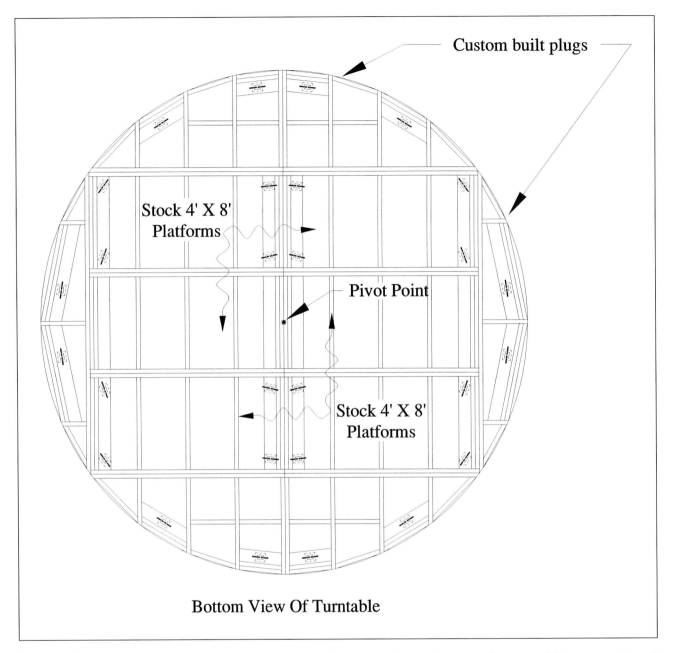

FIGURE 6-44
Orientation of casters for a turntable (the number and position of casters is based on the specific loading conditions of the turntable)

caster plate can be of many shapes and sizes, as long as it is capable of transferring the weight on the wagon from the support frame directly and wholly to the caster, which has now become the platform leg. Figure 6-40 illustrates some common applications of a caster plate on the basic 2×4 platform described previously. In each example, the caster plate, whether wood or metal, is fastened to the support frame of the platform. A prevalent mistake occurs when the caster is bolted directly to the platform deck. This approach circumvents the platform support frame, which

provides the platform with its strength, and greatly reduces the maximum-load capacity of the wagon.

A legged platform can also be converted into a wagon using caster plates. The example in Figure 6-41, on page 157, uses a 2×6 plank as the caster plate under each pair of legs. The 2×6 is $4'0''$ long—the width of the platform. The casters are bolted to the bottom face of the caster plate. They are positioned $3''$ in from the end of the caster plate to avoid any conflict between the platform legs and the bolts securing the casters. The platform legs are secured to the top

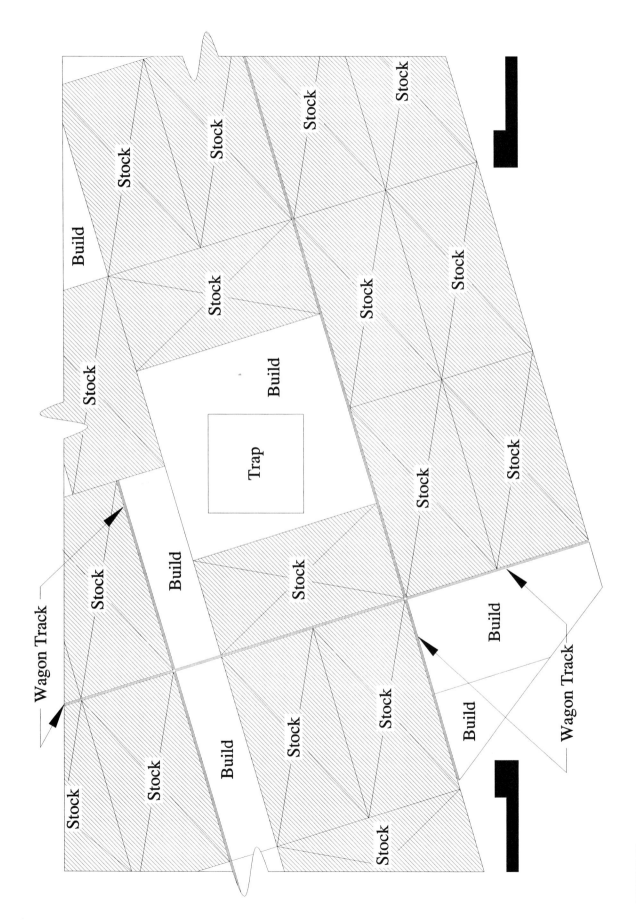

FIGURE 6-45
Assembling a show deck out of stock platforms

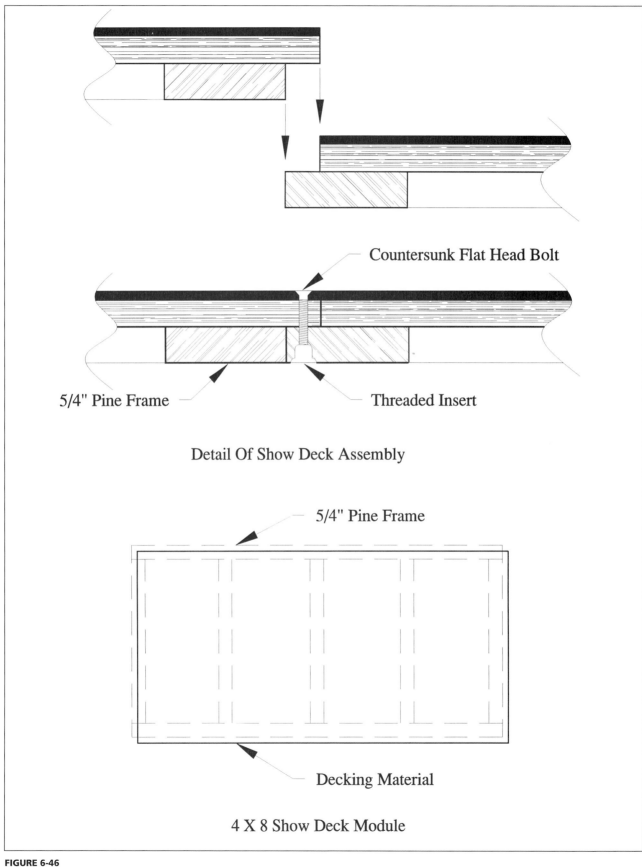

Countersunk Flat Head Bolt

5/4" Pine Frame

Threaded Insert

Detail Of Show Deck Assembly

5/4" Pine Frame

Decking Material

4 X 8 Show Deck Module

FIGURE 6-46
Construction technique for a low profile show deck

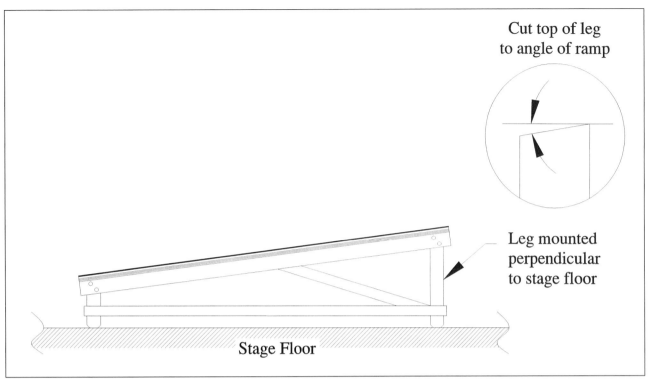

Cut top of leg
to angle of ramp

Leg mounted
perpendicular
to stage floor

Stage Floor

FIGURE 6-47
Legging technique for a ramp

face of the caster plate. An additional 2×4 frame is assembled around the base of the legs to stabilize the legs and caster plates when the wagon is moved.

Slip Stages, Jackknife Wagons and Turntables

The basic concept of a wagon has been adapted into slip stages, jackknife wagons and turntables. They may be moved manually (with the assistance of a hand-operated winch) or motorized. Typically, they have a single line of travel which makes a simple mechanical guide both possible and desirable.

A slip stage can be of any size and shape. A track can be recessed into the show deck or surface-mounted to the stage floor. A show deck is the best choice when multiple crossing wagons are desired. The show deck's recessed track also provides an unobstructed surface when the slip stage or wagon is offstage. A surface-mounted track, while easy and inexpensive, can be problematic. It is a visual and physical obstruction that makes it virtually impossible to use the stage floor without a slip stage in place. Additionally, other wagons cannot

cross the track unless a series of breaks in the track are planned to create a clear path for the other wagons' casters. This system works when full-stage noncrossing wagons are desired.

To complete the tracking mechanism, a guide which rides in the track is mounted on the wagon. Figure 6-42 on page 158 illustrates one method. Rigid casters are used in this system and oriented for the wagon's line of travel.

A jackknife wagon uses a single pivot point as the anchor for the unit. The pivot is set at the center point of the arc that defines the path of the wagon. The pivot can be as simple as a steel pin fastened to the wagon and set into a hole drilled into the stage floor. More sophisticated weight-bearing pivots are sometimes necessary. The movement of the wagon along an arc constitutes a single line of travel, which permits the use of rigid casters. The casters are oriented perpendicular to the radius of the arc, as illustrated in Figure 6-43 on page 159.

Turntables are created in a similar fashion. A circular platform can be constructed

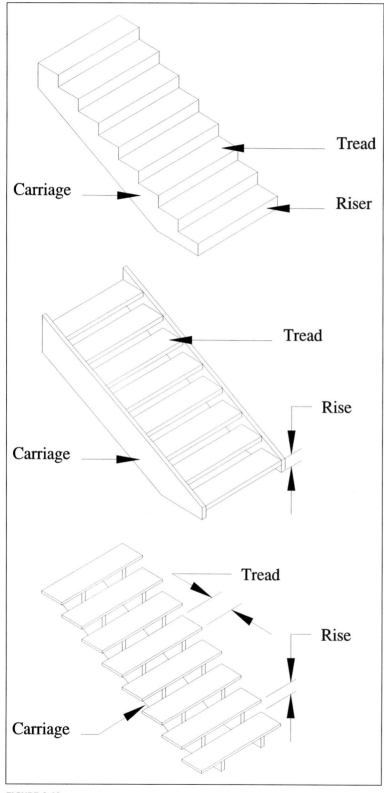

FIGURE 6-48
Standard stair components

from scratch or assembled from a combination of stock platforms and custom-built plugs. The pivot and caster techniques are the same as those described for the jack-knife wagon (see Figure 6-44 on page 160).

Show Decks

A show deck is a temporary floor designed and constructed for a specific production. It is generally employed to facilitate the shifting of scenic units using wagons, slip stages or turntables. It covers the stage floor and contains all the hardware, rigging and tracks required by the design. A simple show deck can be assembled from a combination of stock platforms and custom plugs, as illustrated in Figure 6-45 on page 161.

The basic technique used to construct a show deck is very similar to platform-construction methods. The frame of a show deck typically rests directly on the stage floor, eliminating the need for legs. For a low-profile touring show deck, I recommend a 5/4 support frame. This material is light-weight and rigid enough to ensure a proper fit after repeated installations. See Figure 6-46 on page 162 for an illustration of such a show deck.

Ramps and Raked Stages

A ramp is a platform with a surface that rises at an angle over its length. A maximum angle of 7.5 percent is considered safe, but many stage settings have employed ramps with steeper angles. The legs of a ramp are mitered at the top to the desired angle and fastened to the support frame so they are perpendicular to the stage floor (see Figure 6-47 on page 163).

A raked stage is like a large or full-stage ramp. The entire floor is set at an angle, or *rake*, to the stage floor. This technique is used to provide better sightlines, to emphasize perspective, or for its visual and psychological impact.

Stairs

Stairs consist of three components, as shown in Figure 6-48. The *carriage* is the

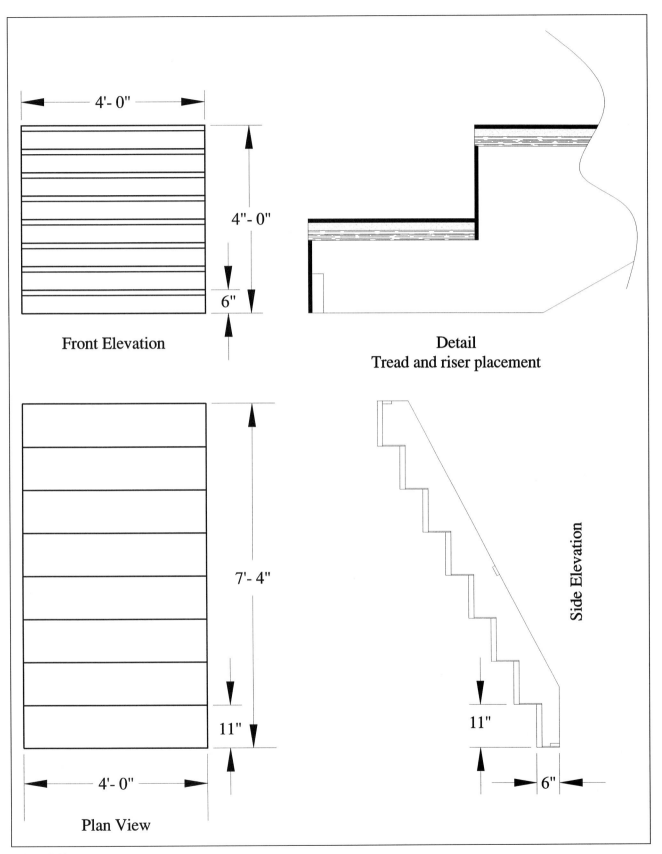

4'- 0"

4"- 0"

6"

Front Elevation

Detail
Tread and riser placement

7'- 4"

11"

4'- 0"

Plan View

11"

6"

Side Elevation

FIGURE 6-49

Construction drawing of a stair unit

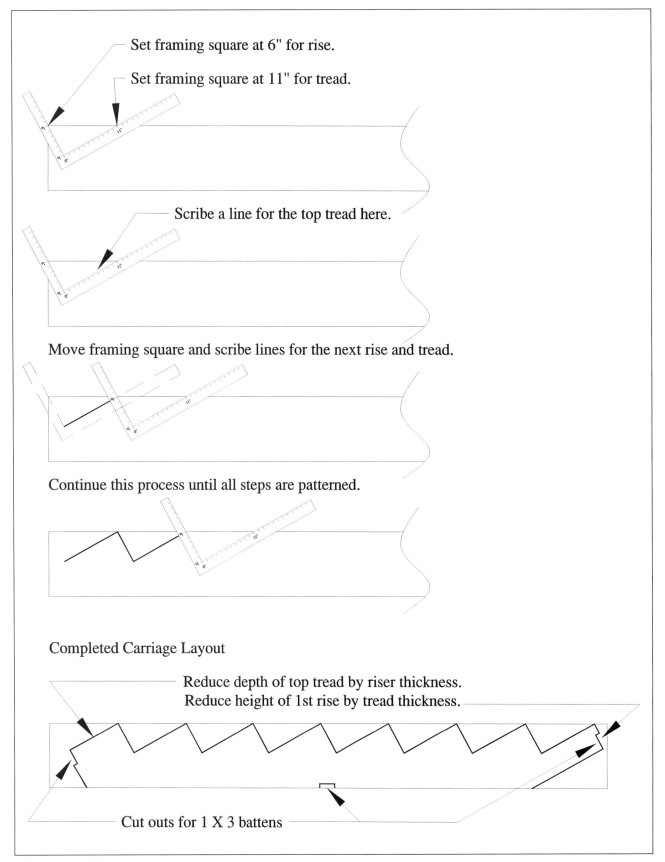

Set framing square at 6" for rise.

Set framing square at 11" for tread.

Scribe a line for the top tread here.

Move framing square and scribe lines for the next rise and tread.

Continue this process until all steps are patterned.

Completed Carriage Layout

Reduce depth of top tread by riser thickness.
Reduce height of 1st rise by tread thickness.

Cut outs for 1 X 3 battens

FIGURE 6-50
Laying out a stair carriage using a framing square

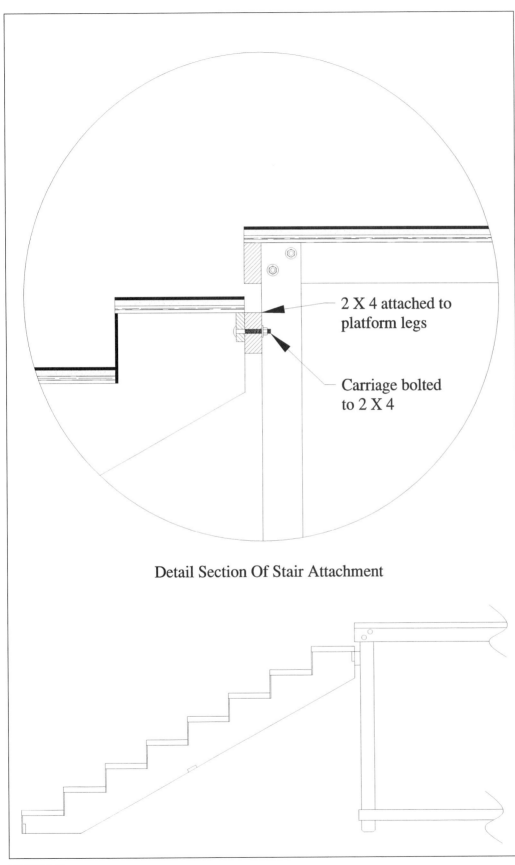

2 X 4 attached to
platform legs

Carriage bolted
to 2 X 4

Detail Section Of Stair Attachment

FIGURE 6-51
Technique for attaching a stair unit to a platform

main structural element of a stair unit. One or more are required, and they are designed and constructed in a variety of shapes and sizes. The *tread* is the horizontal surface of the stair on which a person would step. The *riser* is the vertical surface under the lead edge of each tread. The relationship between the depth of the tread and the height of the riser determines the angle of the stair unit. The standard rule of thumb for determining a safe and comfortable angle for a stair unit specifies the depth of the tread plus the height of the riser should equal 17″ to 18″. The construction plans described here use only a few of the many construction techniques that have been developed for the fabrication of stair units. They illustrate a number of basic principles that may be adapted or modified to fit your specific needs.

The stair unit illustrated in Figure 6-49 has an 11″ tread and a 6″ rise. The overall height of the unit is 4′ and the width is 4′. Its basic construction is outlined in the following steps:

1 To fabricate the carriages, mark the tread-and-rise pattern of the stair unit on three pieces of 1 × 12 pine. You will need approximately 8½′ of 1 × 12 for each carriage. A framing square is used to pattern the tread and rise of each step. Mark the short arm of the square for the rise at 6″ and the long arm for the tread at 11″. Clamp-on guides are manufactured for this purpose, if desired.

Beginning at the top of the carriage, orient the square so that the two marked dimensions align with the top edge of the 1 × 12, as illustrated in Figure 6-50, and scribe a line for the top tread. Move the square along the edge of the carriage to mark the next tread and rise. Continue this process until the appropriate number of steps have been patterned. In this example, eight steps are required to reach the overall height of four feet.

2 Adjust the depth of the top tread to account for the thickness of the material used

for the riser facing. In our example, the riser facing is fabricated from ¼″ Masonite. The depth of the top tread is reduced to 10¾″. This, plus the ¼″ Masonite riser facing, equals the required 11″ tread.

3 Scribe a line parallel to the riser from the rear of the top tread down to the bottom edge of the 1 × 12 carriage.

4 Adjust the height of the bottom riser to account for the thickness of the tread. The layered-decking technique described for platforms is used here for the stair treads. This means ⅝″ CDX plywood plus ½″ Homosote plus ¼″ Masonite, for a total tread thickness of 1⅜″. The height of the bottom riser is reduced to 4⅝″. This height, plus the 1⅜″ thickness of the tread, equals the required 6″.

5 Scribe a line parallel to the tread from the bottom of the first riser to the bottom edge of the 1 × 12 carriage.

6 Mark the carriages for the cutouts to accommodate 1 × 3 battens at the top, bottom and intermediate locations, as illustrated.

7 Cut three carriages using the completed layout.

8 Cut eight pieces of ⅝″ CDX plywood, 4′0″ wide by 11″ deep for the treads. The grain of the plywood must run parallel to the width.

9 Cut seven pieces of ¼″ Masonite, 4′0″ wide by 6″ high for the riser facings.

10 Cut one piece of ¼″ Masonite, 4′0″ wide by 4⅝″ high. This is for the bottom riser facing.

11 Cut three pieces of 1 × 3 stock, 4′0″ long.

12 Position the 1 × 3 framing members in the notched locations of the carriages and attach using glue and either nails or staples. The 1 × 3 should be flush to the outside of two of the carriages, with the third carriage positioned in the center of the 1 × 3.

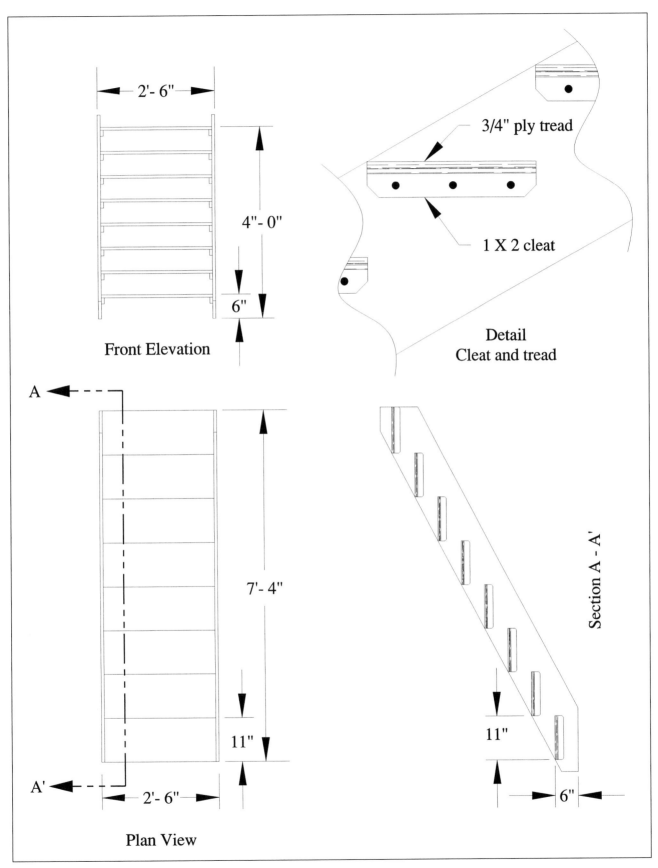

2'- 6"

4"- 0"

6"

Front Elevation

3/4" ply tread

1 X 2 cleat

Detail
Cleat and tread

A

7'- 4"

11"

A'

2'- 6"

Plan View

Section A - A'

11"

6"

FIGURE 6-52
Construction technique for a cleated stair unit

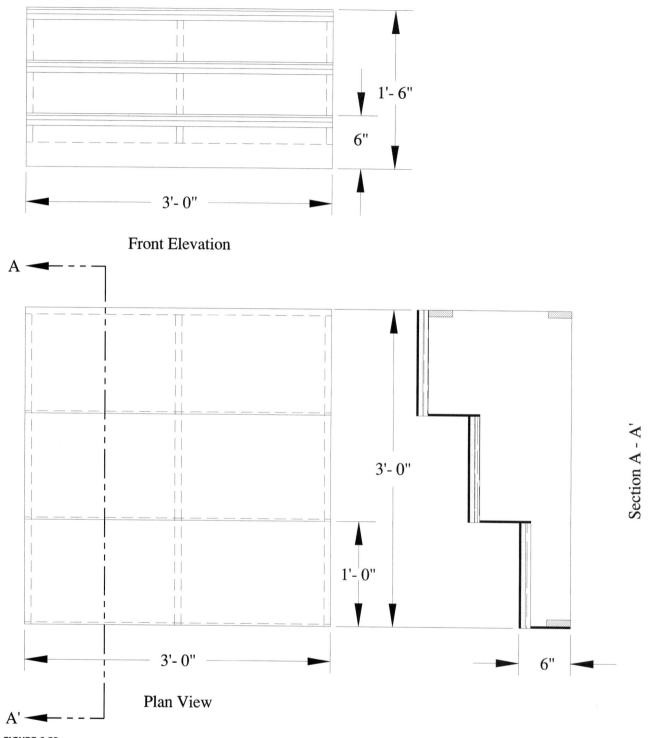

Front Elevation

Plan View

Section A - A'

FIGURE 6-53
Construction drawing for a self-standing stair unit

13 Attach the ¼″ Masonite riser facings to the risers of the carriages. Square the carriages as you proceed.

14 Attach the ⅝″ CDX plywood tread to the carriages.

15 Cut eight pieces each of ½″ Homosote and ¼″ Masonite, 4′0″ wide by 11″ deep.

16 Fasten these layers to the treads.

Legs may be bolted to the top of the carriage to support the stair unit, or the unit may be bolted to the face of a platform through the 1 × 3 batten at the top of the carriage, as illustrated in Figure 6-51.

An alternative to this technique makes construction very simple. Cleats attached to the inside of the 1 × 12 carriages are used to support the treads, eliminating the need to cut the tread and rise into the carriage. In this adaptation, only two carriages can be used, making a narrower stair unit or more substantial construction materials necessary. The stair unit depicted in Figure 6-52 has the same tread, rise and overall height as the previous example, but the width of this unit is reduced to thirty inches.

1 Mark the 1 × 12 carriages for the tread and rise. Position the layout 1″ below the top edge of the carriage and then continue as described for the alternate method. Riser facings are not typically used in this method, so no adjustment to the depth of the top tread is required. The bottom rise must still be adjusted for the thickness of the first tread. In this example, only ¾″ plywood is used for the tread, making the bottom rise 5¼″.

2 Scribe a line parallel to the rise at the rear of the top tread.

3 Scribe a line parallel to the tread at the bottom of the first rise.

4 Cut the carriages to length along these lines at the top and bottom of the carriages.

5 Cut sixteen pieces of 1 × 2, 11″ long, for the tread cleats.

6 Position the top edge of the cleats along the tread layout lines scribed in step 1. Fasten the tread cleats to the inside of the carriages using glue and either nails or staples.

7 Cut eight pieces of ¾″ plywood, 30″ wide by 11″ deep.

8 Attach the plywood treads to the tread cleats with glue and either nails or staples. Square the carriage as you go.

Smaller stair units can be built as self-standing units by fabricating the carriages from ¾″ plywood (as illustrated in Figure 6-53).

PAINT PREPARATION

Most scenic units require some preparation for the painting process. This may be as simple as applying a prime coat to a unit constructed of wood or metal to create a consistent and suitable foundation for the finish paint. In other circumstances, a specific problem or painting technique may need to be addressed.

Soft-covered flats and muslin drops must be sized, or primed, before painting. This process tightens the covering material, fills the pores of the fabric and provides a suitable and consistent texture for paint. A size coat is one without pigment. It is made only of a binder and the vehicle that carries the binder (usually water). Translucent effects require a size coat; starch and water make an excellent choice for this purpose. A prime coat adds pigment and is generally colored to approximate the base color of the final paint job. The type of binder used will determine the texture of the foundation. A hard finish is good for watercolor techniques or those that require the color to puddle or flow easily. A softer, more absorbent texture is desirable for techniques that feature stencils, printing techniques or painterly brushstrokes.

Dimensional lumber and plywood are used as the basic construction materials for scenic units that will ultimately appear to be made of stone, plaster, marble, plastic and many other materials. For this reason, it is often desirable to obscure the wood grain and fill the pores of the wood used in the construction of these scenic units. Fill large blemishes, nicks, gouges, holes and scratches with spackle, a commercially available wood filler or auto body filler. Sand smooth and flush with the wood surface. A good sanding and an appropriate prime coat may be sufficient with some types of wood and with some painting techniques. Others may require one of the commercially available grain killers. A homemade version can be mixed with shellac and titanium white.

Masonite, or hardboard, requires a prime coat that will seal the material and inhibit moisture absorption. It is also the material of choice to represent hard-finished materials such as polished stone or metal. For this reason, use a hard prime coat. A gloss vinyl or shellac will work well. Be sure to prime both sides of the material. For best results, allow the Masonite to acclimate to the humidity levels in the theater before priming.

Apply a primer to all metal to prevent rust and to provide a surface to which paint will adhere. Commercially manufactured primers have binders formulated for nonporous materials and provide a good surface texture on which to apply subsequent layers of paint. Many also have agents which prevent rust. Thoroughly clean metal of all oil and flux before applying a primer. Use auto body filler to fill any nicks or gouges.

CHAPTER 7

INSTALLATION AND RIGGING

The technicians who install and rig scenery are often not the technicians who have built it. This is particularly true in professional and large operations where independent or separate scenic studios exist. Smaller theaters and universities generally use all or part of the construction crew to load-in the set. Regardless of which environment you find yourself working in, it is very important for the scenic carpenter to know and understand the techniques and methods commonly used to install and rig scenery in the theater. A set should arrive for installation with everything required to join, stiffen, brace and rig the scenery in the theater. The scenic construction shop must determine the appropriate apparatus and provide, install and test all the hardware required to meet the specific installation and rigging needs of the scenery.

JOINING SCENERY TOGETHER

Individual flats are regularly connected together to make larger units, and these units assembled to create a diverse array of stage settings. Flats are typically coupled together in one of three basic configurations: (1) edge-to-edge, making one larger continuous plane, (2) as inside corners where the angle between the two adjoining faces is less than 180°, or (3) as outside corners where the angle between faces is greater than 180° (see Figure 7-1). The fastening method used to join the flats or other scenic elements together may be categorized as temporary, semipermanent or permanent.

Joining Traditional Theatrical Flats

Permanent joints are created in the scene shop and remain intact until the set is broken up. Permanent joints should be used whenever possible to reduce the number of individual scenic units which need to be handled. They also generally provide a stronger and more stable joint, and one which more acceptably conceals any visual indication of the joint. One-and-a-half or two-inch tight-pin back-flap hinges are the most commonly used device for permanently joining individual flats edge to edge. When joined together, the flats form a single larger unit such as an interior wall or exterior facade. Two or more flats, when hinged, can be folded together into a more manageable unit for transportation or storage. The largest of the individual flats is positioned in the middle when three flats are hinged together (as illustrated in Figure 7-2). The unit, when folded, should be no larger then the smallest opening through which the scenery must be maneuvered. Hinges are placed on the front of the flat every four feet along the adjoining edges, as illustrated, and secured with no. 9 wood screws. Stove bolts can be substituted for wood screws to provide maximum strength under extreme conditions.

If the outside flats of a three-fold unit overlap, a tumbler is required to allow the individual flats to fold flat and prevent the hinges from binding and being torn from the frame. The tumbler is simply a length of 1 × 3 pine hinged to the center flat and one of the outside flats. The tumbler

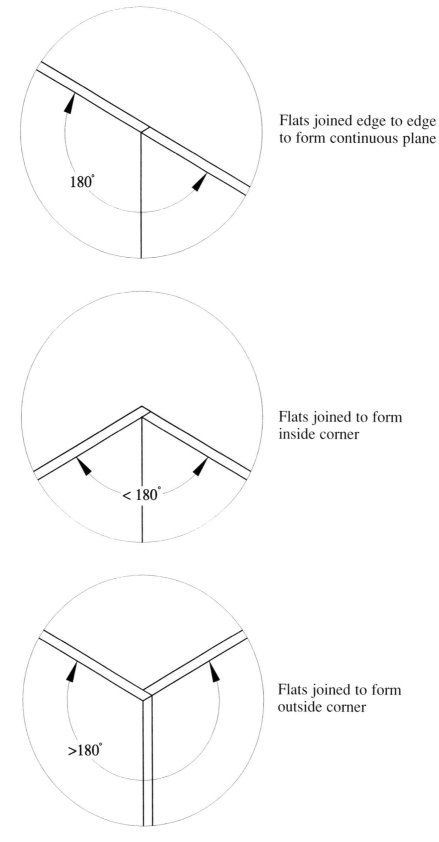

Flats joined edge to edge
to form continuous plane

Flats joined to form
inside corner

Flats joined to form
outside corner

FIGURE 7-1
*Joining flats to form a contin-
uous plan, inside corners and
outside corners*

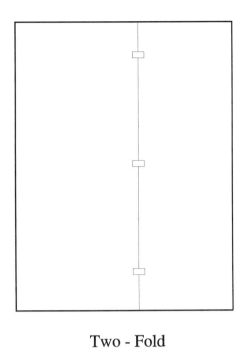

Two - Fold

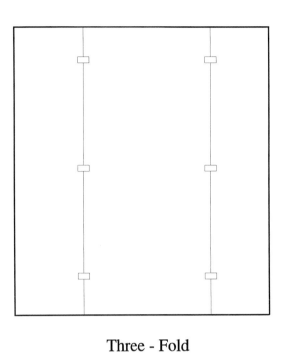

Three - Fold

provides a spacer, allowing one flat to fold over the other. Figure 7-3 illustrates the use of a tumbler.

To conceal the joint, the seam and hinges are covered with a narrow strip of muslin or canvas, called a *dutchman*, which is painted along with the rest of the flat. An acceptable dutchman requires practice and finesse. Use the same material that covers the flat to obtain the best results. The key to a successful dutchman is in the time and effort spent in feathering out the edges. The vertical threads are removed from each edge of the dutchman to soften and obscure the edge. The fabric strip is dipped into a diluted white glue and applied over the seam. Work the feathered edges out well to avoid any bunching of the threads.

Under some circumstances it may be necessary to countersink the hinges to eliminate any shadows caused by the stage lights. This is particularly true when heavy side lighting is anticipated, the finished wall is a light color with little or no pattern to camouflage the underlying hinge, or when the audience is in close proximity to the scenery.

In situations where the set can be constructed in place on the stage or transported to the stage in large pieces and there is no need to move it for the run of the show, flats may be joined together edge-to-edge with a simple wood or metal plate. The plate is positioned on the back of the flat across the seam and screwed into the frame. A dutchman is then applied to the front of the flat to hide the seam.

Inside and outside corner joints are easier to manage. Scenic carpenters, if not the show's designer, should plan for the orientation of these joints with respect to

FIGURE 7-2
Arrangements for a two-fold and three-fold flat

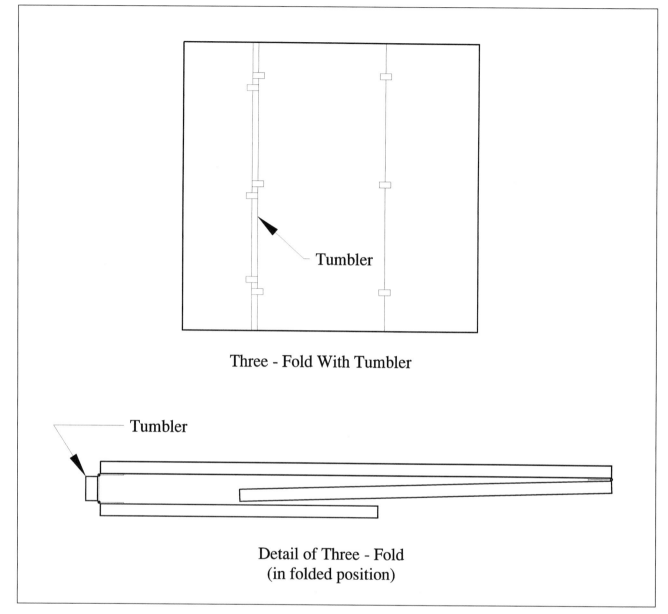

Three - Fold With Tumbler

Tumbler

Detail of Three - Fold
(in folded position)

FIGURE 7-3
Using a tumbler on a three-fold flat

the view of the audience. The seam of the joint should run parallel to the proscenium whenever possible. This is the least visually obtrusive position and reduces the likelihood of the audience seeing any backstage light leaking through the crack. A permanent joint for a 90° inside corner or 270° outside corner is easily made by nailing the flats together from the rear with duplex nails or from the front with finish nails. Drywall screws are also a good choice if you own a cordless drill or screw gun. You will recognize this joint as a face-to-edge butt joint. A corner other than 90° or 270° requires one or both of the flats to

be built with the adjoining edge beveled to the appropriate angle. The flats can then be nailed or screwed together.

Semipermanent joints are those that stay together as long as the set is in one location. They are made up and tested in the scene shop for fit and accuracy, and then separated for transportation to the theater. The joints are remade as the set is installed in the theater and remain together for as long as the production runs. Loose-pin back-flap hinges are generally used for this type of joining. The hinges are located every four feet along the seam on the back of the flats. Bolts may also be used in some

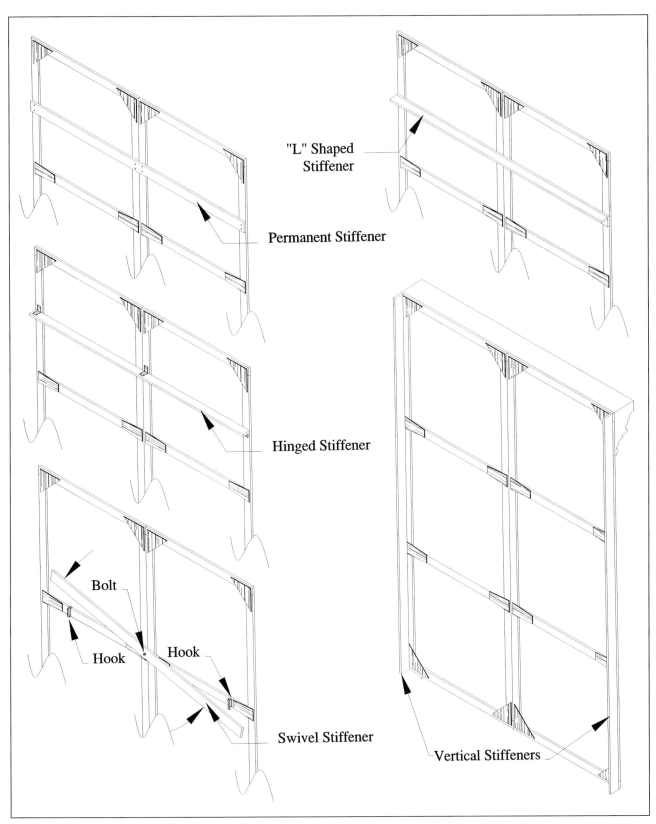

FIGURE 7-4
Various stiffening techniques

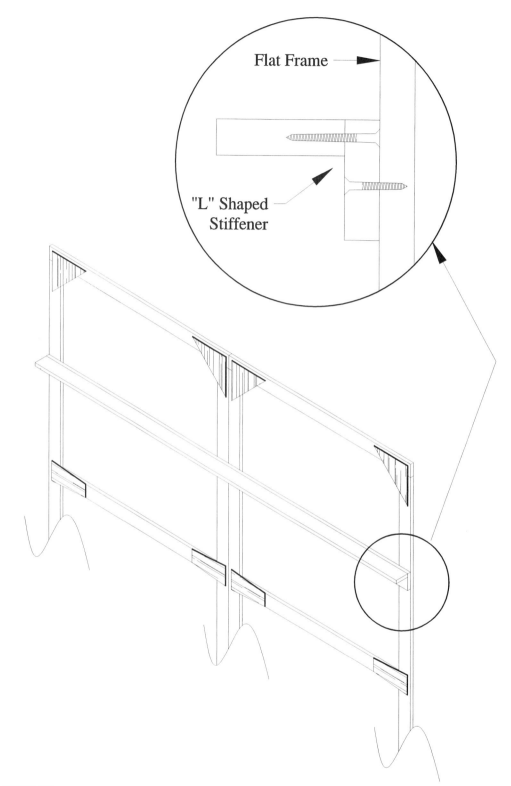

Flat Frame

"L" Shaped
Stiffener

FIGURE 7-5
Using an L *stiffener*

situations, particularly for joining three-dimensional scenic units.

Temporary joining techniques are required when large scenic units must be bro-

ken down for rapidly shifting from one scene to another. This can be achieved by lashing the flats together, as discussed in chapter five, or more commonly by joining

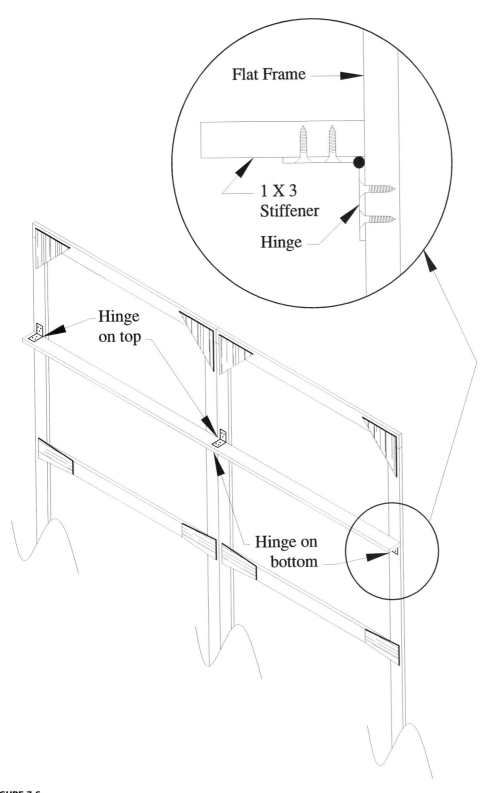

FIGURE 7-6
Using a hinged stiffener

the flats using loose-pin hinges. Under these conditions, the pin is often replaced with pin wire to facilitate rapid assembly or disassembly of the joint.

Stiffening

Scenic units that are subject to bending stresses due to heavy or concentrated loads, or those that are assembled using hinges, often require stiffening to make them rigid. Flats hinged together edge-to-edge, forming larger units, require some horizontal stiffening device to be applied across the joint to ensure a stable and structurally sound scenic unit while in performance. In other cases, where a heavy cornice or other architectural detail may cause the flat to bend under the weight of the detail, a vertical stiffener is required. Flats can act as stiffeners when joined to other flats at 90° angles. Likewise, flats constructed with thickness pieces (or returns, as they are sometimes called), are stiffened by these components. Several stiffening methods are pictured in Figure 7-4.

For scenic units assembled from two or more individual flats that need not fold during the run of the production, a semipermanent stiffener can be used. Figure 7-5 illustrates this technique. The stiffener is constructed of two pieces of 1 × 3 pine long enough to span the width of the scenic unit. The pieces are joined face-to-edge to form an *L* shape as depicted in Figure 7-5. The stiffener is positioned horizontally across the back of the flats and screwed into the flat frames using drywall screws. The strength of the stiffener is provided by the 1 × 3, which is oriented with its faces perpendicular to the face of the flat. This position places the strongest cross section of the 1 × 3 opposing any force that might tend to fold the flat.

Another option uses hinges to fasten a single 1 × 3 batten to the scenic unit as the stiffener. The hinges are positioned on alternate sides of the stiffener (as illustrated in Figure 7-6). Using loose-pin hinges allows the stiffener to be removed so the flats can be folded for shifting or storage. These techniques may be used horizontally, as described above, or vertically to stiffen a flat.

Bracing

Most two-dimensional scenery needs some type of auxiliary support in order to stand erect. Vertical support is provided by stage braces or jacks. A stage brace (Figure 7-7) is a diagonal brace that is attached near the top of the flat and to the stage floor. Traditional stage braces are adjustable in length. The connection to the flat is by means of a double-pronged hook on one end of the stage brace, which mates to a metal plate, known as a *brace cleat*, attached to the flat frame. The foot of the stage brace is secured to the stage floor with a stage screw. The "improved" stage screw works with a threaded insert that is set into the stage floor at the appropriate location. This enhancement enables the stage screw to be inserted or removed repeatedly during scene shifts without wearing away at the hole.

Fixed-length stage braces are also available and are secured to both the flat and the stage floor with drywall screws through metal angle brackets on each end of the stage brace (see Figure 7-7).

Jacks are another device used to provide vertical support. They are generally constructed in the form of a triangle for greatest rigidity, but can take other shapes to accommodate the scenic-unit construction. The stile of the jack should be at least two-thirds the height of the flat it is to support. The stile, rail and diagonal framing members of the jack are joined using cornerblocks on one or both sides, as illustrated in Figure 7-8 on page 182.

Hinges are used to fasten the jack to one of the stiles of the flat. Either a foot iron and stage screw or hinges can be used to secure the jack to the stage floor. As an alternative to a positive attachment to the floor, sandbags or stage weights can be fitted over the rail to provide the ballast to hold the scenic unit erect.

Jacks can also be constructed on wheels and in a variety of configurations that are semipermanently attached to the flat. The total assembly is then moved as a single unit during scene shifts. Figure 7-9, on page 183, depicts a typical application.

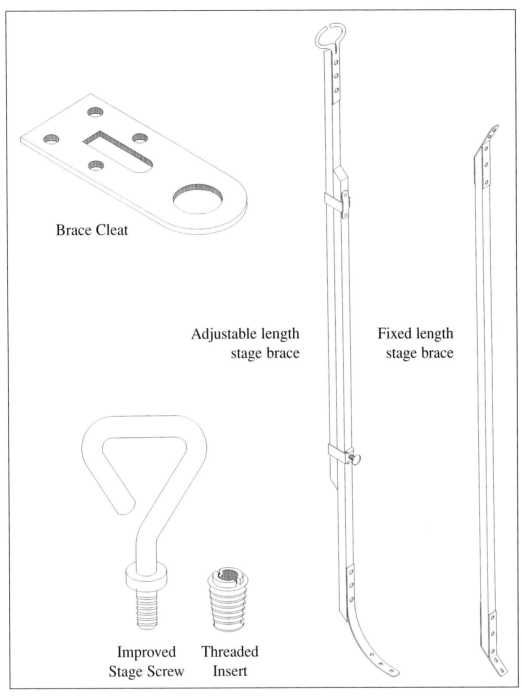

Brace Cleat

Adjustable length
stage brace

Fixed length
stage brace

Improved   Threaded
Stage Screw   Insert

FIGURE 7-7
Stage braces and attachment hardware

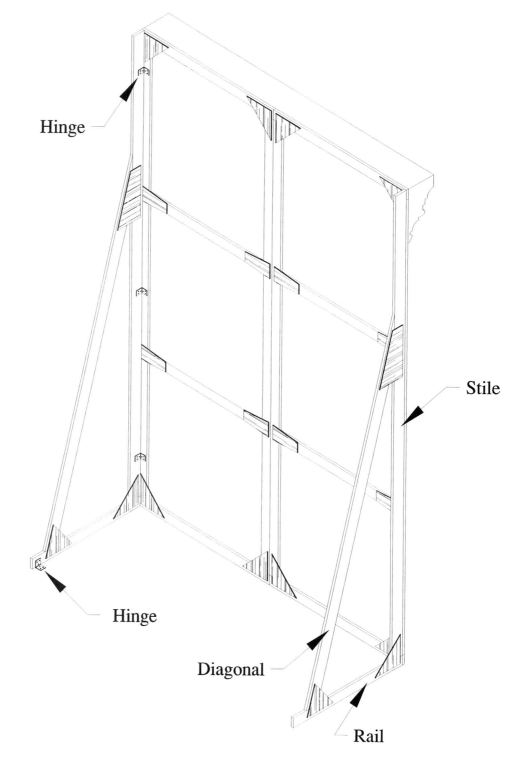

Hinge

Hinge

Stile

Diagonal

Rail

FIGURE 7-8
Using jacks for vertical support of a flat

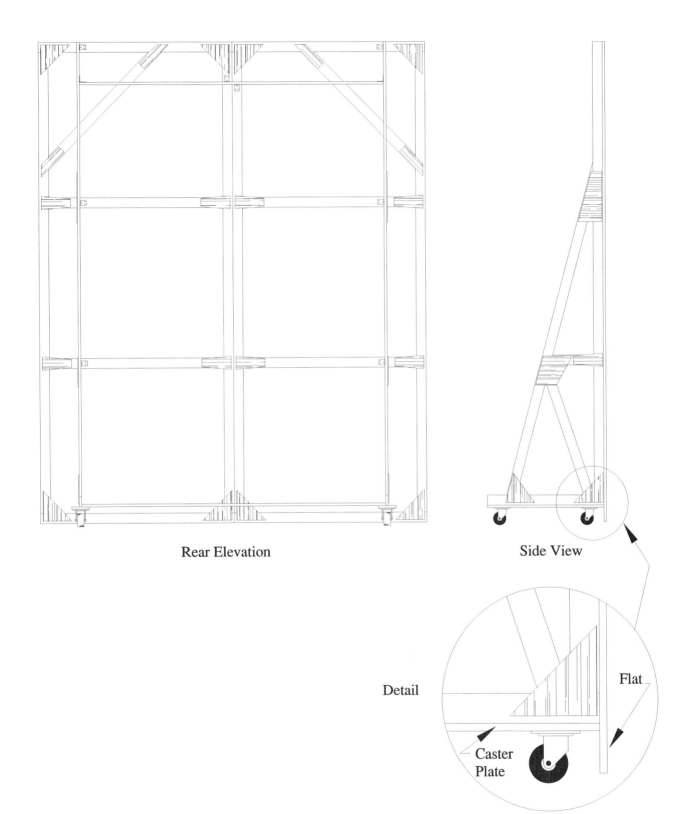

Rear Elevation

Side View

Detail

Flat

Caster
Plate

FIGURE 7-9
Creating a rolling unit using jacks on a caster plate

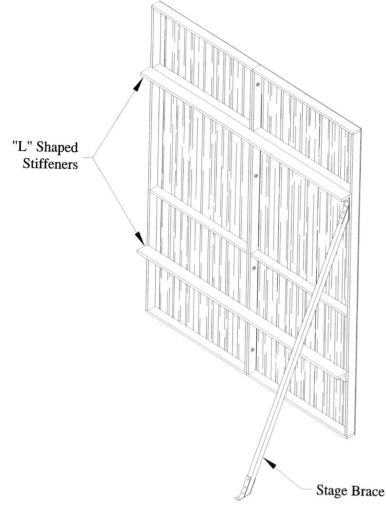

"L" Shaped
Stiffeners

Stage Brace

FIGURE 7-10
Using a stage brace for vertical support of a studio flat

Studio Flats

Unlike traditional flats, hinges are rarely used to join studio flats. Screws, bolts and clamps are regularly used to join studio flats edge-to-edge or edge-to-face. The framing technique used for studio flats lessens the needs for stiffening. When required, an *L*-shaped stiffener is screwed to the back of the flat. Vertical support is once again provided by stage braces or jacks, as illustrated in Figure 7-10.

INSTALLING THE SINGLE SET

Installation of a single-set production, one in which the setting does not move or shift during the run of the production, requires the set to be secured to the stage floor and supported vertically. To attach a set assembled from traditional flats to the stage floor, one of the following methods can be used.

1. A length of 1×3 stock is laid on the stage floor against the rear face of the flat's bottom rail. Duplex nails or screws are used to fasten the 1×3 cleat to the stage floor. Finish nails are used from the face of the flat to secure the flat to the cleat. The small heads of the finish nails can be easily hidden with a little paint of the appropriate color or, in some situations, simply countersunk into the flat frame with a nail set. This technique is another example of why the cornerblocks used on the flat joints are held back 1″ from the edge. This setback allows the 1×3 to be positioned snugly against the flat frame.

2. Tight-pin back-flap hinges are screwed to the rear face of the flat's bottom rail and to the stage floor. When working with studio flats, nail or screw through the bottom rail into the stage floor.

A good deal of vertical support naturally occurs as flats are attached to one another per the designer's plans. In Figure 7-11, flats *A* and *B*, joined at right angles, provide vertical support for each other. Reveals, returns and backing flats can be additional sources of support. Any portion of the set that is not supported by other elements of the set or those that require reinforcement, such as door or window flats, can be supported with jacks or stage braces. Another option is to support the scenic unit from above using the theater's rigging system. One end of the lift lines is attached to the scenic unit, while the other is fastened to a batten or some other overhead structure. With the unit secured to the stage floor, tension is applied to the lift lines. This technique is not as structurally sound as utilizing jacks or stage braces, but can be useful when floor space upstage of the unit is at a premium and nothing comes in contact with the scenic unit.

SHIFTING SCENERY

Multiple-set productions, or those that play in repertory, require that some plan be devised to facilitate the shifting of scenery from one set to the following set or one production to the next. The theater's permanent equipment and backstage layout will be a significant influence to the development of this plan. Chapter two introduced a variety of equipment that might be permanently installed in a theater for this purpose. The availability of a rigging system, turntable, slip stages, elevators or other such devices provides significant mechanical tools to accomplish a scene shift with relative ease.

Shifting on the Deck

Any combination of turntables and wagons will allow for all or a significant portion of a set to be installed for the run of the show. There is no need to break down and carry off individual pieces of scenery and replace them with those which form a subsequent setting. The scene shift is accomplished when the turntable is rotated or the wagons exchange places on stage, carrying one set off as the other comes on. When employing these devices, the scenery may be installed onto the deck of the device in the same manner as the single-set installation instructions given above. If the set must be exchanged for another when it is in its offstage position, temporary attachments such as stage screws and foot irons should be utilized.

Turntables and wagons can also be purchased, rented or constructed as part of a production's specific scenery requirements to enable this type of scene shift. Chapter six provides general construction information for these devices. Under some circumstances, it may be more practical, desirable or economical to build portions of the set on small wagons or to directly caster small sections of the set. Every attempt should be made to keep the number of individual pieces to a minimum and to provide mechanical assistance—eliminating the need to employ weightlifters as stagehands.

Rigging to Fly

Scenery is rigged to fly to facilitate scene shifts or create special effects. Scenery

FIGURE 7-11
Flats can provide vertical support for each other

which is not in use for a scene is raised to its storage position above the stage in the fly loft. The height to which the unit is lifted is known as its *high trim* or *out trim*. When the scenery is required in a scene, it is lowered to its specified position on the stage. This position is naturally called the *low trim* or *in trim*. Stage technicians refer to the act of raising a piece of scenery or equipment as "flying it out." To lower it is referred to as "flying it in." You can think of this in terms of "in" use or "out" of use or "in" sight or "out" of sight. Rigging systems are also used to simply suspend or support scenery and equipment in stationary positions for the duration of the production.

Flying or suspending scenery or overhead lifting requires special knowledge of the materials, equipment, techniques and procedures used in theatrical rigging to ensure the safety of everyone participating in the production. For this reason, I suggest a single qualified individual have overall responsibility for all flying scenery and equipment. All of the equipment and materials used in flying scenery and theatrical equipment must be designed, manufactured and tested to support the weight of these items with a significant margin of safety. A safety factor of eight to ten is standard, but should be increased if a particular situation demands. As an example, suppose you are required to rig an item that weighs 100 pounds. The application of the standard safety factor requires that the system, including all components, joints, fasteners and hardware, be capable of supporting 800 to 1,000 pounds. These safety factors are employed to compensate for errors in load estimates and calculations, component manufacturing variables, wear and tear on the equipment and, most importantly, to account for the increase in forces acting on the system as a result of dynamic loads (those which are in motion), and shock loading.

The forces generated by the weight of a particular scenic unit can multiply quickly under conditions that are present whenever scenery and equipment are flown. The mere act of raising or lowering a scenic unit develops forces greater than the forces generated by the weight of a stationary object. We have all experienced this physical reality on various occasions. Perhaps you have stood on a stick of wood in an attempt to break it, only to find it would not break under your weight alone. The solution is to jump on the piece of wood, adding the force of movement to that of your weight, which often generates enough total force to cause the wood to break. The movement that occurs as part of the function of flying a scenic unit similarly magnifies the force being applied to the system well beyond those that are present when the unit is stationary. The extreme condition of this scenario is known as *shock loading*. Imagine

a scenic unit in its storage position over the stage. When the time arrives for it to be flown in, the unit hangs up on another piece of scenery or equipment, momentarily causing the lift lines to go slack. Before the operator can react, the unit comes free and drops until it reaches the end of its rope. The force applied to the system when the scenery is caught by the lift lines is multiplied several-fold and could cause damage or failure if the system was not designed with a substantial safety factor.

The three most common systems for flying scenery—found in theaters today—the hemp system, counterweight system, and motorized-winch system were described in chapter two. This section of the text is concerned with properly connecting the scenery to one of these systems. The main components required to make this connection consist of the lifting lines, linking hardware, a trimming device and hanging hardware. The lifting lines may be wire rope or fiber rope. Wire rope is the standard in professional operations and will be the focus of this text; the use of fiber rope will be taken up later in this chapter.

Rigging wood-frame scenery to fly requires the use of standard hanging hardware. The bottom hanging iron is designed to support the flat frame from under the bottom rail. The bend in the hanging iron hooks under the bottom rail as pictured in Figure 7-12. This way, the framing members and joints are subject to compression stress only, and the fasteners that secure the hanging hardware do not directly support the weight of the unit. In other words, hanging the unit in this manner subjects the structure and its components to stresses that are no different than those which are present when the unit is standing upright on the stage floor. These are the conditions under which the structural components and construction techniques for wood-frame scenery were engineered. If the unit were hung from the top rail, as I have too often seen, tensile stresses, which are much more likely to weaken the unit and create a po-

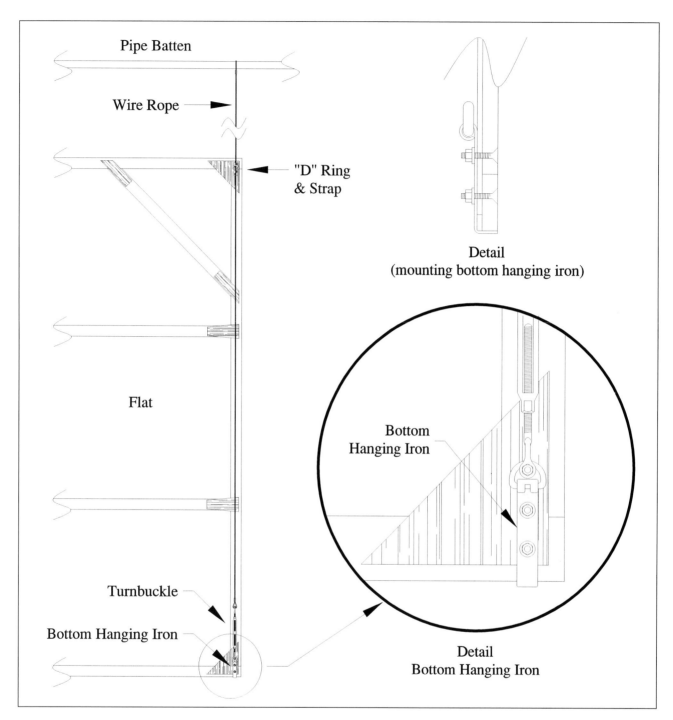

Pipe Batten

Wire Rope

"D" Ring
& Strap

Detail
(mounting bottom hanging iron)

Flat

Bottom
Hanging Iron

Turnbuckle

Bottom Hanging Iron

Detail
Bottom Hanging Iron

tential safety hazard, developed. Additionally, the fasteners that secure the hanging hardware to the frame must bear the entire weight of the unit. If rigged properly, the primary function of these fasteners is simply to hold the hanging iron in position. This is a much easier task.

A trimming device is attached to the ring of the bottom hanging iron to provide a means to adjust or trim the height of the unit. A turnbuckle or trim chain can be used for this purpose. These items should be rated by the manufacturer to support the load of the flying unit. I prefer the use of jaw-to-jaw turnbuckles (as illustrated in Figure 7-13, page 188). The lift line is attached to the top of the turnbuckle using a thimble and nicopress sleeves. Cable clips can be used, but remember: They reduce the lifting capacity of the wire rope by

FIGURE 7-12
Using a hanging iron to bottom-hang a flat

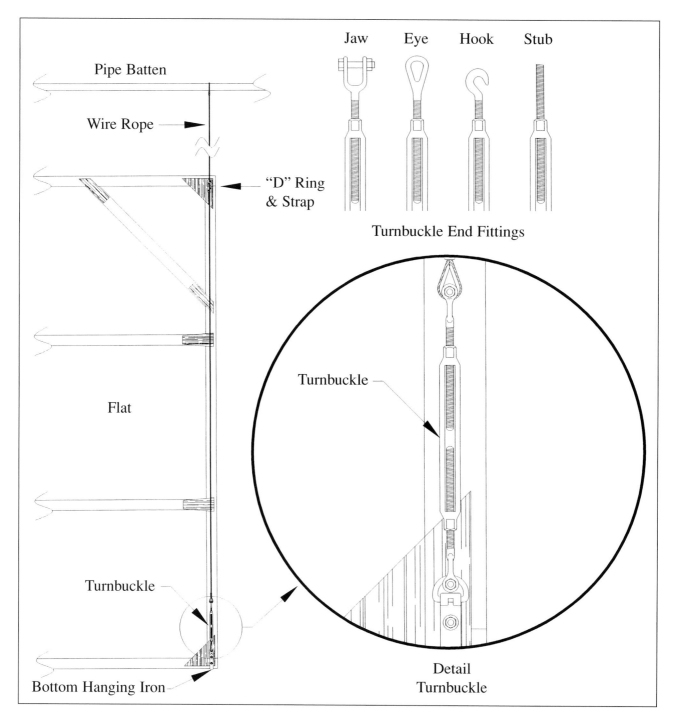

Jaw   Eye   Hook   Stub

Pipe Batten

Wire Rope

"D" Ring & Strap

Turnbuckle End Fittings

Flat

Turnbuckle

Turnbuckle

Bottom Hanging Iron

Detail
Turnbuckle

FIGURE 7-13

Using a turnbuckle to provide a means to trim the height of a hanging flat

20 percent. Figure 7-14 illustrates this connection. The lifting line continues up the frame and through the ring of a top hanging iron or D-ring and strap at the top of the flat. This hardware is used to guide the lift line and keep the scenic unit in a vertical position. All hanging irons should be bolted to the flat frame to ensure a sound connection under the most severe conditions. Use

flathead stove bolts inserted through and countersunk into the face of the flat.

The lift line continues up to the batten of the theater's rigging system. The length of the lift line is determined with the help of a centerline section of the theater. The length should be such that the rigging system batten remains out of sightlines when the scenic unit is at its low trim and the

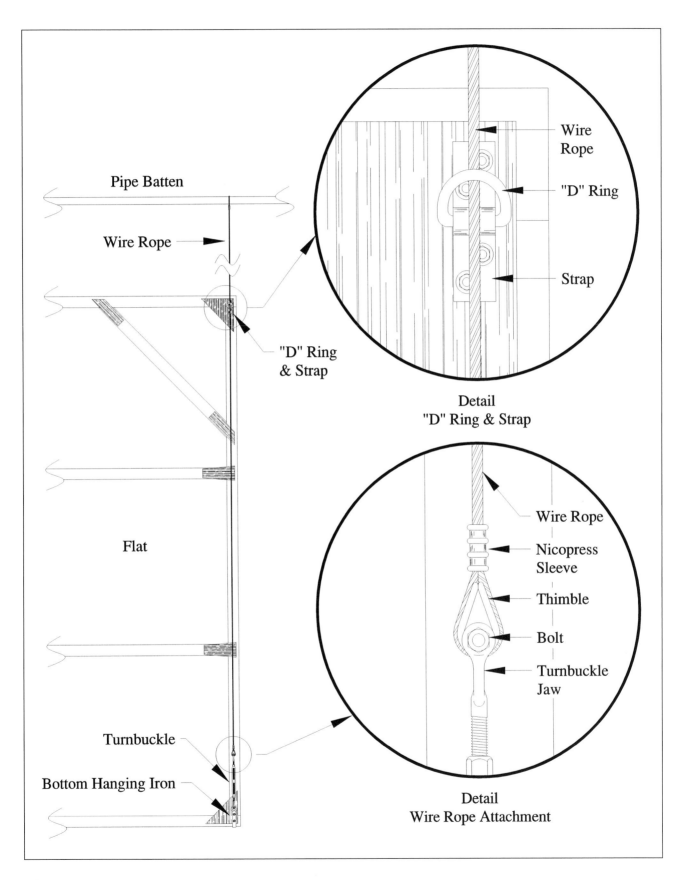

Pipe Batten

Wire Rope

"D" Ring
& Strap

Flat

Turnbuckle

Bottom Hanging Iron

Wire
Rope

"D" Ring

Strap

Detail
"D" Ring & Strap

Wire Rope

Nicopress
Sleeve

Thimble

Bolt

Turnbuckle
Jaw

Detail
Wire Rope Attachment

FIGURE 7-14
The connection of the wire rope to the turnbuckle and the use of a D ring as a keeper

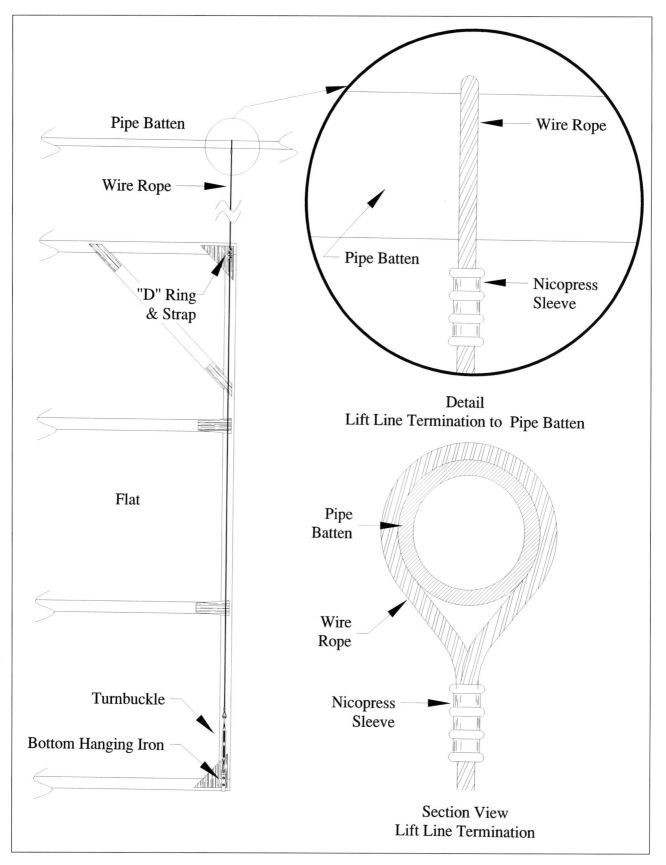

Pipe Batten

Wire Rope

"D" Ring & Strap

Flat

Turnbuckle

Bottom Hanging Iron

Wire Rope

Pipe Batten

Nicopress Sleeve

Detail
Lift Line Termination to Pipe Batten

Pipe Batten

Wire Rope

Nicopress Sleeve

Section View
Lift Line Termination

FIGURE 7-15
The connection of the wire rope to the batten

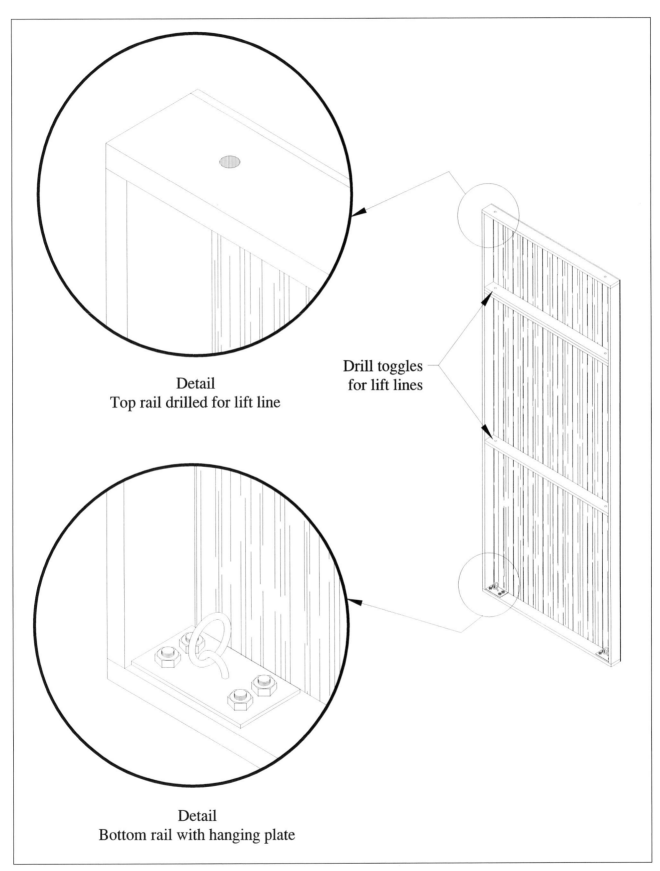

Detail
Top rail drilled for lift line

Drill toggles
for lift lines

Detail
Bottom rail with hanging plate

FIGURE 7-16
A technique for hanging a studio flat

scenic unit is out of sight when at high trim. A loop is made over the pipe batten and the end of the wire rope is fastened to itself with nicopress sleeves or cable clips (see Figure 7-15 on page 190). Some technicians attempt to tie a clove hitch with the wire rope around the pipe batten, or make several loops around the batten. No strength is added by these methods and, in some cases, they can reduce the weight capacity of the wire rope. The simpler, the better. Keep the number of components and connections to a minimum.

Trim chains are used around the pipe batten to facilitate installation. The lift lines are precut and attached to the trim chain. When using chain for overhead rigging, be sure to purchase rated chain, as with all the other components of a rigging system.

As stated, lifting a scenic unit from the bottom should be the primary goal. However, this is not always possible or practical. Ceilings are a typical example. In this case, a ceiling plate is used in place of the hanging iron. The larger metal plate helps distribute the load over the framing member. A sufficient number of ceiling plates and lift lines should be used to distribute the weight of the scenic piece. Again, be sure to bolt the ceiling plate to the frame.

The basic rigging concepts outlined above should be applied to rigging three-dimensional scenery, studio flats and scenery constructed from other materials. A little more latitude is available when hanging metal-framed scenery due to its superior strength and joining techniques. Hanging hardware can be welded directly to the frame, making it possible to hang from the top of the unit in some circumstances.

Studio flats are a little more awkward to hang than traditional theatrical flats. Satisfactory results can be obtained by bolting a ceiling plate or other large plate and ring to the bottom rail. Holes are drilled through the intervening toggles and the top rail, allowing the wire rope to pass through the frame (see Figure 7-16, page 191). With very heavy loads, a piece of strap metal is secured to the underside of the bottom rail. The ring assembly is bolted to the metal strap, sandwiching the bottom rail between the two.

The permanently installed equipment for theatrical rigging cannot be all things to all scenery. At times, it is not always in the right place or designed to accommodate the size or weight of every piece of scenery that comes along. A few common rigging techniques are available to deal with the most common problems in theatrical rigging.

A technique known as *breasting* will allow for some horizontal movement of a flying piece of scenery. This may be required when a batten is not exactly over the stage position of the flying scenery. It can also be required when storage space is not available directly over the scenery's playing position. The basic concept is to attach the scenery to two sets of lift lines that are separated by some distance. Figure 7-17 illustrates this concept.

When a drop is too tall to fly out of sight-lines or the grid is too low to accommodate its height, the bottom of the drop can be attached to a second set of lift lines and raised (as illustrated in Figure 7-18). This technique is known as *tripping* and effectively folds the drop in half.

Please note that when breasting or tripping techniques are utilized, the weight of the load is shared by two or more sets of lift lines. Additionally, the load shifts between these lift lines as a direct result of employing either of these techniques. Caution should be taken to ensure control of the load is maintained at all times and safety restraints are employed as required.

Bridling is a technique employed to distribute a concentrated load over a greater area or to transfer a concentrated load to the lift lines of a rigging system. It is also used to more accurately position a scenic item without regard to the specific location of the rigging-system components. Figure 7-19 (page 195) illustrates this technique. The technique can also be used to distribute or position dead-hung loads. Additionally,

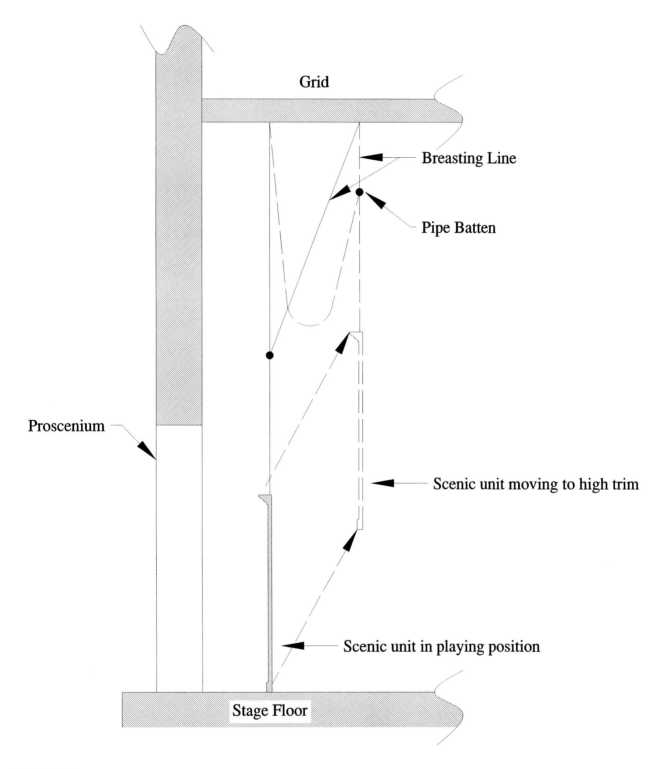

FIGURE 7-17
Breasting technique used to adjust the horizontal position of a flying unit

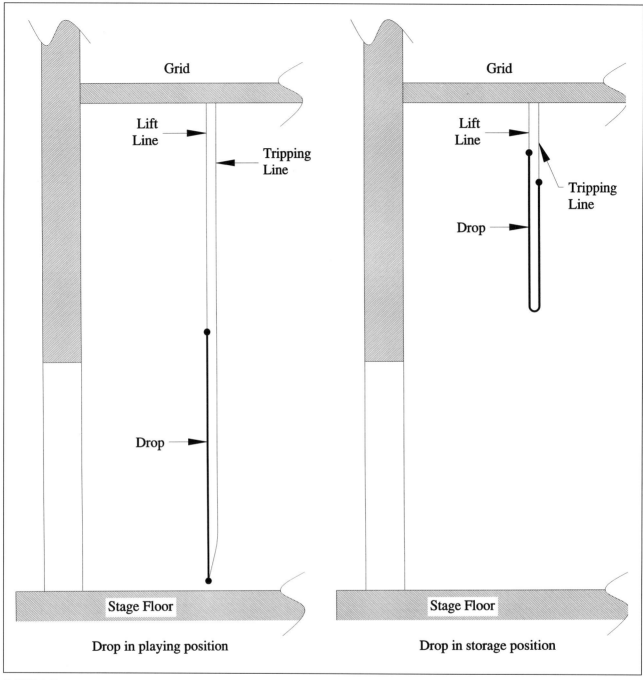

FIGURE 7-18
Tripping technique used to store soft goods that are too tall for fly loft

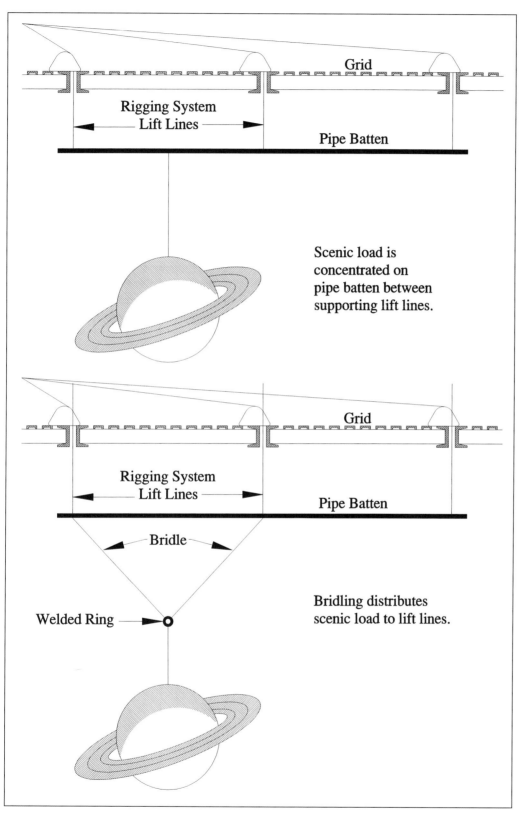

FIGURE 7-19
Bridling technique used to distribute loads

bridling is a useful method to rig scenic items that hang from a single point, such as a chandelier. When suspended from two points, the chandelier will not easily spin.

USING FIBER ROPE

While wire rope is used for the lion's share of rigging applications, fiber rope still has a significant place in the theater. Additionally, without access to the special tools and hardware required for using wire rope, fiber rope may be your only option. Every stage technician must have a working knowledge of fiber rope and the ability to tie a handful of useful knots. Knots are designed for a specific purpose. Choosing and properly tying the appropriate knot will ensure a safe application. Knots cause stress, damage rope fibers and reduce rope strength by as much as 50 percent. This is another reason to work with an appropriate safety factor when choosing materials for rigging.

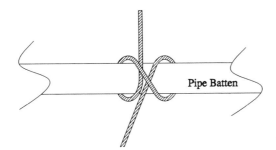

FIGURE 7-20 *A bowline ties a loop in the end of a rope.*

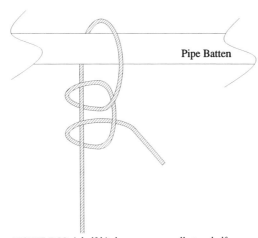

FIGURE 7-21 *A clove hitch is used to tie a rope to a rigid object such as pipe batten.*

FIGURE 7-22 *A half hitch, or more usually two half-hitches, is also used to secure a rope to a rigid object.*

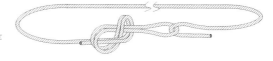

FIGURE 7-23 *A trucker's hitch provides a means for adjusting the length of the rope.*

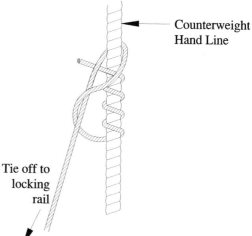

Counterweight Hand Line

Tie off to locking rail

FIGURE 7-24 *A stopper hitch is used to tie a safety line to the hand line of a counterweight.*

FIGURE 7-25 *A square knot is used to join two equal-size ropes together.*

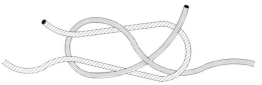

FIGURE 7-26 *A sheet bend joins two ropes of differing sizes.*

CHAPTER 8

STOCK SCENERY

The use of stock scenery is as old as the theater itself. The Greeks performed their dramas in front of a permanent background, which represented a series of buildings, a temple or palace and fulfilled the requirements of most the dramatic literature of the time. Some scholars believe a set of stock scenery was used to represent other locales such as a forest or cave. Much debate has taken place concerning the use of periaktoi by the Romans. Vitruvius believed that each of the three panels which made up the periaktoi was painted with a different scene generically suitable for tragic, comic or satyric presentations. Throughout history, stock scenery has adapted to meet the styles and conventions of the time.

During this century, stock scenery has existed in two forms. Many opera and ballet companies, which have maintained a standard repertory of productions, have maintained complete stock sets for this repertory. The sets are designed for the specific opera or ballet, but not so specific as to make it unusable for another company's production. The conventions of these theatrical forms have depended less on the potential emotional and intellectual contributions of scenery than the theater. As with the Greeks and Romans, scenery has traditionally served opera and ballet as a general background for the performer. This is not to say that the scenery has not been spectacular or visually rich, but merely less interactive with the performer.

The theater has chosen to maintain a stock of individual components that can be assembled into a variety of configurations, trimmed, repainted and dressed to meet the needs of each new production. This technique became particularly useful with the rise in popularity of the box set. The settings of a substantial portion of the dramatic literature of the early twentieth century focused predominantly on realistic interiors that were well served by box-set designs. The traditional wood-frame flat became the standard building block for the box set.

The box set, constructed of wood-frame flats, continues to be a popular approach to design and construction in professional, educational and community theaters today. However, a broad array of new theatrical literature and styles, audience tastes and expectations, and the visual influence of film, television, computer graphics and other entertainments have made certain types of stock scenery more difficult to utilize and less aesthetically desirable. However, there are still significant reasons to maintain and employ stock scenery. Your success will depend on your ability to assess the scenic needs and goals of your particular producing organization.

The visual style and physical characteristics of your theater will provide important clues to the type, quantity and suitable application of stock scenery in your productions. If your theater produces a significant number of plays that require realistic interior settings, you will have little trouble utilizing stock scenery, as so many other theaters have during recent decades. On the other hand, if you tend to produce more avant-garde theatrical forms, embrace a more metaphorical visual style or work in a less conventional performance space, you will need to be a bit more creative in developing and putting stock scenery in service.

The use of stock scenery can greatly

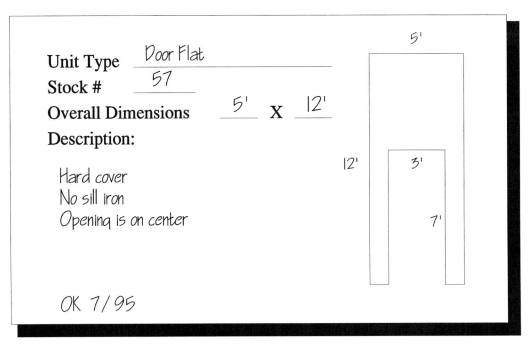

FIGURE 8-1

An example catalog card for stock scenery units

reduce certain repetitive scenery costs and is generally found to be beneficial in most resident-theater environments. The idea behind maintaining an inventory of stock scenic components is to reduce the material and labor costs of constructing scenery for each of the theater's productions. Additionally, it is simply wasteful to discard a perfectly good piece of scenery at the end of a production's run. Environmentalism and conservation have rekindled an interest in stock scenery. However, stock scenery comes at a cost. Storage space, which is usually at a premium, must be dedicated to the stock inventory. Additionally, the visual elements of the theater's productions can be adversely affected by the use of stock scenery. Experienced and talented designers and technicians will be able to disguise the use of stock scenery, but others may allow the scenery to dictate the design. Eventually, everything begins to look the same and the design of a production is relegated to meeting only the simple physical requirements of a production instead of informing the production using a visual language that creates a world specific to the characters, themes and ideas of the play.

Some argue that the use of stock is only another in a series of limitations imposed on the design, like budget and space limitations. My experience with young designers at UCLA has suggested that too often the design is driven by what is available in the stock inventory rather than the needs of the script. This is particularly true when money is in short supply—one of the conditions which stock scenery is intended to mitigate.

In using and maintaining stock scenery, the scene shop must know not only how to build scenery that will withstand repetitive use, but also how and when to use it. Designers will often entrust decisions on the use of stock scenery to the scene shop. It becomes the shop's responsibility to determine which units can be constructed with stock scenery and which pieces require new construction. When new construction is required, consideration should be given to building in such a manner as to add to the theater's stock inventory. A catalog of the theater's stock is necessary for optimum use. Figure 8-1 provides an example of a catalog card that may be utilized for this purpose. A sketch of the item, along with critical dimensions and an evaluation of the item's general condition, should be included. Additionally, the storage location and some type of inventory identification number are very helpful.

Determining your theater's stock scenery needs requires you to consider the distinct types of scenery and their uses. Soft goods are easy to store and are easily re-used. As stated previously in this text, masking should be a part of any theater's permanent equipment. This usually takes the form of black velour legs, borders and drops in sizes and quantities to complement the theater's physical characteristics. Additional masking and scenic backings are often required for productions and generally can be produced from stock components without compromising the visual style of the production. The design and visual aspects of these scenic elements are usually less demanding than more prominent elements of the set, making them ideal candidates for stock scenery. Drops can also be repainted for use in more than one production. The buildup of paint is the limiting factor in the useful life of a drop: Eventually the paint will inhibit the drop from hanging smooth and the paint will begin to crack.

The usefulness of other vertical scenery, primarily walls, will depend on a number of factors, as stated above. The visual language of many modern theater artists has taken on such a diverse vocabulary that vertical scenery, walls, and backdrops, may be difficult to supply from stock items. Figure 8-2, page 200, illustrates a designer's elevation for a set of walls constructed in traditional wood framing. This type of scenery can make significant use of an inventory of stock flats. Figure 8-3, page 201, illustrates the potential for all or part of these walls to be from stock. Notice the unit that is to be built to add a stock flat to the theater's inventory. UCLA maintains very little flat stock for use as the principal scenic components of a set due to the predominant style of its design program. I do believe a theater should always maintain a certain number of stock flats for scenic backings and masking pieces for reasons

stated earlier—which we do.

My experience has shown that weight-bearing units are the most successful stock-scenery items. This category includes platforms, wagons, show decks, scaffolding, stairs and ramps. These items are easily adapted to a variety of visual styles with inexpensive coverings. Their fundamental structural requirements ensure their suitability for repetitive use and adaptability to many situations. They also tend to be costly to construct, making reuse a definite advantage. Some commercially available products are available for use as stock stage, platforms and stairs. The best of these items are well suited for general staging requirements for concerts, assemblies and outdoor venues, but I have not had much success in employing these products in theatrical applications where flexibility and visual characteristics are primary factors.

The wood- or steel-frame platforms described in chapter six can be useful stock items. Their construction as stock scenic items requires a significant level of uniformity to ensure their usefulness. Templates should be developed and employed for mounting the hardware required to join stock units together into larger units. The goal of the template is to allow the units to be assembled in almost any configuration and joined to any other unit without modification. Similarly, a template should be established to fasten legs to the supporting frame. Again, any leg should be interchangeable with any other leg and able to attach to any supporting frame without additional fitting. Platforms are assembled and legs fabricated to the distinct dimensions of each new design. Specific shapes and any requirement to pierce a platform for access to the traps or installation of an elevator are achieved with the construction of show-specific platforms added to the stock units. Figure 8-4, page 202, illustrates one example.

UCLA maintains a small stock of 1×6 wood-frame platforms and a substantial

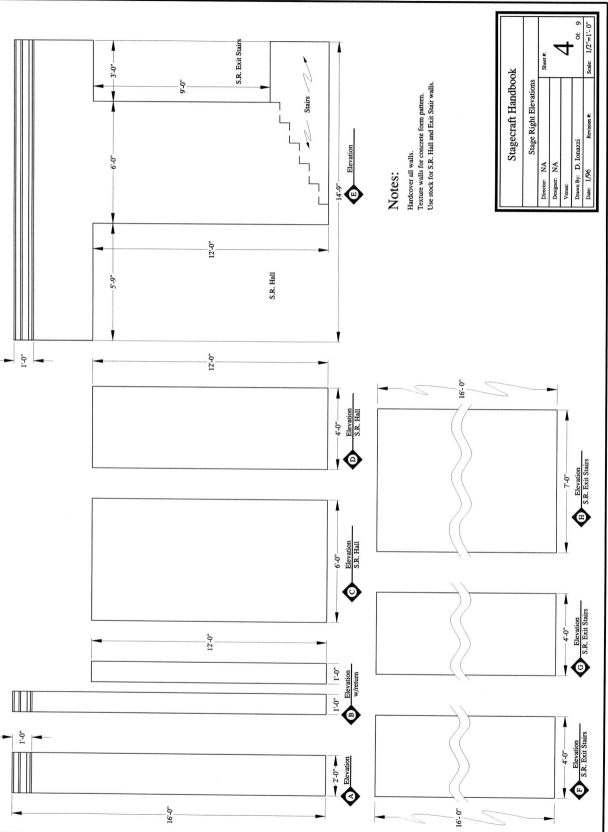

FIGURE 8-2

A typical sheet of designer's elevation

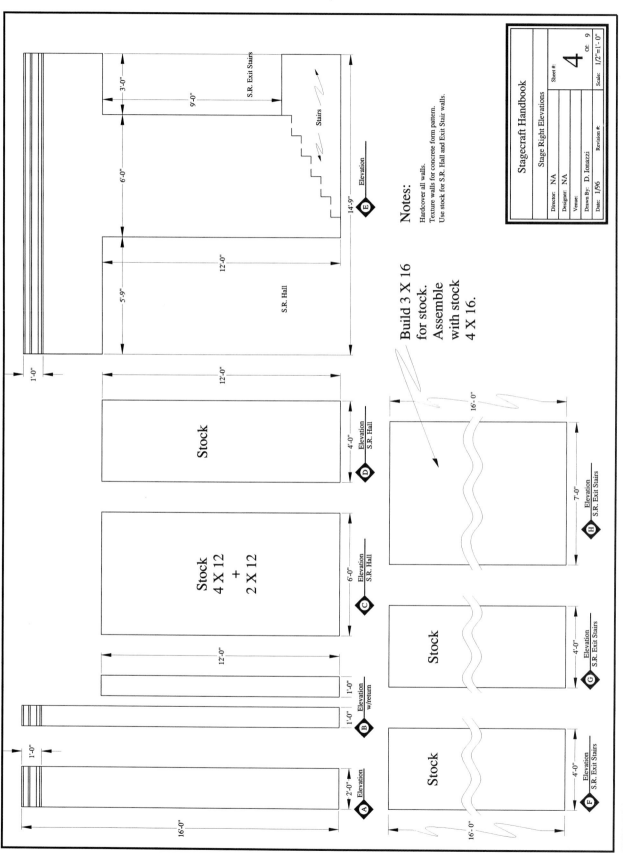

FIGURE 8-3
Using stock flats for the flats in Figure 8-2

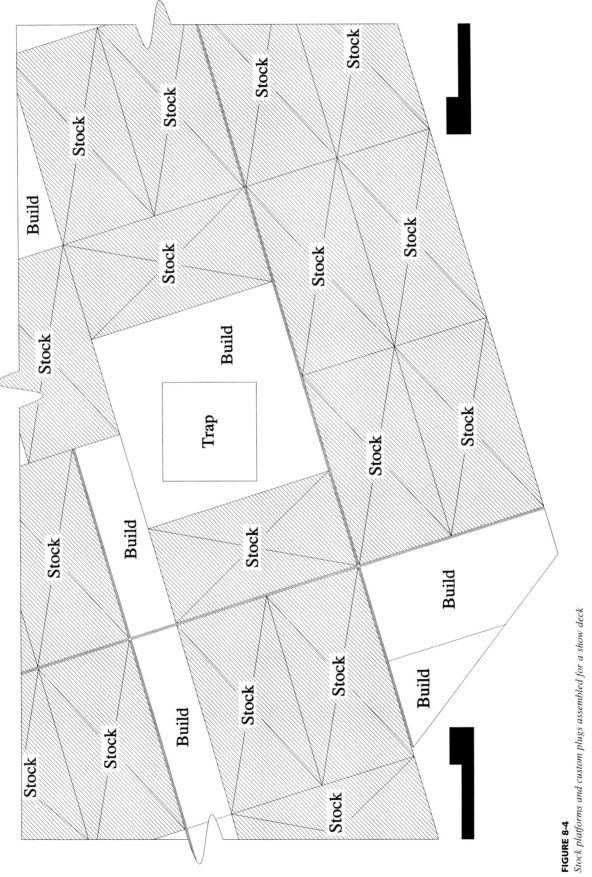

FIGURE 8-4

Stock platforms and custom plugs assembled for a show deck

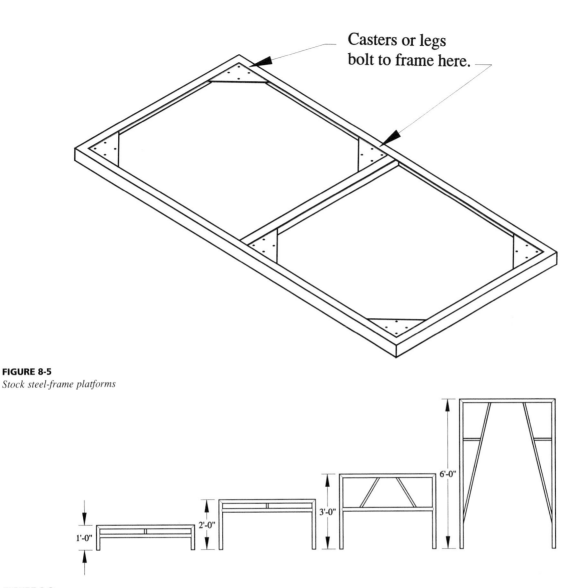

Casters or legs
bold to frame here.

FIGURE 8-5
Stock steel-frame platforms

FIGURE 8-6
Stock scaffold end frames used to create elevated platforms

inventory of 4′×8′ steel-frame platforms designed to utilize one-inch plywood as the base decking. These frames are constructed of 3″×3″ angle iron and designed to accept a round steel tube leg or caster bolted to a steel plate that is part of the frame assembly, as illustrated in Figure 8-5. We have also experimented with an aluminum version of the frame, which, as you can imagine, is much lighter.

Properly designed and constructed scaffolding can be a valuable asset to the stock inventory of a theater. It can save valuable construction time when elevated platforming is required, even when stock platforms are available. The most useful scaffolding

I have experienced has been custom designed and fabricated for use at UCLA. Figure 8-6 illustrates the standard end frames, which are joined together with X shaped braces to form 4′×4′ modules. The end frames are assembled in one-foot increments up to ten feet. Six-inch spacers can be installed between removable base plates and the end frame legs to achieve six-inch increments. Six-inch truss is used for clear spans of up to twelve feet. One-inch plywood is used as the base decking material.

In recent years, the UCLA shop has built a number of raked decks for our productions. As this trend became obvious, we

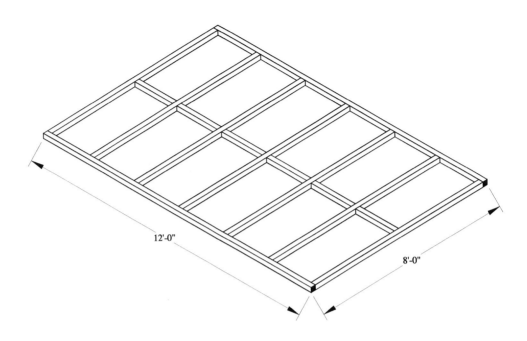

FIGURE 8-7
Two-inch square steel tube frames for platforms and rakes

considered a stock solution, which has been very efficient and convenient. Several 8' × 12' steel frames fabricated from two-inch square steel tube, as illustrated in Figure 8-7, above, were constructed. They store vertically in very little space and are easily assembled into full-stage decks for either of our two proscenium theaters. Square steel tube legs are cut per the design specifications of the production and welded to the frame. Our stock of 1" plywood is used as the base decking material and custom pieces are constructed to achieve any irregular contours. The finish layer of the deck is constructed per the specific requirements of the design. This illustrates the need for the shop to keep an eye open for trends and potential stock items that may be useful in your circumstances.

Stairs are a little more difficult to maintain in stock. First, they are awkward and clumsy to store. They also visually act more like vertical scenery, such as walls, than they do platforms, requiring them to conform to the specific visual style of the design. However, there is often great demand for stairs offstage, out of sightline, for escapes. Remember that any staircase that appears onstage usually requires another staircase offstage. This is a principal application of a stock stair unit.

The best development of stock scenery is a result of organic growth. The stock comes out of the units designed and built for specific productions and their performance spaces, with the idea of creating stock as part of the construction criteria. Years ago, I could have recommended building a set of flats of a height to complement a specific theater and in a variety of standard widths. I would have great confidence that these items would be very useful in fulfilling the scenic requirements of most productions. Today, with the wide variety of scenic and visual styles being explored and the equally diverse array of literature and directorial concepts being produced, that would be impossible. My best advice is to look for those items which tend to be repeatedly requested for your productions. These will most likely be found in the items required to support the design offstage and in show decks and elevated levels.

I hope the information presented in this text will provide you with a strong foundation for the planning and construction of quality scenery. My final thought on the construction of scenery takes me back to the beginning of the process. There are many solutions to each scenic-construction problem. No one method or technique is best suited for every production or every theater. Design and production styles, audience sightlines and proximity to the scenery, and the actors' physical interaction with the scenery are just some of the external criteria which will influence the construction methods and materials you will use. Many times, the unique combination of factors present within a production will lead you to a totally new construction solution.

The most valuable tool available to every scenic carpenter is thorough planning. No level of skill, no tool and no amount of money will make up for a lack of planning. Understanding the external criteria and being able to visualize the entire construction process from start to finish before the first piece of wood is cut are the first and most important steps in building not only quality scenery, but scenery suitable to your circumstances.

Remember that good scenery should be economical, mobile, compact and simple. This set of characteristics is relatively easy to achieve when you recognize a significant advantage you have when working in the theater. The theater is made of illusions. All scenery is an illusion. Scenery is meant to be experienced in the very controlled environment of the theater. In this environment, the theater artist has control of the audience's view, the quantity and quality of light, and how the scenery is used. This control makes it possible to create the illusion for the audience that what they see is real. Add to this mix the ability of talented actors to take the audience into their world, the world of the play, and it is difficult for any of us not to believe we are seeing the real thing.